MAKING AUTISM A GIFT

MAKING AUTISM
A GIFT

*Inspiring Children to Believe in Themselves
and Lead Happy, Fulfilling Lives*

ROBERT EVERT CIMERA

A Rowman & Littlefield Education Book

ROWMAN & LITTLEFIELD PUBLISHERS, INC.
Lanham • Boulder • New York • Toronto • Plymouth, UK

A Rowman & Littlefield Education Book

ROWMAN & LITTLEFIELD PUBLISHERS, INC.

Published in the United States of America
by Rowman & Littlefield Publishers, Inc.
A wholly owned subsidiary of The Rowman & Littlefield Publishing Group, Inc.
4501 Forbes Boulevard, Suite 200, Lanham, Maryland 20706
www.rowmanlittlefield.com

Estover Road, Plymouth PL6 7PY, United Kingdom

Distributed by NATIONAL BOOK NETWORK

British Library Cataloguing in Publication Information Available

Library of Congress Cataloging-in-Publication Data
Cimera, Robert E.
  Making autism a gift : inspiring children to believe in themselves and lead happy, ful-
filling lives / Robert Evert Cimera.
    p.   cm.
  ISBN-13: 978-0-7425-5299-9 (cloth : alk. paper)
  ISBN-10: 0-7425-5299-3 (cloth : alk. paper)
  ISBN-13: 978-0-7425-5288-3 (pbk. : alk. paper)
  ISBN-10: 0-7425-5288-8 (pbk. : alk. paper)
  1. Autism in children. 2. Autism. I. Title.
  RJ506.A9C485 2007
  618.92'85882—dc22

                                                                2006026302

Printed in the United States of America

⊗™The paper used in this publication meets the minimum requirements of
American National Standard for Information Sciences—Permanence of Paper for
Printed Library Materials, ANSI/NISO Z39.48-1992.

This book is dedicated to my wonderful wife, who loves me for all my many oddities; to all the homeless animals at the Humane Society shelters; and to the professionals and family members who work with individuals who have autism.

Contents

Robert Evert Cimera

ONE

"Well . . . I DO Like to Draw!"*:
The Art of Defining Autism

If you are reading this book, you are probably either a teacher or a parent of a child with some form of autism. Perhaps you are even both. Either way, you probably have a great many questions regarding how you can help your child. Hopefully, I can be of assistance.

My name is Robert Cimera. I have a Ph.D. in special education and I have taught students with autism at elementary school, middle school, high school, and college levels. Yes, college! Believe it or not, people with autism can actually go on to Big Ten universities and earn their graduate degrees! But I will talk about that a little later.

I am writing this book for three reasons. The first is that the incidence rate of "autism" appears to be escalating dramatically. Recent studies indicate that the prevalence of autism has risen over 300 percent since 1995! In fact, several reports have called the increase a "pandemic." So clearly, the topic of autism and its related disorders is an important one. (I'll discuss why the incidence of autism is increasing in the third chapter.)

---

* I probably should explain my choice of chapter titles. You see, I had an aide who worked out this comedy routine with one of my students. The aide would introduce the student by saying, "This is Alex . . . he is autistic." To which Alex would reply, "Well . . . I DO like to draw!" It was very funny. It also illustrates how defining autism is as much an art as it is a science, as you will soon learn!

The second reason why I am writing this book is that everybody talks so negatively about autism, almost as if it were cancer or a death sentence or something horrible from the Dark Ages. Autism isn't horrible. It isn't a death sentence. People with autism aren't destined to be failures. They aren't a burden on society. They aren't stupid or crazy! They're merely people who are, in some ways, different than the "typical" person.

One of my main goals for this book is to inform you about what autism is and isn't. But I also want to give you hope. You see, people with autism can be successful! They can lead great lives! They can live independently in the community, go on to get their Ph.D.s, write books, have terrific high-paying jobs, fall in and out of love, and do everything that you and I can do. As I will say repeatedly throughout this book, having autism (in and of itself) isn't a bad thing. It is simply a difference.

As a teacher, I think that the biggest obstacles that my students had to overcome didn't involve their disability. The biggest obstacles involved how they were treated and raised. Let me explain.

There is a famous research study where a professor gave each of her students a rat. The professor told half of the students that their rats were "inbred" and "mentally retarded." The remaining students were told that their rats were "genetically superior" and "cognitively gifted." The students then had to train their rats to run through a maze and do various feats.

As you might imagine, the students who had the "mentally retarded" rats claimed that they couldn't get their rats to accomplish anything. The "genetically superior" rats, however, learned how to run through mazes, climb ladders, and so forth. But there was no difference between the rats. Further, they were randomly assigned to students. Do you see the point?

Making Autism a Gift

Many of my students with disabilities failed academically, socially, and vocationally not because they didn't have the abilities to succeed, but because they were told since birth that they would never be like "normal" people. They failed because they expected to fail. They failed because their parents, teachers, and everybody in their lives told them things like, "Oh . . . that is okay. You have a disability and that means you can't do things like other kids!" I'll give you one more example and then I'll move on.

I used to be a director of a program that transitioned students with disabilities out of school and into the community. Basically, I found jobs for high schoolers who had mental retardation, autism, and other disabilities.

I had one student (John) who wanted to work at McDonald's, so I got him a position cleaning the lobby of the McDonald's a block away from his home. As I was teaching John how to clean tables, he kept saying, "I can't do that."

"Oh yes, you can!" I said reassuringly in my Pollyannaish, special education–teacher voice. "All you have to do is squirt the tables with this bottle and then wipe the table with this towel. It is easy!"

I kept showing him how to clean the tables. But after each time, John would say the same thing, "I can't do that!"

Finally, I got a bit disgusted. I mean, he wasn't even trying to clean the tables and he certainly had the physical and cognitive abilities to complete the task successfully!

"Why?" I said, a bit snippy. "Why can't you clean these tables?"

John looked at me and said very frankly, "I can't do that! I have mental retardation. I have a full-scale IQ of sixty-seven!"

John was eighteen at the time, and I could tell that throughout his entire life, people had focused almost exclusively on his mental retardation. Nobody ever reinforced the idea that he could learn and do things for himself. Consequently, he never tried. He wouldn't even attempt to squirt a table with a bottle of cleaning solution and then wipe it with a damp cloth. John's disability wasn't mental retardation. It was his learned helplessness.

So, as I said before, I want this book to give you some hope that your children can succeed. After all, if you don't believe in your children, who will? Further, if you don't convey to your children that they can succeed, they won't. They will fail. They will live the lives that many adults with autism live—in poverty, without jobs, with their elderly parents or in group homes with little social contact with other members of the community.

However, hope isn't enough. You can't just "hope" that your child will be happy, healthy, and involved in the community. You have to teach your child the skills that he or she* will need.

My final goal for this book is to give you strategies that will help you teach your child these skills. I will be discussing methods for addressing aggressive behaviors, increasing socialization, enhancing communication skills, and many other areas critical to your child's success.

As with any book, some of what I will be discussing might not apply to your situation. For example, maybe your child doesn't throw temper tantrums. If that is the case, then skip or skim those sections. In other words, take what you need to improve your child's life and ignore the rest.

At the end of this book are many pages of resources. There, you can find even more information and support. If all else fails, feel free to contact me. My e-mail address is in the back. I don't know every-

---

* From now on I will refer to your child as "he." I don't mean to be sexist. It is simply easier than to keep saying "he or she." Further, as I will discuss at length later, most individuals with autism are male.

thing by a long shot, but I can certainly listen and help you find what you need.

So that is what this book is about and why I wrote it. By the time you get to its last pages, you will not only know what autism is, but you will know a good deal about how to prepare your child for life! So let's get started.

WHAT IS "AUTISM"?

The first question that you probably have is, "What *exactly* is 'autism'?" Well, this seems like as good a place as any to begin our time together. Therefore, let's address this question in some detail.

Unfortunately, answering the question, "What is autism?" is much like answering the question, "What is life?" Certainly various people have their thoughts, theories, and opinions. Moreover, some people believe very firmly that only their view is completely correct. However, it is really impossible to say, "*THIS* is what autism is!" You can't say that autism is any one thing in all cases. This is probably puzzling you, so let me elaborate.

Autism is a very subjective, human-defined condition. Further, what it is changes over time. What do I mean by that?

Autism is a term that has been coined in order to describe a wide variety of people who are different from the norm. Let me put it this way: autism isn't like cancer or a tumor or a tree. If you had never heard of cancer or tumors or trees, they would still exist. Moreover, you could look under a microscope or at an x-ray or out your window and see a cancerous cell, a tumor, or a tree. They exist even if humans don't know about them. Are you with me so far?

Autism is a concept or term used to describe a group of people who have a set of similar characteristics. The number and type of characteristics that autism describes depends largely on whom you ask. In other words, autism, in some respects, is much like a philosophy or subjective "label."

Are you beginning to see why it is so difficult to answer the question, "What is autism?" Plus, just to make matters even more confusing, there are many different names for autism and the conditions that are closely affiliated with it. For example, there is, of course, "autism." But there are also other terms: "autism spectrum disorder" (ASD), "Asperger's syndrome" (AS), "pervasive developmental disorder" (PDD), "pervasive developmental disorder–not otherwise specified" (PDD-NOS), "high functioning autism," "infantile autism," "educational autism," "classical autism," "childhood autism," "Kanner's autism," "childhood schizophrenia," and so on and on and on.

Unfortunately, many of these terms are used synonymously when they shouldn't be. For example, Asperger's syndrome, or AS, is often used to indicate somebody with "mild" or "high functioning" autism. However, many professionals now consider it to be a completely different, though related, condition. If you don't know what Asperger's is, don't worry. I'll talk about it in greater detail in later chapters.

At any rate, hopefully, you can see how talking about autism or PDD or ASD can get a bit confusing! Which, as I said before, is why I wanted to write this book. Hopefully, I can clear the air a bit.

Before we get too far, I want you to understand that I will be using the term "autism" the way many people use the phrase "autism spectrum disorder," or ASD. Basically, I believe (as do many authorities nowadays) that autism isn't just one homogenous condition where "if you have seen one kid with autism, you have seen them all!" I don't think that in the slightest! I believe that autism is a vast continuum of related conditions that are loosely linked by a set of, sometimes vaguely defined, characteristics.

Making Autism a Gift

VARIOUS DEFINITIONS OF AUTISM

You are probably sitting there saying in an exasperated voice, "I understand that autism is something that is very subjective and that it is just a label that we use to categorize people who share similar characteristics. But what is the actual *definition* of autism?! What are the characteristics?!"

Well, as you might expect, these questions aren't easy to answer either. The problem is that there are many definitions of autism that are currently being utilized. Some certainly overlap, but there are also huge gaps. Let me show you what I mean.

ASA's Definition of Autism

I want to share with you three definitions of autism that are currently very popular. The first comes from the Autism Society of America (ASA).

ASA is one of the largest and most respected organizations that focus on autism. When I was a teacher, ASA's help was invaluable to my success. I highly recommend that you join this organization. For more information about its mission and programs, please go to the resource section at the back of this book. ASA can provide you with a great deal of help.

At any rate, according to ASA, autism is a

complex developmental disability that typically appears during the first three years of life. The result of a neurological disorder that affects the functioning of the brain, autism impacts the normal development of the brain in the areas of social interaction and communication skills. Children and adults with autism typically have difficulties in verbal and non-verbal communication, social interactions, and leisure or play activities." (www.autism-society.org/)

Got that? Let's move on to our second definition of autism!

Autism According to IDEA

The second definition of autism that I want to discuss can be found in the Individuals with Disabilities Education Act (IDEA). If you don't know much about IDEA, you will by the end of our time together! I am going to dedicate an entire chapter to some of the legalities it outlines. But for now, just understand that IDEA is the federal law that governs special education. It is a biggie! So if you have a child with autism, you'll have to know a lot about it!

According to IDEA,

> Autism means a developmental disability significantly affecting verbal and nonverbal communication and social interaction, generally evident before age 3, that adversely affects educational performance. Other characteristics often associated with autism are engagement in repetitive activities and stereotyped movements, resistance to environmental changes or changes in daily routines, and unusual responses to sensory experiences. The term does not apply if a child's educational performance is adversely affected primarily because the child has a serious emotional disturbance (34 C.F.R., Part 300, § 300.7 [b][1])

Even though IDEA's definition of autism is only three sentences long, it contains a great deal of information! But don't worry if you didn't get it all. I'll be reviewing what all this information means in a few pages. Hang in there. Let me cover one last definition.

Making Autism a Gift

APA's Definition of Autism

The American Psychiatric Association (APA) produces a book called the *Diagnostic and Statistical Manual of Mental Disorders*, or *DSM*. It is the "bible" of clinical diagnoses for psychiatrists, psychologists, and other such professionals. Every few years or so, APA updates the *DSM*. The fourth version of the DSM is often referred to as *DSM-IV-TR*, which stands for the text revision (TR) of the fourth edition (IV).

According to the *DSM-IV-TR*, a person with autism is defined as having

A. A total of six (or more) characteristics from (1), (2), and (3), with at least two characteristics from (1), and one from both (2) and (3):

  (1) Qualitative impairment in social interaction, as manifested by at least two of the following:

    i. Marked impairment in the use of multiple nonverbal behaviors, such as eye-to-eye gaze, facial expression, body postures, and gestures to regulate social interaction.

    ii. Failure to develop peer relationships appropriate to developmental level.

    iii. A lack of spontaneous seeking to share enjoyment, interests, or achievements with other people (e.g., by a lack of showing, bringing, or pointing out objects of interest).

    iv. Lack of social or emotional reciprocity.

  (2) Qualitative impairments in communication as manifested by at least one of the following:

    i. Delay in, or total lack of, the development of spoken language (not accompanied by an attempt to

Robert Evert Cimera

       compensate through alternative modes of communication such as gesture or mime).

    ii. In individuals with adequate speech, marked impairment in the ability to initiate or sustain a conversation with others.

   iii. Stereotyped and repetitive use of language or idiosyncratic language.

   iv. Lack of varied, spontaneous make-believe play or social imitative play appropriate to developmental level.

(3) Restricted, repetitive, and stereotyped patterns of behavior, interests, and activities as manifested by at least one of the following:

     i. Encompassing preoccupation with one or more stereotyped and restricted patterns of interest that is abnormal either in intensity or focus.

    ii. Apparently inflexible adherence to specific, nonfunctional routines or rituals.

   iii. Stereotyped and repetitive motor mannerisms (e.g., hand or finger flapping or twisting, or complex who-body movements).

   iv. Persistent preoccupation with parts of objects.

B. Delays or abnormal functioning in at least one of the following areas, with onset prior to age three years:

(1) Social interaction,

(2) Language as used in social communication, or

(3) Symbolic or imaginative play.

C. The disturbance is not better accounted for by Rett's Disorder or Childhood Disintegrative Disorder.

Well, there you have it—three of the chief definitions of autism! Now, I know there is a great deal there, so let me break it down into more manageable pieces. Then I will go back and talk about the entire "definition" just so we are on the same page.

SO, WHAT IS AUTISM?

Okay, with three different yet widely accepted definitions of autism under our belts, let's start figuring out what they each mean. Then we can find out what they all have in common. And, hopefully, we can finally come to some sort of general understanding about what autism *is*!

Summary of ASA's Definition

If you go back for a moment and reread what ASA said autism was, you'll notice that there are several key words and phrases. Let me talk about each of them in turn.

Developmental disability. If you read much about autism, you are going to come across the term "developmental disability." This means that autism manifests itself during the individual's "developmental period," which is usually thought to be from conception through age eighteen. So, in other words, people cannot develop autism when they are adults. If they begin to experience autistic-like symptoms after age eighteen, they probably have other issues, such as schizophrenia or a brain injury.

You might be wondering whether people can develop autism when they are children. That is, can a child be born "normal" and then *acquire* autism a few years later? Many experts would say, "No, you are more or less born with autism." However, there are others who would strongly disagree. They claim that autism is caused by environmental factors and toxins, including the MMR (measles, mumps, and rubella) shots that children get when they are toddlers.

Robert Evert Cimera

(I'll talk about this issue in a little bit.) They also point to a condition called "childhood disintegrative disorder," or CDD, where apparently normal children become "autistic-like." (I'll also talk about CDD later.)

The point is that, generally speaking, children are thought to be born with autism. I know several families who knew almost immediately after birth that their children were autistic. The way they described it, their children were just not responsive to touch and other stimuli the way most newborns are.

But this is not to say that autistic children are clearly autistic as soon as they come out of the womb! It is very likely that parents might think that their child is normal until a teacher says something to the contrary. Still, the main idea here is that a child is autistic from birth or shortly thereafter. Adults, and even adolescents, don't suddenly develop autism.

Neurological disorder. The second key feature of ASA's definition of autism is "neurological disorder." As you might suspect, many people believe autism is caused by a neurological issue, where the brain doesn't function the way that it should. Specifically, the people at ASA believe that the brain of a person with autism didn't develop normally. There are also many people who believe that the brain of a person with autism developed correctly, but that there is something in it, such as toxins from the environment, that is preventing the brain from functioning effectively. I'll talk about the suspected causes of autism in greater detail later.

Communication and social skills. The final defining characteristic associated with autism, according to ASA, is that individuals with autism typically have significant difficulties with verbal and non-verbal communication and appropriate social interaction. As you will soon see, this doesn't mean that people with autism can't talk or that they can't interact with other people. Some clearly can. Yet, according to ASA, these skill areas are atypical compared to their non-disabled peers.

Summary of IDEA's Definition of Autism

Okay, so that was ASA's definition of autism. Now let's look at what the federal government says autism is. If you go back and look at what IDEA says autism is, you will see several important words and phrases, some similar to the ones used by ASA, others quite different.

Developmental disability. As in ASA's definition, the first key phrase of IDEA's definition of autism is "developmental disability." By now, you should know what that means. You should also be getting a sense that there is general agreement that autism is something children have at a very young age, if not right at birth.

Generally evident by age three. This part of IDEA's definition of autism is probably pretty self-explanatory. Generally speaking, the symptoms of autism are present by age three. Although, that is not to say that children cannot be diagnosed at later ages. I know an eleven year old who is just being diagnosed with autism. I am sure that there are some people who are diagnosed when they are adults.

Still, according to IDEA, the symptoms of autism are *usually* evident by age three. If a teenage boy suddenly starts exhibiting symptoms of autism, he probably doesn't have autism. He might have mental health issues, or maybe he is on drugs or has suffered a traumatic brain injury.

So what are the symptoms of autism? Good question. Let's move on to the next component of IDEA's definition!

Communication. As in ASA's definition, IDEA's definition states that in order for people to have autism, their verbal and nonverbal communication skills must be significantly impaired. Now, I am sure that you have a whole bunch of questions about this. For example, you might be thinking, "But my child has autism and he can speak!" and that is probably true.

IDEA isn't saying that people with autism are mute or that they can't communicate. It isn't saying that at all! According to IDEA, people with autism can have any number of difficulties with verbal or non-verbal communication. For instance, they might experience delays in language acquisition so that by four or five years old, they are still only talking in single words or short phrases. I'll go into greater detail about the communication issues in chapter eight.

Repetitive behavior. Okay, so one of the defining characteristics of individuals with autism, according to IDEA, is that they have problems with verbal and non-verbal communication. Another characteristic linked to autism is repetitive or stereotypic behavior. For instance, individuals with autism might rock back and forth, or twirl things, or wave their hands in front of their eyes, or do a hundred and one other things over and over again.

Keep in mind that these repetitious behaviors might be very subtle, so you might not notice them at first. For example, one of my students used to stroke his left arm as if he were cold. Another one of my students would tap his right foot very gingerly over and over again, almost as if he were testing the temperature of water in a pool. I'll talk about repetitious behaviors in chapter nine.

Resistance to environmental change. The final defining characteristic associated with autism, at least according to IDEA, is that individuals with autism tend to be very resistant to changes within their environment or their routines. For instance, one of my students needed to have the trash can in a certain corner of our classroom before he could sit down and work on his assignments. If the trash can was not in its "appropriate" location or was gone altogether, he would get very agitated, sometimes even violent.

Making Autism a Gift

Other students of mine were very regimented regarding their schedules. They had to do certain things at very specific moments in the day. For example, one student might have had to meet with the occupational therapist at 10:30 every Monday morning. If the occupational therapist was ill or couldn't make the appointment, my student would get very anxious.

Adversely affects education. Okay, this is going to sound a bit strange, so just relax and take a moment to think about what I am about to say. According to IDEA, even if a child has all of the characteristics that I have just described, he still might not have autism. That is because, again, according to IDEA, in order to have autism, individuals must have these characteristics (i.e., poor verbal and nonverbal skills, resistance to environmental change, and repetitious behavior) to such a degree that their education is affected. Specifically, their ability to receive an "appropriate" education is adversely impaired. (I'll talk about what IDEA defines as an appropriate education in chapter eleven.)

In other words, having the characteristics of autism is only part of the issue. These characteristics must be so severe that your child's ability to learn is impacted.

You might be wondering, "Is it possible for people to have autism and *not* have their education affected?" But the answer is a bit complicated.

According to IDEA, in order for people to have autism, their education must be hindered, so the short answer is, "No, people can't have autism and not have their education affected." However, if you look at autism as other people define it, then the answer is, "Yes, sometimes."

So technically, you can have a child who was diagnosed with autism by a medical doctor or some sort of specialist, but your local school officials might say, "That kid doesn't have autism! He is doing fine in school!" And they could deny your child special education services.

As a matter of fact, I just finished working as an "expert witness" on a case where a school district didn't want to furnish supports to a child who was previously diagnosed with high functioning autism. The school believed that the supports were unnecessary due to the progress that the student had recently made. The student's parents disagreed. I'll tell you more about this situation when I talk about special education and your rights as a parent of a child with special needs (see chapter eleven).

<u>Not caused by a serious emotional disturbance.</u> So, according to IDEA, autism is a disability that occurs early on in a person's life. It usually manifests itself by age three. It is associated with three key defining characteristics: (i) difficulty with communication, (ii) repetitive behavior, and (iii) abnormal resistance to changes, either in a routine or within an environment. Moreover, these characteristics have to be so severe that they adversely affect the child's ability to learn. But not everybody who meets these criteria has autism!

IDEA also says that if these characteristics were caused by an emotional disturbance, it isn't autism. For example, suppose that an individual just lived through a horrific event. Maybe that person survived an airplane crash or was a hostage and was about to be executed, or something equally harrowing. Such individuals might exhibit many of the symptoms that I have just described. They might be withdrawn and non-communicative. They might rock back and forth in an effort to comfort themselves. They might even fly off the handle if something changed around them. According to IDEA, these people would not have autism.

Summary of APA's Definition of Autism

Two down! One more to go! Now let's dissect APA's definition of autism. When we are done, we will put everything together and see what autism *really* is!

Number of characteristics. The first part of APA's definition that we need to investigate involves the number of characteristics that people need to display in order to have autism. At first glance, this seems pretty straightforward, right? I mean, in order to have autism, they have to have six or more of the characteristics. Further, they must have at least two symptoms in section one and at least one symptom in both section two and three. Hopefully, so far, this all makes sense. But wait! There is more to this than mere numbers!

The number of characteristics needed for someone to have autism isn't magical. It isn't as if having five characteristics is normal and having six means that someone has autism! A total of six characteristics is just what the people at APA *believe* is indicative of autism.

Again, what I am trying to illustrate is the notion that autism isn't an exact thing. It isn't like people have autism or they don't. There is a lot of subjectivity to how autism is defined. APA could have said, "Someone needs to have these thirty-seven characteristics to have autism!" Or, "Someone needs to have these two characteristics!"

It is much like defining a tree as having two or more of the following: (i) a tall frame, (ii) leaves, and (iii) birds' nests. Yes, these things often describe trees. But they hardly define what a tree is. Moreover, there are things that are tall, leafy, and have birds' nests but aren't trees. For example, they might be big bushes! Also, just because a tree doesn't have leaves or a bird's nest doesn't mean it is any less of a tree!

The characteristics. Much like the definitions provided by ASA and IDEA, APA's definition lists several characteristics associated with autism. However, unlike other definitions, APA's definition provides a great deal of flexibility for how a person with autism behaves. Basically, APA lists thirteen characteristics and says that an individual only needs to have six of them in order to have autism. But let's take a look at the types of characteristics that, according to APA, could indicate autism.

The first group of characteristics outlined by APA involves impairments in social interactions. These social impairments include impediments with non-verbal communication, such as using and interpreting facial expressions and body language, as well as general difficulty with developing and maintaining social relationships. For instance, one of my college students who had autism would walk up to his professors (usually interrupting them as they were already speaking to somebody else), ask a question, and then walk away as the professors were trying to answer what he had asked. It was almost as if my student got what he wanted and was through with the conversation, so he just walked away. Such behavior is pretty common among high functioning autistics or individuals with Asperger's.

The second group of behaviors that might indicate autism, according to APA, involves communication skills. For instance, children with autism might not develop spoken language as quickly as their peers. In fact, they might not develop any verbal language at all. Moreover, even if individuals with autism do speak, they are likely to have problems communicating effectively with others. Their speech can often be rather mechanical and stilted. They can also use the same apparently meaningless words or phrases over and over again, especially words and phrases that they have just heard. For example, a student may hear the phrase "butter toast" while watching the cartoon *Ed, Edd, and Eddy* and end up saying "butter toast," "butter toast," "butter toast" all day long.

The final group of characteristics that APA says must be present for a person to have autism involves "restrictive, repetitious, or stereotyped behaviors, interests, or activities." This is very much like what IDEA mentioned, but on a grander scale. Not only may students with autism rock back and forth, stroke their arms, or tap their feet, but they may also perseverate on various topics of conversation. For instance, a teacher friend of mine has a student who talks constantly about the bathrooms on airplanes. It doesn't matter if anybody is listening or even there, he'll just sit and talk to himself about bathrooms on airplanes for hours and hours (e.g., how small and noisy they are, how the toilets aren't like the toilets at school, and so forth). One of my students always prattled on about colors—what color something was, and how it was a better color than something else, and what foods were what colors. You get the idea.

Additionally, individuals with autism may perform the same actions repeatedly. For example, one of my students would get up from his chair and go open and close the door to the classroom. He would do this exactly three times. If somebody came into or out of the room, he would have to get up, walk over to the door, and open and close it three more times.

<u>Some symptoms by age three.</u> As with all of the other definitions that I have discussed, APA believes that autism is a developmental disability and that at least some of the symptoms described above must be present by age three.

<u>Not caused by other conditions.</u> Finally, according to the American Psychiatric Association, in order for autism to be present, the symptoms cannot be caused by other conditions—specifically, Rett's or childhood disintegrative disorder. I'll talk about what they are in chapter four.

Robert Evert Cimera

A GENERALLY ACCEPTED
DEFINITION OF AUTISM

So there you have it—three different definitions of autism! Notice that they have several things in common, as well as some variations. Let's go over some of the similarities, and then you should have a working definition of autism.

First of all, all three definitions agree that autism is a developmental disability. Again, this means that people can't "develop" autism when they are adults. Moreover, most of the definitions indicate that at least some of the symptoms of autism must be present by age three.

So what are the symptoms of autism? Well, the list of symptoms that a person must have in order to be "autistic" varies from definition; however, by and large, each definition focuses on three areas of abnormality.

The first area involves communication skills—both verbal and non-verbal. As I have said, this isn't to say that people with autism can't speak or hold conversations. They may. It is just that their ability to convey and interpret the subtle meanings that are often involved in typical communication is impaired or underdeveloped.

The second area of abnormality involves social interaction. Individuals with autism don't interact with other people "normally." It is almost as if they simply don't "get" how to socialize. Perhaps a better way of explaining it is that they don't understand the unwritten "rules" of how to interact.

Finally, people with autism generally display repetitious behaviors, including "self-stimulation" behaviors, such as rocking back and forth or staring at things that twirl. Other examples include dwelling on certain topics, engaging in compulsive behavior, or seeking out environmental predictability.

Making Autism a Gift

SUMMARY

I suppose that we could just stop there and leave everything where it is. We could simply say that autism is a condition characterized by impairments in language, abnormal social skills, and repetitious behaviors that typically manifest themselves by age three. But somehow, something is lost in such a summary. It makes it sound as if autism is only part of a person or that it only affects three areas of the person's life. This isn't accurate.

You see, autism isn't part of a person. It isn't like having a certain hair color. You can't shave off autism from the child. A person with autism cannot stop being autistic any more than I can stop being Norwegian or male or a product of the twentieth century.

Think of autism as a state of being. It is a completely different place than the one most people live. It is neither good nor bad. There is nothing inherently wrong about being autistic. It is merely different.

Moreover, just as people with autism are very different from the "typical" population, people with autism can be incredibly different from each other. One child with autism can grow up, run a Fortune 500 company, and be one of the richest men in the world (Bill Gates, by the way, has always been rumored to have Asperger's syndrome). Another child with autism might have profound mental retardation, never utter a word, and require constant supervision throughout his entire life. Again, people with autism (as a group) are incredibly diverse.

My job is to help you understand autism (in a broad sense) and give you strategies for teaching your child—regardless of his "functioning level"—so that your child can have the best possible future. In essence, you might think of me as your tour guide to the planet autism. Buckle up! It is going to be a wild ride!

TWO

"But He Is Too Active to Have Autism!"*: Characteristics of Autism

In the last chapter, I talked about what autism is. Unfortunately, the answers that I provided probably weren't as clear-cut as you might have wanted. Even after being introduced to several definitions of "autism," you probably still have *many* questions. So rather than trying to define autism in absolute terms, let's now focus on the characteristics that individuals with autism tend to display. Perhaps that will give you a better idea of what autism is all about.

But before we go any further, I want to make sure that you understand something very important. "Autism" or "autism spectrum disorder" or whatever term you want to use is an "umbrella category." Basically this means that it includes a variety of different people who may share some characteristics, but not others.

As you might guess, autism is an extremely large umbrella category. There is incredible diversity within this population. So when I

---

* As a very young child, my niece used to rock back and forth in her high chair. For a while my brother, her father, thought that she might have autism. One day he mentioned this to our mother, who replied, "But she is too active to have autism! She is always running around like a normal child!" Evidently, my mother thought kids with autism usually sat in one place self-stimming. However, this isn't true at all! People with autism can be just as active as anybody else! Further, there is more to autism that just rocking back and forth, as you will see from this chapter.

talk about specific characteristics, remember that your child might not exhibit some of them. Moreover, your child might have some characteristics that are more mild or severe than what other children with autism exhibit.

With all of this in mind, let me talk about some of the "symptoms" or "traits" of people with autism. When possible, I will try to tell stories involving my own students. Hopefully, they will illustrate how the severity of these characteristics can fluctuate.

GENDER

The first characteristic of autistic individuals that I want to discuss involves gender. People with autism are overwhelmingly male. Estimates differ, but recent research has found that autism is four to seven times more likely to occur in males than females.

Why more males? Nobody knows. Maybe it has something to do with the prenatal hormones to which females are exposed. Maybe it is because of the differences in brain development that males and females experience. Some experts even suggest that there is a genetic link that makes autism more likely in males. Again, researchers really don't know for sure why autism is more prevalent in males than females.

It is important to keep in mind that females *can* have autism. Moreover, females who have autism are far more likely to have severe mental retardation than males who have autism. This leads me to the second characteristic.

MENTAL RETARDATION

First of all, not all people who have autism are also mentally retarded. In fact, many people with autism are cognitively gifted! This is particularly the case with those individuals who are labeled with Asperger's or "high functioning" autism.

When I was at the University of Illinois at Chicago, there were two students with autism in one of our graduate programs. They were studying computer programming or technology or something of that nature. Apparently one of them was considered to be a "superstar." I remember one of his professors said that he was *the* best student that the professor had ever had! So please don't think that ALL individuals with autism are also mentally retarded.

However, with that said, many individuals with autism are likely to also have mental retardation. In fact, one recent study that reviewed the literature in the field suggested that as many as 70 percent of children with autism in the United States also have some degree of mental retardation.

But I personally believe that this number is just a stab in the dark—a "guestimate," if you will. As you learned from the previous chapter, individuals with autism often have difficulty communicating and interacting appropriately with the world around them. So how can test administrators measure somebody's intelligence if the person is not responsive to their questions?! They can't!

Yes, there are a great many children with autism who also have cognitive impairments, such as mental retardation. But I think that it is impossible to say exactly how many children have both diagnoses, especially in the cases where the children with autism are unwilling or unable to interact with the administrators of intelligence tests.

Because mental retardation is so frequently part of the autistic world, I will talk about it in greater depth in chapter four. There are also multiple resources on mental retardation in the back of this book. If you are *really* interested in understanding mental retardation, you might want to consider getting *Mental Retardation Doesn't*

Making Autism a Gift

Mean "STUPID!": A Guide For Parents and Teachers. It might help you.

STEREOTYPIC BEHAVIOR

Another central characteristic of autism that I discussed in the last chapter involves stereotypic, or repetitive, behaviors. For example, students of mine would frequently rock back and forth in their chairs and flap their hands in front of their unblinking eyes. Why did they do this? Well, find out for yourself.

Take a moment and set this book down. Rock back and forth very slightly (and slowly) and stare off into space ahead of you. Now flap or wave your hand limply four or five inches in front of your eyes. Go ahead. Nobody is going to laugh at you.

Well, if you actually had the guts to pretend that you had autism, you might have found something kind of surprising. If you are like most people, you probably felt calm or relaxed, or maybe as if you were being hypnotized. Perhaps that is why people with autism do such things. It comforts them. It is also a way of blocking out all of the stimuli from the world around them.

This makes sense. After all, how does a mother soothe a crying baby? She puts the baby on her shoulder and rocks the child slowly back and forth.

The same thing is true for good masseuses. No, the masseuse doesn't put you over his shoulder and rock you. But he does rock your body back and forth ever so slightly as he is trying to get the stress out of your muscles.

So, when your child starts rocking back and forth, stroking his arm, flicking his fingers, or whatever, he is probably trying to relax and drown out the world around him. I could always tell if my students were bothered if I watched how they self-stimmed (that's special-ed jargon for "self-stimulate"). The faster they rocked or stroked or flicked, the more anxious they were.

LACK OF IMAGINATIVE PLAY

If you give typical children a box, they can have hours of fun playing with it. They can pretend that it is a fort or a rocket ship or a television or a gateway to other planets or a million and one other fun things! Typical children can use their imaginations to turn the box into anything they want.

Children with autism aren't like this. It isn't that they can't "play." They can. But they aren't as imaginative as their peers. For example, they are likely to put things in the box because that is what they have seen done with boxes. In other words, they won't usually use things in novel ways.

As soon as I say this at workshops, many parents seem to sigh in relief. They will then talk about how their children don't have autism because they play with things in unusual ways. For instance, they will take a plate and try to spin it like a top.

Although this is a "novel" way of playing with a plate or a pen or picture frame, it really doesn't "prove" that a child doesn't have autism. Actually, the presence of such behavior could prove quite the opposite. As I have explained to several parents over the years, the obsession with spinning objects (especially bright shiny objects) is a common feature of autistic behavior. It falls under the repetitious, or stereotypic, behavior that I discussed earlier.

"LACK" OF EMOTION

One of the often-cited characteristics of individuals with autism is a "lack" of emotion. First of all, nobody *lacks* emotions. All humans have them. It is just that people with autism tend to have flatter affects than do other people. They tend to have a blank expression on their faces and their eyes seem to look "through" you, that is, when they make any eye contact at all.

David Letterman once said of comedian and actor Andy Kaufman, "I look into Andy's eyes and I am not sure anybody is looking back at me."

That is how I always felt with my students who had autism. I knew that there was somebody inside the head of each student, but I couldn't feel the connection. I got the sense that they weren't really "seeing" me. It was almost as if to them, I wasn't there.

However, to say that individuals with autism express no emotion is certainly not accurate! Rather, they tend to show emotions in a different way than do non-autistic people. For example, as I discussed briefly above, many individuals with autism will show that they are anxious or nervous or uncomfortable by rocking back and forth or by flicking their fingers in front of their eyes or by tapping their feet quickly. Non-autistic children usually don't do this.

Moreover, as I am about to discuss, individuals with autism are very capable of showing anger. So please do not buy into the stereotype that children with autism are like androids who don't feel anything. They do. They can even express love! It is just that they do so in very unusual ways.

For example, a parent of a child with autism told me this incredible story about how she had been trying to get her son to show more emotion. I think, like most such parents, she was frustrated because her child never said, "I love you Mommy," or performed other acts of affection.

She tried getting her son to give her hugs, but he couldn't tolerate being held. She tried to get him to smile and say, "I love you," but he would only do so if she prompted him. Further, when he did, he said it in a flat, monotone voice that lacked conviction.

Robert Evert Cimera

Finally, right when this mother was about to give up, she and her son were walking side by side when his pinky reached out and wrapped around hers. He apparently had seen that in a movie or on television show. A couple was holding "pinkies" and swinging their arms back and forth as they walked romantically down a beach. At any rate, her son saw this somewhere and he emulated it with her. She cries every time she tells people that story, which brings me to a slightly tangential point.

Studies have found that the most difficult part of having a child with autism isn't the presence of aggressive behavior (which I am about to discuss), but the absence of affection. I know from my own personal experiences that it would be very hard to have a child who didn't want to crawl into my lap, cuddle with me on the sofa, and say, "I love you Daddy!" I'll discuss how you can address this issue in subsequent chapters.

AGGRESSIVE OR SELF-INJURIOUS BEHAVIOR (SIB)

Although individuals with autism do not always show affection appropriately, they can be very quick to use violence, both against others as well as against themselves. Let me give you some examples.

My first job as a special educator involved working with a student who put his aide in a coma. The school's staff members don't really know what happened, but they found the student sitting in the school's parking lot rocking back and forth and beating his aide's unconscious head against the concrete.

Another one of my students, Ron, was very aggressive. During a forty-five-minute observation, he hit, pinched, grabbed, or bit his aide 214 times. That is nearly five aggressions every minute or one every 12.6 seconds!

Making Autism a Gift

This particular student used to grab his aide's breasts and twist. He did it so often that she eventually started wearing a chest protector (i.e., what catchers on baseball teams wear).

Once, Ron grabbed my . . . well . . . testicles. I have to say that I have never been in so much pain in my life. He just grabbed and squeezed. I immediately collapsed and was unable to get up for several minutes. From then on, whenever I worked with Ron, I wore an athletic cup.

Last semester, one of my student teachers had her finger broken by a student with autism. Evidently, he grabbed her finger and snapped it backward.

Two years ago, one of my student teachers had her eye scratched by a pre-school–aged child with autism. I don't mean the area around the eye or the eyelid, but the actual eyeball! I could go on and on, but I think that you get the idea.

Then there are individuals who are aggressive toward themselves. This is usually referred to in special education lingo as SIB, or "self-injurious behavior." Ron, for example, used to hit himself in the temple and eye. Some of my other students used to bite themselves or pull out their hair.

I even know of students who banged their heads on the wall with such force that they would cause severe damage if they didn't wear protective helmets all of the time. In fact, sadly, there was a little boy named Brandon who lived in a nearby institution a few years back who would run into walls at full speed. He would also throw tantrums and bang his head on the floor.

Brandon was so self-destructive that he literally pulverized the front part of his skull. I am not exaggerating when I say "pulverized." He actually broke his skull to such a degree that he had operations to put metal plates to protect his brain. His forehead was kind of concaved in the middle.

He wore this oversized helmet that was inflated with air, kind of like a balloon. Whenever he hit his head, air escaped through a small valve. I guess it was supposed to cushion his head and prevent the numerous impacts from causing more injury.

Unfortunately, it didn't work. Brandon died from self-inflicted brain damage when he was around twelve years old. You might have heard about it on the news. It was a nationwide story for a little bit.

There was a big argument about what should have been done to stop Brandon from self-abusing. The faculty tried a long list of behavior modification strategies. They tried rewarding appropriate behaviors and punishing him when he started to self-abuse. But nothing worked. A few doctors at the institution actually wanted to use "shock therapy." But that was seen as being very extreme and immoral. In the end, as I said, nothing worked and he eventually died from his injuries.

I don't mean to make it sound like kids with autism are inherently dangerous and need to be locked up. I know many students with autism who never laid a finger on themselves or other people. Still, it is an all too common trait of the population as a whole.

This leads me to the question of why? Why do people with autism tend to be aggressive?

Well, think about it. One of their defining characteristics is poor communication skills, right? If you had trouble communicating and something was bothering you, what would be the quickest and most effective way of getting people's attention? Probably grabbing them in rather sensitive places!

Again, please keep in mind that people with autism aren't stupid. They aren't vegetables or unthinking robots. They think and reason and learn. Sometimes a person who is not autistic has to learn what they are thinking in order to really appreciate what is going on. I'll talk extensively about aggressive behavior in chapter seven.

Making Autism a Gift

LACK OF SOCIAL OR EMOTIONAL RECIPROCITY

Social and emotional reciprocity means that people are able to inter-relate with others. They are able to take turns when talking to some-body and be sympathetic listeners. In short, it is the ability to be empathetic and follow the unwritten rules of social interaction.

For example, many of my students couldn't make "small talk"; that is, they often had difficulty chit-chatting about nothing in par-ticular. They usually didn't say things like, "My! What a beautiful day it is!" or "How about those Cubs!" Their conversations tended to be direct and to the point.

They also might treat people like objects. For example, I know a child with autism who won't say that he is thirsty and that he wants milk. Instead, he will walk up to his mother, take her by the hand, and lead her to the refrigerator. He will then put her hand on the handle of the refrigerator, have her open it, and put her hand on the milk. After he gets his milk, he stops interacting with her—at least until he wants something else.

ECHOLALIA

Echolalia is a term that means the repetition of sounds, words, or phrases. For example, in the movie *Rainman*, Dustin Hoffman's character (who had autism) frequently repeated things that he had heard. In one scene he hears a radio station give its call letters and slogan. He ends up spending the rest of the day saying, "WMNX . . . BAD! The future of rock and roll . . . WMNX . . . BAD! The future of rock and roll! WMNX . . ." Well, that might not be an exact quote from the movie, but I think you get the idea.

Actually, I have a funny story about echolalia. I worked in a workshop for people with disabilities very briefly. (If you don't know what workshops are, that is okay. I'll be talking about them when I discuss employment options for people with autism.) Anyway, there were maybe fifty or sixty people with disabilities all working in the same room; probably a dozen of them had autism.

Periodically, a worker by the name of James T. (people always had to call him by both his first name and middle initial or he'd get angry) would call out, "Birdhead!" Don't ask me why. It was just what James T. did. Everything would be very quiet and all of a sudden he would scream, "Birdhead!"

Well, the people with autism would start repeating it over and over again. "Birdhead!" "Birdhead!" "Birdhead!" would echo throughout the room.

Then Glenn, another individual with disabilities who was working in the workshop, would get angry and start yelling, "Am not!" And, of course, the echoes of "Am not!" "Am not!" "Am not!" would begin popping up all over the place.

This would go on and on day after day. "Birdhead!" "Am not!" "Birdhead!" "Am not!" It makes me smile now, but I have to tell you, it drove most of the staff to become chain smokers.

There are two different types of echolalia: "mitigated echolalia" and "delayed echolalia." Delayed echolalia is when a person with autism repeats something for hours, days, or maybe even weeks after first hearing it. Mitigated echolalia, on the other hand, is when a person hears something and begins repeating it right away, as was the case with the "birdhead" and "am not!" story.

According to a recent publication, roughly 75 percent of individuals with autism display some form of echolalia from time to time. The question you are probably asking yourself is, "Why?" Why do they do this? Is it a means of communicating something? Is it something that is just nonsensical?

Making Autism a Gift

It used to be thought that echolalia was kind of an automated outburst that didn't have any function: kind of like a hiccup, but with words. However, that view is no longer popular. Now, echolalia is thought to be the person's way of dealing with unwanted stimuli.

So when an individual with autism is feeling overwhelmed, perhaps by people talking to him, he may start repeating the same thing over and over again as a way of blocking the stimuli. It is much like how people who meditate will say "oommmmmmm" to relax. Saying the same thing over and over again is a good way of tuning everybody else out.

Other people believe that echolalia is a way for individuals with autism to get attention. Perhaps they want something, but they don't know how to express their desires, so they start repeating whatever words or phrases come to mind.

My own experiences seem to support the drowning out theory. Most of my students would enter into echolalic phases when something was wrong. If it was too noisy in the room, for example, they would rock back and forth, rubbing their hands and repeating the same thing over and over again. When I removed whatever was bothering them so that the was room quieter, they stopped. However, perhaps there were times when my students merely wanted my attention and I didn't realize it.

DELAYED AND ATYPICAL SPEECH

Researchers have found that although 50 percent of autistic children eventually develop functional speech, 80 percent of them will do so at a delayed rate; that is, few individuals with autism will speak at the developmentally appropriate times. So it is very likely that your child will be behind his peers with regard to verbal language acquisition.

Robert Evert Cimera

Further, when your child does develop language, it is likely to be somewhat abnormal or not "age appropriate." For example, many of my students who could talk confused the rules of grammar and spoke as if they were learning the language for the first time. They frequently referred to themselves in the third person and would say things like, "Gregory would like to go to recess," rather than saying, "I would like to go to recess."

My students also often left out articles and would put words together in what appeared to be a random order. For example, they might hand me a book and say, "Story read you." Or they would say, "Going three o'clock home."

LITERAL INTERPRETATION

In addition to having expressive language delays, individuals with autism also tend to have receptive language delays. That is, they are likely to misinterpret what people tell them. It isn't that they can't acquire the vocabulary or understand the meaning of words. It is just that they tend to take things very literally or at face value. For instance, if you say that it is raining cats and dogs, they might actually think that cats and dogs are falling from the sky.

Additionally, people with autism typically don't understand sarcasm or humor. Suppose, for example, that your child comes up to you and asks, "Are you reading a book?" (when clearly you are), and you respond, "Why no! I am reading an elephant!" If your child had autism, he might be a bit perplexed. After all, he knows what an elephant is, and he sees that you certainly are not reading one! You are reading a book! So why would you say that you are reading an elephant when you aren't?

Personally, I think that this is one of the greatest deficits that many people with autism have. If you think about it, much of how humans interact with others involves the subtle hidden meanings that are present in jokes and sarcastic comments. Now picture trying to function in the world when you don't understand such hidden meanings! Think about how socially isolated you would be. Think about how vulnerable you would be. I believe that this inability to understand underlying meanings is why people with autism are frequently taken advantage of by other people.

PREOCCUPATION WITH PREDICTABILITY

Individuals with autism are also notorious for needing consistency. They seem to crave predictability, not just in their own actions but also in their environment and the behavior of others. Let me give you some examples.

I had a classroom with double doors. If anybody came in through the door on the left, one of my students would get aggravated. He would lead the person by the hand out of the classroom (through the left-hand door) and bring this person back in through the door on the right.

Another one of my students could only sit in certain locations. He had to sit in the second row of the bus and to the left. He had to sit by the wall two seats from the door in my classroom. And he had to sit at the end of the last table in the lunchroom. If these seats were already occupied, he would stand and glare at the intruders until they moved.

Larry needed to have all of his pencils lined up from longest to shortest on top of his desk before he could begin working. Scott needed to wear gray T-shirts. Russell couldn't function unless everything was very quiet.

Moreover, most of my students were very regimented as far as their schedules went. At such and such time, they had to go to recess or start on their English homework. Whenever their schedules were altered, they had a very difficult time adjusting to the change.

And it wasn't just their long-standing schedules, such as their school day routines, that couldn't change. They had trouble dealing with changes to recently expected events. For instance, suppose that you told your child that you were going to take him to get some ice cream at Dairy Queen. However, when you get to Dairy Queen, you find that it is closed, so you begin driving to another place. Immediately your child begins to get upset. You explain that you are still going to get ice cream, but just not at Dairy Queen, since it is closed. But your child keeps focusing upon the fact that you lied and that you said that you were going to take him for ice cream at Dairy Queen.

In other words, individuals with autism seem to get a tremendous amount of comfort from knowing what to expect. When things change and they can't predict what will happen, their world appears to collapse. By knowing what kinds of factors your child latches onto, you can create environments, situations, and strategies that promote learning. You can also reduce the likelihood of temper tantrums and meltdowns!

HYPERFOCUSED

Much as with self-stimming behavior (such as rocking back and forth or staring at shiny objects), many people with autism can become hyperfocused; that is, they become so absorbed by what they are doing that they can't tear themselves away. A person might even have great difficulty trying to get their attention.

Now, everyone is like this from time to time. I might be so into writing to you that I can't hear my wife calling my name. Or you might be so deep into your thoughts that somebody can actually wave a hand in front of your unseeing eyes. So please don't think that you are autistic! This is merely one possible characteristic that people with autism tend to display.

HYPERSENSITIVITY

Nearly all of the people with autism that I know are hypersensitive to certain stimuli. For example, many of my students couldn't be touched. They simply couldn't bear it. Others were intolerant of various noises, such as the rumble of trucks going by the house or high-pitched sounds.

Several of my students were very sensitive to how their clothes felt. One of my students, Ryan, couldn't stand wearing certain types of socks and underwear. His mother had to shave the inside seam of his socks. If she didn't, he would throw a fit of biblical proportions.

The same thing was true with the tag in his underwear. His mother had to not only remove it but also let him wear the underwear inside out so that the seam pointed away from his skin. He used to scream, "My butt itches!" if his underwear didn't fit him just right.

Ryan also had to have his shoes tied a certain way. They couldn't be too loose or too tight. Plus both of his shoes had to have the *exact* same amount of tension and the "loops" from the knots had to be the exact same size. If one shoe was tied a little tighter than the other, or if one loop was a little longer than the other, he could not function.

As you can imagine, putting his shoes on when he was younger was quite the ordeal. I still feel very sorry for his mother. She had no clue how he liked his shoes tied. She had to keep trying over and over until she got both of them to the same degree of tautness.

Another one of my students, Roger, was very sensitive to certain smells. He had to sniff his food and wouldn't eat things that he couldn't smell or that smelled funny. Consequently, he had a very limited diet.

Roger was also repulsed by most perfumes, aftershaves, fabric softeners, laundry detergents, and even soaps! Once the staff realized this, some of his odd behaviors made sense. For instance, he had this one aide whom he obviously didn't like. Whenever she came into the room, Roger would rock back and forth, rub his face, slap his hands together, and sway his head back and forth. If this aide remained around him, he would get very aggressive and nobody could figure out why. He would grab her by the hair and try to bite her. It was an awful scene.

Eventually the staff figured out that he didn't like the shampoo that she used. Apparently it smelled funny to him. What was odd was that he could smell it from not only across the room, but when she was outside in the hall! She must have been thirty feet away and Roger would still smell her coming!

Light is also problematic for many kids with autism. One of my student teachers is currently working with a child who has to wear specially tinted goggles whenever he is outside or by a window. The light bothers him, much like smells bothered Roger.

Once you know about your child's "triggers," that is, what he is sensitive to, you will be able to minimize many of the impediments that he will face. It took Angie, Ryan's mother, a long time to figure out that he had to have his socks and underwear the right way. Once she did, his behavior improved immensely.

GIFTS OF AUTISM

Did I just say "gifts of autism"? Yup! Believe it or not, having autism isn't all bad. It really isn't. In fact, you might find that your child has many positive qualities as a result of his autism. These dramatic

Making Autism a Gift

strengths are often called "splinter skills." You might have heard of the terms "savant" or maybe "idiot savant." These terms basically mean the same thing; however, the term "idiot savant" is demeaning and shouldn't be used.

Individuals with autism can have superb, even photographic memories. For instance, there is a guy with autism who works at my local humane society. He enters data into the computer. He has a little office in the back and wears industrial-sized earphones (the kind that people who work on airport runways wear) so that the barking of the dogs doesn't bother him. He sits at his desk and enters in all kinds of accounting information.

At any rate, I volunteer at the humane society and play with the dogs. One day, this gentleman walked up to me and said my full name, home address, the names of my landlord and a few of my friends, the name of my cat, the type of cat that I have, when I adopted her, and even the number of the check that I used to pay for her! He then ambled away, leaving me rather perplexed.

Well, like I said, this guy spends several hours a day entering data for the shelter and he must have entered the data from the application that I filled out when I adopted my cat Nixon. As it turns out, he memorizes everything that he types. It is really quite remarkable! It isn't as if he tries to memorize everything. He isn't "studying" every detail that he is entering. He simply remembers it whether he wants to or not!

Other people with autism whom I know are very good at remembering specific facts. For example, I could give one of my students any date, such as May 3, 1822, and he could tell me what day of the week it was. I could even try to trip him up by saying a leap year or a date that is millions of years away. He is always able to tell me exactly what day of the week it is.

The other day our local news did a story on a child with autism who is a skilled pianist. He was brilliant! I can't remember how old he was, maybe six or seven, but he could play like a classically trained musician; however, he never had a lesson. He simply sat down at somebody's piano one day and started playing.

One of my colleagues knows a young man with autism who is an artist. He draws these beautiful pictures that are extremely lifelike! In typical autistic fashion, he only draws pictures of horses. Apparently, he is infatuated with them.

People with autism can even be skilled athletes! For example, Jason McElwain was the manager of his high school basketball team. His coach put him into the last game of the season, and Jason ended up scoring twenty points in something like four minutes. He even made six three-pointers! Moreover, he outscored everybody on both teams. I can imagine Jason practicing hour after hour, shooting hoops with obsessive determination like only a person with autism can.

And, finally, people with autism can be fantastic motivational speakers and authors, such as James Williams. James is only seventeen years old and has already written two incredible books (*The Self-Help Guide for Special Kids and Their Parents* and *Out To Get Jack*). He also tours the country enlightening "normal" people about what it is like to have autism. If you would like to learn more about James and what he does, please go to http://www.jamesmw.com.

The point that I want to make is that people with autism can have a great deal going for them. For instance, Dr. Temple Grandin is a professor of animal science at Colorado State University and she has autism! Dr. Ian Huser is an astronomer with autism! Liane Willey is an author who has autism! Maybe Jason McElwain will some day become a famous NBA player! And James Williams is already a famous writer and speaker! So please don't think that your child won't succeed or do something special with his life because of his diagnosis. He can *if* you help prepare him!

The trick is finding ways of utilizing the strengths that your child has. For example, if your child is very precise and good with numbers, what is stopping him from becoming an accountant? Or maybe he is great with computers! Then maybe he will be a world-renowned computer programmer!

Again, think about all of the characteristics that I have discussed in this chapter. Many of them are very useful to have! Think about how far you could go in life if you were completely focused on one thing and were able to devote all of your energies to thinking about and working on that one area of expertise! When I get to chapter twelve, I will talk about how to turn some of these strengths into vocational success stories!

SUMMARY

Autism is a very heterogeneous condition. Get a hundred people with autism together in the same room and they will likely behave in remarkably diverse ways. However, there are a few characteristics that people with autism typically display. In this chapter I have talked about some of them. But please keep in mind that everybody is different. Moreover, some characteristics might be more severe in some people than others. One child with autism might self-abuse nearly every moment of every day. Others might only hit themselves if there are loud noises or if they are scared. Still others may not self-abuse at all.

By understanding your child's characteristics, you will be better able to address your child's needs. So take a few minutes and apply what you have learned in this chapter to your child. Think about the things he does and how he behaves. Further into this book, I'll begin to talk about how to eliminate or change "bad" or "disruptive" characteristics and how to increase or enhance those that are positive.

THREE

"Funny, I Don't Feel Sick!"*: Diagnosing Autism

Okay, by now you should understand that "autism" is really an umbrella term for a bunch of conditions that share somewhat similar characteristics. These characteristics vary depending upon the definition used; however, they basically fall into three categories:

Poor Communication Skills
Abnormal Social Skills
Repetitious Behavior

Hopefully, you also know that the severity of these symptoms varies greatly from one person to another. So it is impossible to accurately describe or define autism in such a way that it covers everybody with that label. Some children with autism will have mental

---

* I was at an IEP meeting once where the school psychologist was summarizing past diagnostic reports. He said in an overly professional and patronizing tone as if the student wasn't sitting right next to him, "Randy was diagnosed with autism." To which Randy immediately replied, "Funny, I don't feel sick!" It was the funniest damned thing that I had ever heard! Everybody laughed; everybody, except the school psychologist, who evidently didn't see the humor in the comment.

Please remember, autism isn't an illness. It is simply part of the spectrum of human existence!

retardation and may need constant supervision for the rest of their lives. Many will live in the community and get jobs. Maybe they will even become university professors or writers! In other words, there is a tremendous range of abilities underneath the "autism umbrella."

So let's suppose that you think that your child has autism. What do you do? Or perhaps somebody has already told you that your child has autism. How do you know if that person is right? These are great questions! Fortunately, they are also the focus of this chapter! So keep reading!

WHO CAN DIAGNOSE AUTISM?

As with many things that I am going to be discussing in this book, there is a very short answer to the question, "Who can diagnose autism?" There is also a very long answer. Let me begin with the short one and then go from there.

In order for students to be in special education, they have to be diagnosed by what is sometimes called an "M-Team," or "multi-disciplinary team." This team is also often called a "D-Team," or "diagnostic team." At any rate, in order for a child to be enrolled in special education programs, a team of school officials (including teachers, school psychologists, nurses, and other professionals) must determine whether that child is eligible for services. Part of this eligibility criterion, which I will discuss in chapter eleven, involves a diagnosis. So, technically speaking, all students with autism who are in special education are diagnosed by the school.

Now, you are probably sitting there saying, "Wait a second! That isn't true! My child was diagnosed way before he ever entered school!" And you are probably correct. But keep in mind that what I said above only applies to people who are going to be in special education. There are many individuals who are diagnosed with autism way before they enter school.

You might be wondering, "So how are those children diagnosed with autism?" Well, that is where things get a little hairy. But bear with me and I think that I can clarify things a bit.

You see, anybody can point to your child and say, "Yup! He has autism!" However, not everybody is *qualified* to make such a decision, nor do you have to accept the decision of people who are allegedly experts.

Many people think that pediatricians are qualified to make diagnoses of autism and mental retardation, but they usually aren't. They might be correct when they say that your child has autism, but the final evaluation and diagnosis should come from a child psychologist.

Generally speaking, child psychologists are better trained for this sort of thing. I am not saying that medical doctors aren't skilled professionals! Most are! But you wouldn't take your car into a plumber if it had an oil leak, would you? Medical doctors are great for physiological problems—colds, broken bones, illnesses, that kind of thing. But, as I will discuss later, there really aren't any accepted medical tests for autism. You need somebody who is familiar with the cognitive and social development of children. Your run-of-the-mill MD simply doesn't have that kind of expertise. So rather than going to your family doctor, take your young child to a qualified child psychologist to be officially assessed and diagnosed.

WHAT MAKES SOMEBODY QUALIFIED TO MAKE DIAGNOSES OF AUTISM?

So what makes a child psychologist "qualified"? That is a really good question! Unfortunately, it takes more than a degree to make somebody a skilled professional. Let me give you an example from my own life.

I have a learning disability and ADHD-C. For many years, I didn't know what was "wrong" with me. I couldn't concentrate. I found myself saying things without meaning to. I acted impulsively, often without realizing what I had done. I was very different from my peers and I didn't know why.

At the time, I had never heard of ADHD; I just figured that I was crazy or something. So I started seeing various counselors and psychiatrists who I hoped would help me figure out what was going on.

Some psychiatrists thought that I had an "anxiety disorder." Others thought that I just needed to "try harder to understand other people's perspectives and treat them better." Still others actually thought that I was an "abused" child and that I needed to "work through my feelings about my parents."

The point is, I went to see many, many different professionals who all had the correct credentials and degrees, but I really don't think that most of them were qualified to help me. They simply saw whatever it is that they wanted to see. They didn't look at me with an open mind.

The person who diagnosed me with an anxiety disorder specialized in anxiety disorders; the person who thought that my parents abused me (which they never did) worked primarily with abused populations.

I really can't stress this enough! You need to go to somebody who is not only knowledgeable but also willing to consider *ALL* other possibilities. Don't be surprised if you have to contact several specialists to finally come up with a diagnosis that makes sense!

In fact, a colleague of mine is working on a study examining how kids with autism are diagnosed and by whom. Her preliminary findings suggest that the average child sees six different "professionals" and receives four different diagnoses before being diagnosed with autism. Six professionals! And four different diagnoses! Pretty shocking, eh?

So, in order to be sure that your child is diagnosed correctly, you need to understand what autism is, how it is diagnosed, and by whom! Which is why I am here.

This leads me back to the original question, "How do you know if somebody is qualified to diagnose your child with autism?"

The first thing to look for obviously is a degree and license. Does the specialist have an actual degree from an accredited university? Is this person licensed to practice in your state? If so, good! That is the first step.

Also look at when this person graduated from school! Was it a long time ago? Was it more than twenty years ago?

I am not implying that older child psychologists are somehow less competent than professionals who are newer to the field. After all, there is a lot to be said for experience. However, the field of autism has changed *so* much that it is very important for you to find a professional who keeps up on the recent research and developments. For example, when I was a child, autism was thought to be caused by overprotective mothers! So make sure that your child's psychologist is staying current in the field.

How do you do that? How do you find out if a psychologist is staying current? Ask. Seriously! Finding a good child psychologist to help your child is probably going to be one of the most important decisions that you will ever make! So spend some time and "interview" each psychologist! Find out why they went into the field and how they keep their knowledge up-to-date! Ask them what conferences they go to and how often. Ask them if they present at any conferences or publish any papers in referred journal articles. In fact, ask them to provide you with a CV, or curriculum vitae.

Making Autism a Gift

I know that this sounds like you are being nosy or overly protective. But this is your child we are talking about! It is perfectly acceptable to ask professionals about their qualifications. And if they seem put out or annoyed or refuse to answer your questions, then find somebody else! Why would you want to work with somebody who doesn't help you make an informed decision?

Of course there are other ways to determine whether psychologists are qualified. For example, look at the professional journals in their offices. Are they new? Do they have anything to do with autism? Do they look read?! Are the pages bent back? Are the bindings broken? Are there notes in the margins? Are the corners dog-eared? Are there Post-it notes on the pages?

Also, ask around! Get to know other persons who are in a similar situation as you and ask if they know anything about the professionals whom you are investigating. Believe it or not, the autism community is pretty close-knit. Parents are often very willing to share information!

If you need help connecting with other families, please consult the support groups and organizations that are listed in the back of this book. You should be able to find some great sources of information regarding professionals in your neighborhood.

Again, what you are trying to do is make sure that the people who work with your child are qualified and have up-to-date knowledge. Please don't feel as if you are spying or intruding or being obnoxious. Ask any parent who has had a bad experience (and unfortunately there are many). It pays to do a little legwork to find the best possible person to work with your child!

HOW IS AUTISM DIAGNOSED?

Okay, so let's suppose that you have found a child psychologist whom you like. He of she is very willing to answer your questions, is

Robert Evert Cimera

open with his or her background, and clearly knows about all differ-ent kinds of disabilities. Now what? What is the diagnostic process? How is autism actually diagnosed?

As I said before, there are no universally accepted medical exams for autism. There are no blood tests or DNA analyses that can tell you for certain whether a child has autism. At the time I am writing this book (summer of 2006), there are some promising research de-velopments related to brain scans that in the future, may help doc-tors identify who has conditions such as autism, learning disabilities, mental retardation, and attention deficit hyperactivity disorders. But right now these tools are still being developed and evaluated.

Consequently, the procedure for diagnosing somebody with autism is as much an art as it is a hard science. Basically, child psy-chologists evaluate whether children meet the criteria that I dis-cussed in the first chapter. Specifically, they will try to ascertain whether a child exhibits (i) delays in communication, (ii) abnormal social skills, and (iii) repetitious behavior.

How this evaluation is done depends largely on the individual child and professional. Many child psychologists will actually sit down and play with children to see how they interact and verbalize or how they adjust to changes in their surroundings. Some child psychologists might ask your child to fill out various questionnaires or surveys. They might even administer certain standardized tests, such as achievement or aptitude tests, in an effort to determine where your child is at academically.

Although child psychologists may use different methods and means to diagnose your child, there are a few things that you need to look for to make sure that they are doing a good job.

For example, there is length of time. I know of several cases in which a "specialist" declared after a fifteen-minute "examination" that a child had autism. In case you don't know, fifteen minutes is a ludicrously brief period!

Making Autism a Gift

As I said earlier, diagnosing autism is as much an art as a science. Making an accurate diagnosis takes time and an in-depth knowledge of the child. No psychologist can get that kind of insight from a fifteen-minute visit!

How long should your child's psychologist take to diagnose your child? Well, it depends. Ask yourself this question: "How long does it take for the psychologist to see your *real* child?" By that I mean, how long does it take for your child to open up and act "normal," or more accurately, "like himself" around this perfect stranger?

This question is critical! If your child is naturally shy, introverted, or awkward around strangers or in new environments, it may take the psychologist several visits to get to know him. So please don't expect a quick decision. I would expect that the average diagnosis time is four to six weeks, with at least one visit to the child psychologist each week.

But that is just my estimate. Other people might expect this process to be longer or shorter. Again, the bottom line is, make sure that the psychologist spends enough time with your child to make an informed diagnosis!

Also, make sure that the psychologist uses a variety of assessment devices. For example, if the psychologist diagnoses your child with autism based only upon a single checklist, find a different psychologist!

IS THE DIAGNOSIS OF AUTISM CORRECT?

As you are probably becoming aware, the term "autism" is very subjective. So too is the diagnosis! I know several children who were diagnosed with autism by one doctor, with ADHD by another, and finally with reactive attachment disorder by a third. So how do you know if the diagnosis of autism is the correct one? Here are some questions to ask yourself.

Have Other Diagnoses Been Ruled Out?

Before accepting any diagnosis, whether it is autism or mental retardation or behavior disorder or whatever, make sure that all other diagnoses can be ruled out! For example, young children with a hearing impairment might look as if they have autism. Their language skills would probably be delayed. They might sway back and forth in an effort to hear what is going on around them. And they may appear a bit standoffish. So it is important that you rule hearing loss out before you accept a diagnosis of autism.

Ask what other diagnoses your child's psychologist considered prior to arriving at a diagnosis of autism. Ask how those conditions were eliminated from consideration. If the psychologist did not consider any other disability or cannot explain how other disabilities were ruled out, get another psychologist! An evaluator who only considers one condition is likely to find it far too often.

Does The Diagnosis Make Sense?

By now, you should have a basic understanding of what autism is and some of its common characteristics. So when the school psychologist diagnoses your child with autism, ask yourself, "Does that make sense? Does autism seem to fit my child?"

Remember, I might have a Ph.D., do research, and write books, and your child's psychologist might come from the best university and be extremely up-to-date about all of the latest trends and treatments. But *you* know your child better than either one of us! You have much better insight about your child than any professional!

So again, take a look at your child, a very honest, objective look. Then go over what I talked about in the first two chapters. Now ask yourself whether most of the pieces fall into place. I am not saying that I have described your child perfectly in the first two chapters, but there should be enough similarities for you to be nodding your head and saying, "Yes, that sounds like him!"

What if I Am Still In Doubt?

Let's suppose that you have met with a psychologist who believes your child has autism. However, you aren't really sure. You have read the first couple of chapters of this book and compared my descriptions to what you see in your child. But something just isn't lining up. You still aren't really sure that your child has autism.

If this is the case, then get a second opinion! Get a third opinion or a fourth! Talk to as many professionals as you need to in order to feel comfortable with the final diagnosis! After all, you don't want your child misdiagnosed! Imagine if your child really had ADHD or bipolar depression or schizophrenia or a hearing impairment, or is actually normal! Think about all of the wasted time and energy that would result from the wrong diagnosis! So if you are in doubt, keep searching for answers!

However, there is a big difference between real doubt and denial! Look, I know that you want the psychologist to come back and say, "Oh, everything is fine! Don't worry!" After all, nobody *wants* a child to have autism. Still, you have to be honest with yourself. Autism does exist and your child may have it. The sooner you get an accurate diagnosis, the better.

AFTER THE DIAGNOSIS

Okay, let us assume that you found a great, highly qualified child psychologist who conducted a thorough examination of your child using multiple measures over an extended period of time. Let us also assume that this child psychologist did in fact diagnose your child as being autistic. What now?

Well, the first thing to do is help yourself. You can't begin helping your child without first taking care of yourself. That probably sounds a bit self-centered, so let me explain.

Researchers have found that having a child diagnosed with a disability is extremely stressful on parents. In fact, it is very much like having a child die. Parents feel profound loss and go through a cycle of grief. You can't begin to help your child deal with his disability until you do! So let me talk about some of the feelings that you or your family members may be having.

Shock

The first feeling that probably hit you when you heard that your child had autism was most likely shock. Even if you suspected that there was a problem before you brought him in to be evaluated, actually hearing the word "autism" for the first time was probably like a kick in the stomach.

Trust me, this feeling will gradually fade. You will regain your breath, take a step back, and begin to evaluate what you have just heard. Don't panic. Everything is going to be fine.

Denial

After the initial shock of hearing that their children have autism wears off, many people go into denial. They simply don't want to believe that their children are "abnormal." A parent might say, "Whatever my child has, it isn't autism!" Or "My child is perfectly fine!" Sound familiar?

Now before we get too far into this conversation, I want to point out that not everybody who says, "My child doesn't have autism" is in denial. After all, maybe that person is correct; maybe the child really doesn't have autism! Remember, parents know their children better than any child psychologist, no matter how good the child psychologist is. So maybe the person isn't in denial. Maybe the person actually has some important insights to share! So listen before assuming that somebody is refusing to face the music.

However, for our purposes here, let's assume that the child really does have autism, but there are family members (perhaps your spouse is one) who simply don't believe it. What do you do? Well, the first thing is to understand why they are in denial.

Most people are in denial for two reasons. One is that they don't understand what autism is. They may think that they do, but in reality they don't. For example, my niece may or may not have autism. She is still being evaluated. However, my mother denies up and down that her granddaughter has anything wrong with her. She says things like, "Amy doesn't have autism! She is so energetic!" For some reason, my mother believes that autistic kids just sit there and stare at walls. Clearly, she is misinformed. In other words, her denial is stemming from a lack of accurate information.

In such situations, it is important for you to educate such family members. Provide them with information about what autism is and isn't. Maybe you could have them visit some of the websites at the back of this book, have them speak to parents who have autistic children, or have them meet actual autistic kids! Maybe you could even lend them a copy of this book! Once they understand what autism is, they are more likely to leave the denial stage.

The second reason people are often in denial is because they don't see their children as exhibiting autistic behavior. That is, they understand what autism is (perhaps you have explained it to them), but they still don't see how it fits their children's characteristics. A parent might say things like, "My child is just a late talker! She'll catch up. I was a late talker too! I am not autistic!"

In such cases, it is good to *discuss* what the family members see in the child and what others have noticed. Notice that I used and emphasized the word "discuss." You can't push people out of denial. You can't "make them see" their error. You have to let them make up their own minds. How do you do this?

Well, like I said, discuss the situation with such family members. Be open and honest and really listen to their beliefs. I would suggest having them sit down with the child psychologist and go point by point over the assessment report. Ask them which of the characteristics they see in the child and which they don't. When they don't see a particular symptom that everybody else perceives, give examples of situations where the child has acted "autistic."

Again, the idea isn't to debate or to "convince." Instead, provide evidence and allow them to eventually come around. Once faced with the facts, people usually see the light—at least eventually. They may need time. They may have to relive the "shock" phase. Don't pressure them to move faster than they are capable. You'll just add to the problem.

When the family members who are in denial offer other suggestions, such as the child is a "late bloomer" or "maybe he has a learning disability," listen and consider what is being said. Then explain why you think that those explanations don't fit the facts.

You have to talk them through it logically. Let them express why they don't think the diagnosis of autism is correct and then address each of their concerns as they arise. When they run out of objections, they are likely to move to the next stage.

Grief

The next phase that people tend to go through when their children are diagnosed with a disability such as autism is grief. Unfortunately, getting people past this stage is easier said than done. However, if you understand why they are feeling the way that they do, you might increase your chances of helping.

Making Autism a Gift

As an expecting father, I am continually having visions of my soon-to-be daughter and me. She isn't even born yet and I still picture her getting her first tooth, going to school for the first time, crying over her first broken heart, winning her first Nobel Peace Prize and so on. I have pictured her entire life in so many ways that it is like we have already lived through so much.

When people hear the word "autism," they often feel like they have lost those visions and dreams. A parent may think, "My child will never fall in love, get married, or win the Nobel Prize." The feelings are very real and very profound.

Even as I sit here typing this while I am imagining my daughter with autism, I feel a growing sense of sadness and loss. In a word, I feel grief. It is as if my little girl, who has been living with me in my imagination for all of these months, has somehow died.

Keep in mind that I am just imagining what it would be like if my daughter had autism. Envision how deep these feelings of sorrow would be if she actually did!

The odd thing about grief is that it can be based upon beliefs that are completely illogical. I am very familiar with autism. I know people with autism who are brilliant, successful, and happy. In short, they are everything that I want my daughter to be. I know in my head that autism doesn't mean a death sentence or a miserable life of despair. Still, I would feel bad if my child was autistic.

Unlike the shock phase, the grief phase never really ends for many people. Many parents end up spending the rest of their lives "mourning" the loss of their "perfect" children. In fact, I know a lot of fathers who are like that. They do whatever they can to avoid addressing their grief. They either throw themselves into their work, spend all of their time with their "non-disabled" children, or play golf. It is very sad.

Robert Evert Cimera

So what can you do if you know some family members who are stuck in the grief stage? Well, first of all, as with people in denial, you can't force them to change. You can't make them see the logic of their situation. Having a child with autism isn't logical. It is an emotional state of being.

So what can you do to help people who are grieving through all of these emotions? Listen. Again, don't try to convince them why they shouldn't feel the way that they do. Don't be all perky and say, "You should be happy that things aren't worse!" Let them vent and talk through their feelings.

If they can't open up and talk with you, you might have them contact somebody else. Maybe you could suggest that they try to find a professional counselor, who can be very helpful. Or have them join a support group, such as those listed in the back of this book! Talking to others who have actually gone through the same ordeal can help people see that they aren't alone.

Anger

Some people who have children with disabilities often feel anger or resentment over their situation. Most of the time, these emotions stem from displaced grief. People are upset and they don't know what to do, so they end up letting their anxiety, frustration, and sadness turn into more hostile emotions.

Usually, people who are angry will be angry at "the world" or "God." Other times, they will even blame their spouses for "causing" the autism. This was true particularly when people thought autism was caused by overprotective parents. As a result, it is very important that someone in anger stage be addressed quickly.

Addressing anger is probably best done by a trained therapist or counselor, especially if the anger is directed toward somebody, such as the other parent or the child. But support groups of other parents can

Making Autism a Gift

also be a big help. If you know people who are in the anger stage, try to be supportive and enable them to talk to somebody about their feelings.

Acceptance

The final stage that people will hopefully reach is acceptance. This is when people accept the fact that their child is different than what they expected. Moreover, they come to believe that being "different" is okay. They learn to see their child as an individual with certain strengths and limitations, just like any other child.

A wonderful example of acceptance comes from Christopher Reeve, the actor who fell from a horse and became a quadriplegic. In an interview before he died, Reeve said something to the effect of, "We [he, his wife, and son] were on one road before the accident. Now we are on a different one. We had dreams before. Now we have different ones."

His point was that just because you aren't where you thought you would be, that doesn't mean life stops. Life gives you certain challenges and you try to overcome them no matter what they are. I suppose that sounds kind of like a cliché. But it is true. The alternative is to just wait for life to end.

Okay, I'll try not to preach. After all, I am probably preaching to the choir. If you are sitting here reading this book, you are most likely well on your way to finding acceptance. However, I want to talk a little bit about what you should do once you are in the acceptance phase.

Coming to terms with your situation isn't the final destination; at least I don't think so. I personally believe that once you have accepted the fact that your child has autism, it is your obligation to help other people who need help facing the same trials. I am sure that people helped you on your journey; hopefully, you are willing to do the same for somebody else.

Robert Evert Cimera

What can you do to help other families? First, you can join support groups and become active in the "autism community." Maybe could even start your own support group or website. Share your experiences and resources. And above all, be willing to help where you can.

CAUSES OF AUTISM

Every month or so, I put on workshops or give presentations about various topics related to special education. After each appearance, I try to stay behind and speak one-on-one with my audience. Nearly every single time I present on mental retardation or autism, a handful of parents will come up to me and ask what caused the disability.

It is a gut-wrenching conversation with a huge impact on the health of the child's family. Basically, parents want to know, "Did I cause my child to be like this?" They want to understand why things turned out that way and they turn to me for definitive answers.

Generally, most experts agree that autism is attributed to abnormalities in the child's brain. Unfortunately, they simply don't know what causes these abnormalities. Yes, there are groups of studies that say this or that. For example, some people point to genetic factors. Others say that autism is caused by environmental toxins or allergic reactions to vaccinations, particularly the MMR shots (measles, mumps, rubella). I even know of some "experts" who claim autism is the result of "God's will."

The problem in the scientific community is that autism is so poorly defined. Further, it really is a spectrum of somewhat related disorders, not one single condition. Consequently, it is exceedingly difficult to determine what actually causes it. After all, if you study a thousand kids with autism, you are likely to find many factors that are common to some, but not others. For instance, some children might have the same genetic markers while other children might have been exposed to mercury or allergenic substances in vaccinations.

Still, people always want to know what causes autism. This is what I tell them.

Although nobody really knows for sure, it seems that autism is caused by a myriad of factors that often interact. There is most likely a genetic component that enables some people to have a greater disposition to having autism. There are also probably environmental agents, such as mercury poisoning and industrial pollutants, that increase the susceptibility of a fetus to develop the brain abnormalities that lead to autism.

The cause of autism most likely isn't an exact recipe where somebody has to have so much of X (e.g., genetic makeup) and then be exposed to so much of Y (e.g., mercury, lead, or MMR shots). There are most likely many different avenues that result in somebody having autism. Some people have autism purely because of their DNA. Other people would have been "normal" had they not gotten such and such vaccination. Still others could have autism because of a combination of the two factors.

What experts *do* know about autism is that it is not caused by parenting styles. Kids don't develop autism because their parents are too lenient or too strict. Despite what some doctors and researchers might say, autism is not caused by overprotective parents. Further, it is not caused by bumps to the head or allergic reactions to food.

In the end, parents cannot "cause" their children to have autism, other than via genetics. So I try to get parents of autistic children to think about the future rather than the past. I ask them: "How are you going to make the most of the situation?" "How are you going to be the best possible parent that you can be?" To me, these are far more important questions than "What causes autism?"

Robert Evert Cimera

PREVALENCE OF AUTISM

In addition to wanting to know what causes autism, people frequently ask me how prevalent it is. This question can answered with a little more certainty—a little more— but not with complete accuracy.

According to the federal government, 65,424 students between the ages of six and twenty-one who were enrolled in special education programs during the 2002–2003 school year had a primary diagnosis of autism. This represents 1.1 percent of all special education students in the United States.

Unfortunately, this number is a bit misleading. It suggests that relatively few people have autism, a situation that is no longer the case, as I will soon discuss. The federal government's number (i.e., 65,424) only includes students with a primary diagnosis of autism. There are many more who are diagnosed with behavior disorders, communication disorders, or mental retardation.

To get a better feel for the prevalence of autism, picture a room filled with 166 newborn babies. Of these children, one will be diagnosed with autism. Stated another way, according to the Centers for Disease Control and Prevention, approximately 0.6 percent of Americans (or 1.5 million) have some form of autism. However, even this statistic doesn't tell the whole story.

Nearly every longitudinal study indicates that the prevalence of autism is increasing and that it is increasing quickly. In fact, a recent review of the scientific literature found that the number of reported cases of autism has increased 10-17 percent each year since 1990. Why?

There are four plausible explanations for this remarkable increase. First, more people are aware of autism. With more people aware of it, children who would have otherwise gone undiagnosed are now being identified.

Making Autism a Gift

Second, the definition of autism and its related conditions is constantly being changed and revised. Consequently, more and more people meet the criteria for autism. In other words, the definitions are being broadened so that they capture individuals who would have not been considered "autistic" thirty years ago.

Third, greater numbers of people are actually "developing" autism. This could be because there are more toxins in the environment that cause autism or because more people are allergic to the new formula used in the MMR vaccinations. These issues, of course, are hotly debated. Obviously, businesses that release mercury in the environment (e.g., paper mills) don't want to be blamed for the increase in disabilities, nor do the pharmaceutical companies who make inoculations.

Finally, the prevalence of autism could be increasing because new technology is enabling medically fragile babies to live well into adulthood. These babies, who would have died at birth had they been born fifteen or twenty years ago, are in essence adding to the number of people who have autism.

So which of these factors is it? What is causing the increase? A significant percentage of credible researchers seem to indicate that it is a combination of all four factors, with the most weight being given to the first three factors (i.e., increased awareness of autism, changes in diagnostic criteria, and an actual increase in new cases). But, again, all of this is hotly debated.

For our purposes, I don't want to focus too much on these issues. The data and the debates around them are interesting if you are a researcher. But if you are a parent of a child with autism, these statistics are meaningless. Your child has autism, so the relevant prevalence rate is 100 percent. Consequently, I would much rather focus on helping you help your child than spend too much time debating numbers. However, I want to end this section with a few facts that might make you feel a little better.

Autism is not associated with any ethnicity or race. You are just as likely to have a child with autism if you are black, white, Jewish, or Hungarian. Autism isn't associated with socioeconomic status either. So rich parents have children with autism at the same rates as parents who are poor or "middle class." Finally, although rates of autism vary from location to location (the area in which I live allegedly has the highest rate of autism in North America), people with autism live in every country, state, and town.

People with autism are everywhere. You, your child, and your family are not alone.

SUMMARY

In this chapter, I talked about issues related to diagnosing individuals with autism. Specifically, if a child is in special education, the *official* diagnosis must come from a group of school personnel that is often called the M-Team. However, many young children are diagnosed before they even enter school. These children should be diagnosed by credible psychologists.

Please make sure your child's psychologist is skilled and has up-to-date information. Ask your child's psychologist about other possible diagnoses and why they have been ruled out. Also make sure that the psychologist spends enough time with your child to make a well-informed decision!

Finally, in this chapter I discussed the causes and prevalence of autism. Although there is considerable debate in the field regarding these two topics, most reliable sources agree on three things. First, autism is most likely caused by several interrelated factors. Second, the number of people with autism is increasing. Third, and most important, parents don't cause their children's autism (other than via genetics).

FOUR

"Of Course, It Could Also Be . . . "*:
Conditions Associated with Autism

One of the main difficulties of writing a book about autism is that I am trying to describe an extremely diverse population. It is like talking about Americans or Norwegians, or people who are left-handed or near-sighted. It is impossible to accurately describe *everybody* who falls under these broad categories. Why? Because there are so many conditions that occur within each of these populations that further diversifies them. For example, you could have a left-handed albino with a learning disability or a black-haired Norwegian who has a stuttering problem.

As I have been saying since page one, your child with autism may be a genius and become a university professor (not that a person has to be a genius to be a university professor!). Or your child with autism could also have profound mental retardation and require lifelong constant supervision. Or your child can fall anywhere else on life's infinite continuum. People with autism are as diverse as

---

* After spending nearly twenty minutes defending her diagnosis of autism, a special education teacher with whom I worked stopped suddenly and looked at the student's devastated parents. "Of course," she muttered, "it could also be QLD syndrome." QLD stood for "queer little duck," which was this teacher's way of saying that sometimes people are just different. It doesn't mean that they have any "disability."

---

people in general. However, maybe I can help you understand general subgroups within this population.

What I would like to do in this chapter is talk about some of the other conditions that are associated with autism. Notice that I said "are associated" and not "always coincide." It is very important for you to understand that people with autism don't always have to have mental retardation or Rett's syndrome or savant syndrome or any of the other conditions that I am about to discuss.

Further, each condition is an eclectic group of symptoms within itself. Obviously I can't tell you everything about mental retardation within a few pages. But maybe I can help you understand the other conditions besides autism that your child might have.

As you read this chapter, you might come across some conditions and think, "No, that's not my child. He doesn't have that." And that is fine. At least you will know a little bit more than you did before. Plus, you will get to rule some things out.

On the other hand, you might come across a few conditions that sound *exactly* like your child or some that might describe him in a vague sense. In which case, you can go to the resource section at the back of this book and learn more about whatever it is that you think that your child has. Regardless of your situation, I hope that this chapter helps you help your child.

MENTAL RETARDATION

The first condition that I want to discuss is mental retardation. As I mentioned in earlier chapters, as many as 70 percent of children with autism are also diagnosed with mental retardation. However, I personally believe that this number is greatly inflated. I mean, how can you measure somebody's intelligence when the person is unwilling to participate in the assessments? But, I am getting ahead of myself. First you need to understand what mental retardation is!

So what is mental retardation? It probably isn't what you think. You probably think it means that people are "eternal children" or that they stop learning after they reach a certain level of knowledge. Maybe you even think that people with mental retardation are "stupid." None of these assumptions are true. People with mental retardation aren't children. They don't stop learning. And they certainly aren't stupid!

Children with mental retardation will grow up and face many of the problems in life that adults without mental retardation face. They will fall in and out of love. They will have sexual feelings. They will even worry about death and dying.

So what is mental retardation? Well, like autism, mental retardation is a term used to describe people with various characteristics. Specifically, a person with mental retardation has

> *Sub-Average Intelligence*
> *Poor Adaptive Skills*
> *Symptoms Before Age Eighteen*

Let me talk about each of these.

Sub-Average Intelligence

You are probably wondering how "sub-average" somebody's intelligence has to be in order for that person to be considered "mentally retarded." But before I talk about cut offs for IQs, let me first talk about what intelligence is and isn't!

Most people seem to think that intelligence is how much someone knows; that is, if someone knows X amount, he is "X" intelligent. Therefore, if somebody else has twice the amount of knowledge as "X," that individual then is twice as intelligent. But this isn't correct.

Robert Evert Cimera

Intelligence isn't about what or how much people know, but how quickly they are able to learn. Think of intelligence as the processing speed of your brain. An intelligent person is able to learn faster than a "less intelligent" person.

"But doesn't processing speed equate to amount of knowledge?" you are probably wondering. After all, a person who can process a lot in a short period of time will undoubtedly acquire more knowledge than somebody who is less intelligent and therefore processes information more slowly than the first person. Not really. Let me give you an example.

Imagine two children. One is super smart. Let's say she has an IQ of 130 (I'll talk about what IQ means a little later). The other child has intelligence that is a little below average. He has an IQ of 90.

The child with a 130 IQ is able to learn very quickly. As soon as her teacher gives an example of a mathematical problem or states a historical fact, she has learned the underlying concepts. When she learned that 2+2 = 4, she also learned that 2 million plus 2 million equals 4 million. In other words, she understands most things right after they are explained to her and she is able to apply the related concepts.

The child with a 90 IQ is able to learn, but does so more slowly than his classmate with a 130 IQ. Rather than understanding the concept of addition after one example (e.g., 2+2 = 4), he requires greater exposure and practice. Once he learns his addition tables up to 10+10, he then comprehends that the principle behind 2+2 is the same as 45,614 + 6.

Again, both students eventually learn the concept of addition. But the child with a higher IQ is able to do it faster and with less intervention from the teacher. The child with the lower IQ needs a little more time and help. But he is still able to learn.

Now back to the earlier question about amount of knowledge and degree of intelligence. It would appear that since the student with a 130 IQ is able to learn so much faster than her peer, she should have more knowledge. But this doesn't always happen.

You see, as the student with the 90 IQ is trying to learn addition, his classmate with a 130 IQ is sitting calmly at her desk waiting, but not learning any more math. So even though she learns more quickly, she is exposed to the same amount of content as the rest of the class. By the end of the school year, she might have picked up some extra pieces of information along the way, but generally, she knows what the rest of the class knows (provided that the rest of the class mastered the material that the teacher covered).

Let me give you another example. As a university professor, I have seen a number of students with various "degrees" of intelligence. Now you would think that my students with "high IQs" would do better and learn more in my classes than students with low IQs. But it is usually the other way around.

Many of my students who have low IQs have always struggled in school, so when they get to college, they are in the habit of working very hard. They read everything very thoroughly, show up to class on time, take notes, and bust their butts to learn what I am teaching.

Many of my "gifted" students have never really had to work hard to learn. Consequently, they often don't try. They might show up for class and they might not. Moreover, they might not learn things on their own. They only focus on "what is on the test." In other words, my "average" students often know more than my "gifted" students because their motivation to learn is higher.

The idea is you might be incredibly smart and able to learn things immensely quickly. However, if you don't want to learn or put yourself in stimulating environments, you won't acquire much knowledge. Consequently, somebody with half of your intelligence might actually know far more than you do. Make sense?

Robert Evert Cimera

Okay, let's start applying this to mental retardation. The average person has an IQ of 100. If you look at the figure below, you will see that an IQ of 100 is located right in the middle of the distribution. Notice how the distribution of IQs bulges up in the middle so that there is kind of a "bell-shaped" curve. That indicates that most people have IQs that are around 100. If you look at the IQ scores that are further away from 100, either above or below, you'll see that there are fewer and fewer people with those IQs. In other words, there are theoretically more people with "average" IQs than really high IQs or really low IQs.

Note that I said "theoretically." There are many people who don't believe in intelligence the way that I am discussing it. Some people believe in multiple types of intelligence. So someone might be really smart in math, but not so smart in social situations, and above average in leadership and so forth. They believe that "intelligence" cannot be reduced to one single score. There are also scientists who don't believe that intelligence can be measured, so why even try to put a number on it. Still, let me continue with this discussion and assume that intelligence exists and that it can be quantified by a single number (e.g., an IQ score).

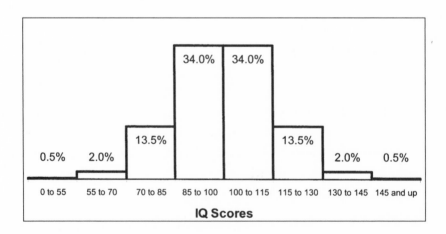

Making Autism a Gift

So you now know that 100 is an average score; that is, if everybody in the world stood in a line starting from the smartest person to . . . well, the not so smart person, the person in the exact middle would have an IQ score of 100. Now I'll answer the question that you probably had earlier: "How 'sub-average' does somebody's IQ have to be in order for the person to be considered 'mentally retarded'?" Good question!

Although the definition of mental retardation differs as frequently as the definition of autism, it is generally agreed that the uppermost IQ for people with mental retardation is around 70. Why 70?

No real reason, actually. Basically, researchers merely felt that roughly 2.5 percent of the population should have mental retardation, and that is the number of people who have IQs below 70. See how I got that? I just added all of the percentages of the two leftmost bars (see the figure). If I were to add up the percentage of people with IQ scores of 100 or below, I would get 50 percent. So, in other words, if researchers set the IQ for mental retardation at 100, half of us would be mentally retarded!

Again, I want to stress that there is nothing magical about an IQ of 70. It isn't like an IQ of 71 is "fine" and an IQ of 70 is somehow really bad. An IQ of 70 is simply an arbitrary cut off point used to designate what mental retardation is. As a matter of fact, this cut off point has been changed considerably over the years. Not too long ago, people with IQs below 85 were considered mentally retarded.

In the future, it is likely that it will change again. Indeed, lawmakers have been discussing lowering the cut off point so that fewer people qualify as mentally retarded; thus, fewer students would be given special education services. In other words, by changing the definition of "mental retardation," lawmakers can reduce the costs of special education. But I am getting a bit off the topic.

Robert Evert Cimera

The main points here are (i) intelligence (as designated by an IQ) is supposed to measure how quickly people learn, not how much they know, and (ii) the IQ range for mental retardation is usually identified at 70 and below. However, this cut off point is completely arbitrary. So, therefore, kids with mental retardation aren't stupid. They don't stop learning. They aren't eternal children. They are simply people who don't learn as quickly as the average person!

Poor Adaptive Skills

So people with mental retardation have sub-average IQs. And "sub-average" is usually considered to be 70 and below. But there is more to mental retardation than just the inability to learn quickly. People with mental retardation must also have poor adaptive skills in multiple areas of life.

"Adaptive skills" are skills that enable people to function in a changing world. They include, but are not limited to, social skills, recreational skills, self-care skills, and vocational skills. Basically, adaptive skills enable people to deal with the unexpected and to reason things out. You might say they are problem-solving skills. Let me give you an example.

Yesterday, for whatever reason, a warning message appeared on my computer that said I was no longer connected to the Internet. While this wasn't the end of the world, it was rather bothersome. I was supposed to appear on National Public Radio in a few days, and I was expecting an important e-mail telling me where I needed to be and when.

At any rate, I had no idea why my Internet service wasn't working. I fiddled with the cord that connected my computer to the phone jack. I rebooted my computer. I reinstalled my Internet program. Eventually, I figured out what was wrong.

Making Autism a Gift

Nobody taught me how to fix this problem. I wasn't following any directions. I was just winging it. I was problem solving. I started with a hypothesis that the computer wasn't connected to the phone jack, checked that possibility out, and then moved on to another idea. I kept adapting.

You do this all of the time. When you are driving to work and the road is closed, you find another way. When you are making dinner and realize that you don't have a key ingredient, you improvise.

These are adaptive skills. For the most part, you and I have fairly good adaptive skills. We might lose our cars from time to time in large parking lots during holiday shopping. Or we might burn our dinners in the oven once in a while. But generally speaking, we can adapt to our environments and deal with life's little challenges.

People with mental retardation, on the other hand, have difficulty dealing with change. It isn't that they can't problem solve. They can. It is just that they have a harder time coming up with successful strategies. For example, they might not think to check if the computer was connected to the phone jack, or they might get lost trying to go around a closed road. If something unexpected happens or their routine changes, people with mental retardation will often have difficulty coping.

Now, you are probably wondering, "Don't poor adaptive skills and sub-average intelligence go together? I mean, doesn't one kind of lead to the other?" Not always. Let me explain.

I had a foster child named Marky. Marky had kind of a tragic history. Among other things, he had been to fourteen different schools in four years. His mother kept moving and getting kicked out of apartments. Needless to say, Marky hadn't learned much in the short amount of time he had been in class. He could read a few words, count to twenty or so, and write his name, but that is about it as far as his academic abilities went.

If you were to give Marky an intelligence test, it would probably reveal his IQ score to be below 70. However, if you were to examine Marky's adaptive skills, you would find them to be excellent. While living on the streets for several years, Marky had learned how to manipulate situations and adapt very quickly. In short, even if he has a low IQ score, he isn't mentally retarded because his adaptive behavior skills aren't underdeveloped.

I'll give you a reverse example. Albert Einstein was brilliant! He was one of the smartest people on the planet. However, he had remarkably poor adaptive behavior skills. He would lose the glasses that he was wearing and set fire to his house by accidentally burning his food; he even got "stuck" on a rowboat because he forgot the oars! Again, he didn't have mental retardation even though he had very poor adaptive behavior skills.

Age of Onset

Okay, so to have mental retardation, an individual must have a slower ability to learn than the average person. A person must also have difficulty dealing with changes and adapting to unexpected events. Finally, in order for you to have mental retardation, you must have the symptoms by a certain age.

As with autism, mental retardation is a "developmental disability." That means it must occur before the child reaches adulthood (usually thought to be by age eighteen). So if an elderly person begins to lose her ability to process information quickly and also develops poor adaptive behavior skills, she doesn't have mental retardation. She is most likely just getting old or she may have Alzheimer's.

Making Autism a Gift

SAVANT SYNDROME

So that is mental retardation. As I said before, many children with autism also have mental retardation. But remember, not all of them do. The next condition that is often associated with autism is sometimes called "savant syndrome." People with this condition have also been called "idiot savants," but that term is considered archaic and derogatory.

If you have seen the movie *Rain Man*, you probably have a general idea of what savant syndrome is all about. Simply put, some individuals with autism possess remarkable abilities or talents in very narrow areas. For example, in the movie *Rain Man*, Dustin Hoffman's character was able to do complex math problems in his head, memorize everything that he read, and count stuff (e.g., cards, toothpicks) within seconds.

While it is rare that somebody would have multiple gifts, savants are not uncommon. Recent studies have found that one out of ten individuals with autism have savant abilities to some degree. These abilities are typically broken down into two categories: splinter skills and prodigious.

"Splinter skills" usually refer to abilities that are above the child's abilities in other areas, but not necessarily above the abilities of other people. So, for example, if a first grader with autism was able to read at the first or second grade level while all of his other abilities were well behind those of his peers, you could say that he had a splinter skill in reading.

Prodigious individuals, on the other hand, would have skills that exceed even exceptional individuals. For example, a prodigious first grader might do college-level calculus!

I should point out that the terms "savant" and "splinter skills" are often used interchangeably, so don't get confused.

Robert Evert Cimera

You might be wondering, "Is it possible for somebody with mental retardation to also be a savant?"

The answer is yes, although it isn't as common individuals with mental retardation. This probably perplexes you, so let me explain.

As I discussed earlier, intelligence isn't how much people know, but how quickly they learn. And although people with mental retardation learn less efficiently than do other people, they *can* learn. So how do people who learn so poorly become savants? Nobody really knows; however, the current school of thought is that they tend to obsess on certain topics and behaviors, which leads to their incredible abilities. In other words, practice makes perfect!

CHILDHOOD DISINTEGRATIVE DISORDER

Also called "disintegrative psychosis" or "Heller's syndrome," childhood disintegrative disorder (CDD) is a condition that is often confused with true autism. The difference between the two is that children with CDD begin life perfectly normal. They laugh, they giggle, they interact, and they reach all of their developmental milestones just like other children. Unfortunately, by around age three or four, they begin losing some of their skills.

Now, when I say that they lose some of their skills, I don't mean like how a student will forget what he learned in algebra class over the summer. What I mean is that they begin to lose vocabulary that they used frequently. They stop making eye contact or interacting with other people. They may even lose motor abilities, such as walking or crawling.

Early warning signs of CDD include increased motor activity, irritability, anxiety, and withdrawal from social contact. Sometimes this regression is gradual and is barely noticeable at first. Other times it is very abrupt and is mistaken for a "phase." Regardless of its progression, by age ten, children with CDD look and act as if they have autism.

Years ago, many professionals doubted that CDD existed. Parents would tell their doctors that their children were regressing, but this was often attributed to parents being "overanxious" or "overprotective" of their children. Sometimes a parent would bring in a child who already appeared to have autism and explain that the child was once "normal." But this belief was chalked up to the parent's wishful thinking.

Now, however, CDD is seen as being very real. Regrettably, its prevalence rate is increasing as fast as autism and nobody understands why.

As with autism in general, some evidence suggests that CDD is caused by a reaction to MMR shots (measles, mumps, and rubella). Other studies seem to indicate that CDD is caused by toxins in the environment, such as mercury. But research is still pretty scant on the subject. The only areas that the research seems to agree upon is that CDD usually leads to profound mental retardation and that it affects more boys than girls.

There have been some breakthroughs where children with CDD have "awakened" from their "autism" and returned to normal. But the number of cases actually documented can probably be counted on one hand. Still, such extremely rare occurrences give hope that future research can determine what is causing the regression and either prevent future children from having trouble or actually reverse the effects that have already transpired.

RETT'S DISORDER

As with CDD, Rett's disorder is often confused with autism. Like CDD, individuals with Rett's disorder begin life appearing and acting

Robert Evert Cimera

like "normal" children. They interact appropriately and reach the developmental milestones on time. However, between five months and two years old, these individuals begin to lose previously acquired skills. Eventually, all receptive and expressive language skills are lost.

Individuals with Rett's disorder also develop stereotyped movements. For example, they typically wring their hands as if they were washing. They may also compulsively lick, tap, or bite their fingers as well as slap themselves.

Unlike individuals with CDD, individuals with Rett's disorder experience a slowing in the growth of their heads so that their head circumference ends up being much smaller than is typical. They also develop poor motor and muscle control so that they may have difficulty walking or controlling their posture.

Although presently a rare condition, recent research seems to suggest that the incidence rate of Rett's syndrome is increasing. Approximately 6 or 7 females per 100,000 will develop this condition. Rett's syndrome does not appear in males.

FRAGILE X SYNDROME

Fragile X syndrome is another condition that often mimics autism. As with individuals with autism, individuals with fragile X syndrome experience significant language delays and dysfunctions, including periods of echolalia. Additionally, individuals with fragile X syndrome will display many stereotypic behaviors (especially hand flapping) and impaired social skills, including excessive shyness.

Physically, individuals with fragile X syndrome can look very different from individuals with autism. They tend to have large oblong-shaped heads and narrow faces with big ears and protruding foreheads. They may also have decreased muscle tone and hypertensibility of their joints.

Making Autism a Gift

Unlike Rett's syndrome, fragile X syndrome affects both males and females; however, the condition affects members of each gender in different ways. Specifically, males with fragile X tend to have moderate mental retardation. Females are more likely to have mild learning difficulties, particularly in math, as well as depression and anxiety.

Fragile X syndrome is caused by a malformation on the tip of the X chromosome—hence the name. Although individuals with this condition often behave as if they have autism, this physiological difference sets the two conditions apart.

ASPERGER'S SYNDROME, OR ASPERGER'S DISORDER

Although officially added to the American Psychiatric Association's (APA's) *Diagnostic and Statistical Manual of Mental Disorders* (*DSM*) only in 1994, Asperger's has become a very hot topic. In fact, it is receiving so much attention that I could write several books on it alone.

So what is it? Well, remember in the first chapter how I described autism as a spectrum of related disorders with somewhat similar characteristics? Think of Asperger's as one of those related disorders.

The best way that I can describe Asperger's is to have you think of an autistic child. Now, give that child average or above-average intelligence. So his IQ is likely to be over 100.

Also, imagine that the child doesn't have delays in language acquisition. So he learns to speak like any of his normal peers. However, although he has age-appropriate (or better) vocabulary, he may have extreme difficulty with receptive language. For example, he may take things very literally, so if somebody says, "It is coming down in buckets outside," he actually expects to see buckets of rain lying around on the sidewalk!

He will also have problems with unspoken cues, such as how people stand or look. People with Asperger's struggle with these non-verbal cues. They might stand too close to people and not realize that they are being annoying. They might misinterpret smiles as signs of hostility.

As with people who have autism, people with Asperger's are likely to display many repetitious and obsessive behaviors. They might rock back and forth, become preoccupied with various topics of conversation or objects, or develop ritualistic routines. They may also have strong attachments to things and environments and will have adverse reactions to changes. Consequently, transitions from one activity to another are often problematic for them.

Moreover, individuals with Asperger's are likely to be extremely sensitive to certain sensory inputs. For example, they might react negatively to various smells, sounds, or tastes. They also are likely to have exceptionalities, such as those described for savant syndrome above.

If you want a more precise definition of Asperger's, here is what APA says it is:

A. Qualitative impairment in social interactions, as manifested by two or more of the following:
   (1) marked impairment in the use of multiple nonverbal behaviors such as maintaining eye contact, facial expression, body postures, and gestures to regulate social interaction.
   (2) failure to develop peer relationships appropriate to developmental level.
   (3) a lack of spontaneous seeking to share enjoyment, interests, or achievements with other people (e.g., by a lack of showing, bringing, or pointing out objects of interest to other people).

Making Autism a Gift

    (4) lack of social or emotional reciprocity.

B. Restricted repetitive and stereotyped patterns of behavior, interests, and activities as manifested by at least one of the following:

    (1) encompassing preoccupation with one or more stereotyped and restrictive patterns of interest that is abnormal either in intensity or focus.

    (2) apparently inflexible adherence to specific, nonfunctional routines or rituals.

    (3) stereotyped and repetitive motor mannerisms (e.g., hand or finger flapping or twisting, or complex whole-body movements).

    (4) persistent preoccupation with parts of objects.

C. The disturbance causes clinically significant impairment in social, occupational, or other important areas of functioning.

D. There is no clinically significant general delay in language (e.g., single words used by age 2, communicative phrases used by age 3).

E. There is no clinically significant delay in cognitive development or in the development of age-appropriate self-help skills, adaptive behavior (other than in social interaction), and curiosity about the environment in childhood.

F. Criteria are not met for another specific Pervasive Developmental Disorder or Schizophrenia.

(DSM-IV-TR, p. 84)

So that is Asperger's syndrome. Does it sound like your child? I should probably point out that there is considerable disagreement in the field as to whether Asperger's is a "type" of autism (e.g., "high functioning autism") or a separate condition altogether. Many people even consider it an example of a non-verbal learning disability.

If you would like more information about Asperger's (or any of the conditions that I am discussing here), please consult the resources at the back of this book. They should be a big help.

Robert Evert Cimera

EPILEPSY

You probably already know what epilepsy is. It is a condition characterized by frequent seizures. A seizure is an "electrical storm" in the brain that causes people to experience an altered state of consciousness. I'll talk about types of seizures shortly.

I want to discuss epilepsy because children with autism are more likely to have epilepsy than their non-disabled peers. Why? Nobody really seems to know. However, some studies suggest that the psychoactive medications that many autistics take to control their behaviors might be partly to blame. Others indicate that abnormalities in the structure of the brain that results in autism also increases a child's risk of having epilepsy.

Regardless of why individuals with autism have seizures, I think that it is critical for you to know something about them. After all, your child could be having seizures without you realizing it. And, if your child *is* having seizures, you will need to know how to address them.

First of all, there are many types of seizures. There is the tonic-clonic seizure (also called "grand mal") that most people think of when they hear the word "seizure." Tonic-clonic seizures are characterized by a loss of consciousness, sudden stiffness throughout the body, and violent convulsions. Individuals experiencing a tonic-clonic seizure may lose bladder or bowel control and could begin foaming at the mouth.

Although most people are familiar with tonic-clonic seizures, they are not the most common types of seizures. For example, far more people have absence seizures (also called "petit mal") than tonic-clonic. Individuals experiencing absence seizures will stare off into space, blinking frequently. Their eyes may look vacant and dreamy. Their heads might bob up and down slightly as if they were saying yes.

Making Autism a Gift

Absence seizures last only a few seconds, after which time the individual regains consciousness. Individuals with absence seizures are likely to have dozens of seizures (often occurring in clusters) per day and never know it.

People who are having myoclonic seizures experience sudden jerking motions, usually in one part of the body. For example, the right arm might abruptly flinch or the left leg might kick to one side. These jerking movements might look like simple muscle spasms, but they are actually seizures.

Atonic seizures are when a person's body goes suddenly limp, like a rag doll or a cooked noodle. Conversely, tonic seizures are characterized by a sudden stiffness throughout the body, as if it has been turned to stone. As with individuals experiencing tonic-clonic and absence seizures, individuals who are experiencing atonic or tonic seizures will not be aware of what is happening to them.

Frontal lobe seizures produce many different effects. Individuals with such seizures may experience an odd feeling in their faces, legs, or hands. They might develop a twitch or their heads will turn abruptly to one side. Unlike individuals experiencing tonic-clonic, absence, tonic, or atonic seizures, individuals with frontal lobe seizures are aware of what is happening to them.

Parietal lobe seizures result in a tingling feeling throughout the person's body. People may also feel as if they are moving (when they are not) or are being choked (again, when they are not).

Finally, there are occipital lobe seizures, which cause partial loss of vision. This loss is only temporary. Vision will return to normal after the seizure. Individuals experiencing occipital lobe seizures might also hallucinate and see things that are not there.

There are many more different types of seizures, but the ones that I have described are probably the most common. Basically, anything that your brain can do can be the result of a seizure. For example,

Robert Evert Cimera

seizures can cause you to smell, hear, taste, feel, and see things that aren't really there. They can also make you walk around, jump, wave your arm, and grimace in pain. See table 4.1 for a summary of these types of seizures.

Table 4.1

Absence Seizures (AKA Petit Mal Seizures)	Individuals experiencing an absence seizure look as if they are staring off into space, much like they are daydreaming, but they will not respond even if you wave your hand in front of their faces. They may blink frequently or their heads might bob up and down, but other than that, they will have a vacant expression. Absence seizures will usually only last a few seconds; however, most individuals will have frequent seizures per day.
Myoclonic Seizures	Myoclonic seizures cause sudden jerking motions, usually of a single muscle or group of muscles. For example, the hand might twitch violently or the upper body might swing forward and then back. Myoclonic seizures should not be confused with normal muscle spasms or Tourette's syndrome.
Atonic Seizures	People having atonic seizures will suddenly lose all muscle tone. They will go limp as if they were rag dolls.

Tonic Seizures	Tonic seizures cause people to go rigid, as if frozen in stone.
Tonic-Clonic Seizures (AKA Grand Mal Seizures)	People with tonic-clonic seizures become very rigid (see tonic seizures). Their bodies then convulse as if being shocked. They will fall to the ground, repeatedly arch their backs, jerk their arms and legs, and roll their eyes back into their heads. They might also urinate, defecate, and foam at the mouth.
Frontal Lobe Seizures	Individuals with frontal lobe seizures may experience a strange twitching or odd feeling in their face, hands, or legs. Sometimes their heads will turn to one side or one of their arms will stiffen. In some cases, their bodies will display a series of bizarre movements. Unlike people having tonic, atonic, absence, or tonic-clonic seizures, people having frontal lobe seizures are aware of what is transpiring.
Parietal Lobe Seizures	Parietal lobe seizures are characterized by a tingling feeling that may spread throughout the body. Individuals may feel like they are moving, sinking, or being choked.
Occipital Lobe Seizures	Individuals who are experiencing occipital lobe seizures will temporarily lose part or all of their vision. They might see flashes of light or have hallucinations. Vision will return to normal after the seizure is over.

So what do you do if somebody is having a seizure? This is a really good question!

First, remain calm. I know that sounds like a cliché or something, but it is very important. As scary as seizures are, there is simply nothing that you can do to stop them. Remaining calm and keeping your head are the best things that you can do.

Next, notice the time. This is going to be crucial, so don't forget! The longer a seizure lasts, the worse off the person is. Moreover, if you call 911, the first thing that the operator is going to ask is, "How long has the person been seizuring?" Many 911 operators will not send an ambulance unless the person has been seizuring for at least five minutes or has never had a seizure before. Again, there is nothing that you (or the paramedics) can do to stop a seizure. Seizures usually stop on their own, so there is normally no need to get help.

Only call an ambulance if

1. *Your child has never had a seizure before.*
2. *The seizure goes on for longer than usual.*
3. *Your child keeps having one seizure after another.*
4. *Your child is hurt while having a seizure.*

Okay, so you notice the time and call 911 if you need to. Now what? Next, you need to get the person on the floor. This is only necessary if the person is having tonic-clonic, tonic, or atonic seizures. By getting people on the floor, you reduce the risks of them falling and hurting themselves. Statistically speaking, most injuries from seizures come from falls, and not the actual seizures.

Once you get the person on the floor, clear the area and cushion the person's head. You don't want him pulling anything on top of himself or smashing his face into the ground, especially if he is on pavement or a tiled floor. Also, tilt the head to one side or have him

Making Autism a Gift

on his stomach. By doing this, you will prevent him from choking on his saliva or vomit.

This brings me to an immensely important point: NEVER put anything in the mouth of somebody who is having a seizure! I know that you probably have heard that people can choke on their tongues. But this is just an old wives' tale! The tongue is attached and cannot be swallowed! So, again, don't put ANYTHING in the person's mouth. I'll tell you a story about why this is so important.

My father used to work in a factory. Back in the 1960s, it was common practice to put things in the mouths of people who were having seizures. One day, as my father told the story, a coworker started convulsing.

In an effort to help, somebody got a metal spoon and attempted to hold down the man's tongue. As I said, back in the 1960s, that was what you were supposed to do, apparently. So the coworker put the metal spoon into this guy's mouth and he bit through it. Literally! Now he had part of a spoon in his mouth and he was choking!

My father and the other workers began panicking. Somebody reached into the person's mouth to get the spoon and, as you might imagine, got the tip of his finger bitten off! So now the man was convulsing, urinating on himself, and choking on not only a spoon but a tip of a human finger!

My father and the other workers began to panic even more, as I am sure that you can appreciate! Finally, to make a long story short, somebody got the bright idea to hang the convulsing worker upside down. So they grabbed his feet and dangled him upside down as he thrashed about. Sure enough, both the spoon and the finger came out! Unfortunately, as legend has it, they accidentally dropped him and broke his nose.

The moral of the story is don't put things into the mouths of people who are having seizures!

Okay! Back to what you *should* do!

Make the person comfortable and wait, keeping an eye on the clock. Loosen all clothing, especially anything around the neck. If there are other children present, try to reassure them that everything is going to be all right.

Once the seizuring person begins to regain consciousness, you may need to explain what happened. The person may be confused and not know where he is, so reorient the person as best as you can. Don't leave him alone! Seizures are like earthquakes; they are likely to occur in groups. Stay with the person for at least an hour after the last seizure has ended. Don't give any food or water until the person is completely cognizant. The person could choke while eating if another seizure occurs.

Finally, allow the person to rest. Having seizures is very tiring and the person might be groggy for the remainder of the day.

So let me recap. This is what you should do if your child is having a seizure:

1. *Remain calm.*
2. *Notice the time.*
3. *Get the person on the floor.*
4. *Cushion the head and tilt it to one side.*
5. *Clear the immediate area.*
6. *Make the person comfortable.*
7. *Call 911 only if this is the person's first seizure, the seizure is longer than normal, the person keeps having seizures, or the person is hurt.*
8. *Reorient the person after the seizure is over.*
9. *Allow the person to rest, if needed.*
10. *Don't leave the person alone for at least an hour after the last seizure.*

Making Autism a Gift

I have one last story for you regarding seizures. It is kind of sad, but it drives an essential point home.

I had a neighbor whose child Chloe frequently wet her bed. Chloe was about six or seven and was horribly embarrassed by what was happening, as were her parents, who thought that she was going through a phase. However, after several months of chronic bedwetting, they finally brought her to the doctor.

The doctor didn't find anything medically wrong with Chloe and suggested that she might have some "unresolved" issues. Consequently, he suggested that she see a child psychologist.

One day, Chloe's father was walking by her bedroom while she was sleeping. He noticed that she was thrashing around, but he couldn't wake her. As it turned out, Chloe was having seizures almost every night. Had they gone on indefinitely, she could have experienced brain damage.

So, if you ever suspect that your child is having a seizure of any variety, tell your doctor! Seizures can be easily detected by electroencephalograms (EEGs). Moreover, they can be effectively treated!

LANDAU-KLEFFNER SYNDROME

Landau-Kleffner syndrome (or LKS) is another condition that is often associated or confused with autism. It is a neurological disorder characterized by a sudden or gradual development of aphasia, which is an inability to understand or use spoken language.

Individuals with LKS develop normally. However, between the ages of three and seven, they lose their language skills. They also may fail to respond to sounds, as if they were deaf. These individuals have abnormal electroencephalogram (EEG) results and often have epilepsy.

Robert Evert Cimera

OBSESSIVE-COMPULSIVE DISORDER

I want to talk about obsessive-compulsive disorder (OCD) briefly because I have found that many parents often confuse it with autism. In fact, several parents whom I know deny that their children have autism and instead claim that the correct diagnosis is OCD. However, while the two conditions are certainly similar in many respects, there are differences that set them apart. Let me tell you what OCD is and then compare it to autism.

OCD is a condition characterized by recurring obsessions or compulsions that are functionally meaningless, yet consume so much time that they impair a person's social, vocational, and daily life. Obsessions are persistent thoughts or beliefs that, if not acted upon, will produce extreme anxiety. Obsessions might include various fears, such as fear of germs or of being carjacked. They might also include fixations with certain objects, such as airplanes or stairs.

Compulsions are repetitious behaviors that a person performs to reduce the anxiety caused by obsessions. For example, a student of mine with OCD had to touch the stairs with each foot in a particular order. His right foot touched the first step, then his left. Then his right foot touched the second step, followed by the left, all the way up to the top.

When he failed to go up or down the stairs in his unique manner, he would become very distressed and couldn't concentrate until he went back to the stairs in question and went up them the correct way.

Other students of mine had to do things the same number of times. For example, one student had to check to see if the doors were closed exactly three times before his anxiety would begin to dissipate. If you ever watched the movie *As Good As It Gets* or the television program *Monk*, you probably have an idea of what OCD is.

Making Autism a Gift

Although your child with autism may have obsessions and compulsions, he is also likely to have the communication and social deficits that I discussed in the first chapter. Individuals with OCD would not necessarily have any delays in language or impairments in social interactions.

In other words, there is considerable overlap between the two conditions. Somebody with autism might have many OCD tendencies but a person with OCD would not have the communication and social skill deficits that a person with autism exhibits.

PERVASIVE DEVELOPMENTAL DISORDER (PDD)

If you have read much about autism, you have undoubtedly come across the term "pervasive developmental disorder," or PDD. PDD is an umbrella term that includes all disorders that are characterized by chronic and profound impairments in social skills and communication as well as stereotypical behavior.

Many people use PDD as if it were interchangeable with autism, but they are technically different. Think about PDD as a huge overarching category of disabilities that includes childhood disintegrative disorder (CDD), Rett's, Asperger's syndrome, and autism.

PERVASIVE DEVELOPMENTAL DISORDER– NOT OTHERWISE SPECIFIED (PDD-NOS)

Pervasive developmental disorder–not otherwise specified (PDD-NOS) is a condition that is included under the PDD umbrella. Basically, PDD-NOS is a "catch-all" category; that is to say, if somebody comes really close to fulfilling the criteria for any of the pervasive developmental disorders but doesn't quite make it, that person could be diagnosed with PDD-NOS. Let me give you an example to illustrate this.

Let's suppose you have a child who acts exactly like the stereotypic autistic child. He has the odd behaviors, poor social skills, problems with communications—the whole nine yards. However, maybe the age of onset for these symptoms was a little later than normal, or maybe he doesn't quite meet the criteria for autism (e.g., his social skills aren't that bad). In such cases, your child could be diagnosed with PDD-NOS, which is sometimes called "atypical autism."

PICA

Pica is a condition characterized by the willful consumption of inedible material. For example, I had students who ate everything that they could get into their mouths, including dirt, rocks, paper, and their own hair and feces. This condition is frequently associated with autism, mental retardation, and other developmental disorders, although in rare cases, it can also be found within normal people.

Now, before you get worried, the eating behavior associated with pica is developmentally inappropriate. In other words, it is something that other children at that age normally wouldn't do. So if your six-month-old keeps putting everything in her mouth, that is okay! That is what six-month-olds do! However, if your sixteen-year-old keeps putting inappropriate things in his mouth, he might have pica.

The cause of pica is unknown. Some people believe that it is an extension of obsessive-compulsive behavior. Others have noted that pica is more prevalent with nutritional deficiencies, such as with iron or zinc. Further, pica can "clear up" if these nutritional deficiencies are addressed. So, if your child has pica, have your doctor conduct a nutritional analysis. You might also want to conduct a functional behavior analysis (FBA) to see if the behavior has a purpose. I'll talk about FBAs in later chapters.

CHILDHOOD-ONSET SCHIZOPHRENIA

I know that the term "schizophrenia" is kind of scary, but it doesn't mean what you probably think it means. Schizophrenia doesn't mean that someone is "crazy." It doesn't mean that the person has "multiple personalities" or is a "psycho killer."

Schizophrenia is a condition where individuals have delusions or hallucinations that alter the way that they perceive and interact with reality. Delusions are incorrect beliefs. For example, a schizophrenic might believe she is the daughter of God or that aliens are out to get her. Hallucinations are sensations that aren't really occurring, such as seeing, hearing, smelling, tasting, or feeling things that aren't there.

There are several different types of schizophrenia. For instance, you might have heard of "paranoid schizophrenia" or "catatonic schizophrenia." There is also something called "childhood-onset schizophrenia," or COS, which is also called "pre-pubertal schizophrenia."

As you can most likely guess, COS is schizophrenia that begins in childhood, usually by age ten. In addition to hallucinations and delusions, children with COS typically have disorganized thoughts and behaviors. They may talk to themselves or an "invisible" friend.

Although rarer than the adult-onset varieties of schizophrenia, COS is thought to affect approximately 1 person out of 100,000. What makes it relevant to this discussion is that it is frequently misdiagnosed as autism and vice versa. In fact, autism used to be referred to as "childhood schizophrenia." However, it is now thought that autism and all forms of schizophrenia are completely different conditions.

COS can be effectively treated through medications. Many individuals with COS grow up and lead completely normal lives, free of delusions and hallucinations.

SENSORY PROCESSING DYSFUNCTION

Sensory processing dysfunction (SPD) is a very new and trendy topic. Some people say that it isn't really a diagnosis, but merely a description of symptoms. The fact that it has yet to be included in the American Psychiatric Association's *Diagnostic and Statistical Manual of Mental Disorders* (*DSM*) strengthens this argument. Still, you will probably hear about it, so you might as well know what it is.

SPD describes individuals who have difficulty processing sensory information, but not because of abnormalities with the sensory organs. For instance, an individual with SPD might get "overwhelmed" by a great deal of auditory information (more so than the average person would). It isn't that something is wrong with the person's ears. She might actually have superb hearing. However, when she enters a room with a bunch of people talking, she might feel inundated and not be able to process everything that she hears.

SPD can involve any sensory input as well as multiple modalities at the same time. Again, it is presently unclear as to whether this is an actual "disability" or simply an explanation as to why some individuals with autism self-stimulate.

SUMMARY

In this chapter, I discussed many conditions that are associated with autism. Some of these conditions, such as mental retardation or

Making Autism a Gift

epilepsy, are likely to occur in addition to autism. Other conditions, such as childhood-onset schizophrenia, are often confused with autism.

If your child has some of these co-existing conditions, it is important that you learn more about them. After all, a child who only has autism is very different from a child with autism *and* mental retardation. Moreover, addressing just the autism and not the mental retardation probably won't produce very satisfactory results. So, if you need more information regarding these ancillary conditions, please consult the resources in the back of the book.

Finally, when your child is diagnosed with autism, ask the psychologist to rule out the conditions that I discussed. For instance, ask the psychologist why your child doesn't have OCD or COS or LKS. Remember, autism is often misdiagnosed! You can help ensure that your child is diagnosed correctly by ruling out similar conditions.

FIVE

"Maybe YOU Need to Be Modified!"*: Strategies for Addressing General Behavioral Issues

Thus far during our time together, I have discussed what autism is, common characteristics of autism, how it is diagnosed, and conditions that are often associated with it. Hopefully, all of this has been interesting and informative, but undoubtedly you are looking for more than just facts and figures! You probably bought this book to find some strategies to help you solve certain difficulties that you and your child face.

To this end, I would like to start talking about addressing general behavior problems. Specifically, I am going to cover how to change behavior by utilizing various types of rewards, punishments, and schedules.

---

* I remember a time when one of my aides was yelling at a student who was misbehaving. She said something to the effect of, "You better stop that or else I'll implement the behavior modification program we developed last week!" To which my student yelled back, "Maybe YOU need to be modified!" It was a funny comment, but also very insightful. You see, often it is the behavior of the teachers and parents that needs to be changed, not that of the child with autism!

Making Autism a Gift

AN OVERVIEW OF
BEHAVIOR MODIFICATION

The term "behavior modification" seems to scare a lot of people. Apparently, images of spankings, shock therapy, mood-altering drugs, and medieval tortures, such as the iron maiden or the rack, come to mind. But behavior modification shouldn't be scary. Nor should it be shunned.

Whether you know it or not, you attempt to modify people's behaviors all of the time. You do it when you need help at a store and look longingly at far-off clerks. You are trying to get them to come over and give you assistance. You attempt to modify people's behavior when you subtly suggest that you don't want any more sweaters for Christmas and that you really would like to have an X-37 Redrider BB gun.

Behavior modification, although it may sound "coercive," is the foundation of effective teaching and parenting. Don't believe me? Well, think of it this way. Do you really want your fourteen-year-old acting like a three-year-old? No! Of course not. That is why you need to teach your child how to act appropriately. You, in effect, *modify* your child's behavior as he grows up.

Moreover, as a teacher, I use behavior modification to "encourage" my students to study and pay attention in class. For instance, if my students are staring off into space or out the window, I call on them and ask them questions. I also give surprise quizzes on the homework I assign. My actions increase the likelihood that my students will perform certain behaviors (i.e., study and pay attention).

So behavior modification isn't something to be feared. It isn't torture or brainwashing or anything like that! It is simply a way of letting your child know what you want him to do and providing incentives for him to do it.

The Functions of Behavior

Before you can alter your child's behavior, you first have to understand why it is occurring. This is often easier said than done, especially when the child might not know or be able to communicate why he does the things that he does.

So how can you determine the function of your child's actions? Where do you begin? First you have to look at the traditional theories of the causes of behavior.

Many scholars believe that behaviors have three basic purposes. The first is to get something that the person wants. For example, your child might throw a temper tantrum to get your attention or to obtain an object that you have denied him.

The second is to avoid something that he does not want. For example, your child might not want you to touch him, so he slaps your hand away or starts screaming or rocking back and forth. Or, he might lie or run away to avoid whatever he deems undesirable.

The third function of behavior, according to many "experts," is a combination of the first two; that is, the person wants to get something and also avoid something. For example, a student might act like a class clown to get kicked out of class so that she doesn't have to participate in a classroom assignment. She might also want to get laughs or respect from her peers.

Now, with that said, I want to add my two cents. I personally don't believe that *all* behavior is willful or has a purpose. For example, imagine that your child is on the kitchen floor screaming and thrashing about. Take a minute and think about all of the possible explanations for that behavior.

One of the plausible explanations that you probably came up with is that your child is having a seizure. Is your child trying to get or avoid anything? No. His body is just reacting to electrical im-

Making Autism a Gift

pulses going crazy in his brain. There is no thought to his actions. There is no purpose.

The same is true for students who stare out the window because they are tired, have ADHD, or are on drugs. Their behavior (i.e., staring out the window) has no premeditated function.

Although this action might not be willful or convey some sort of meaning, it is still important to know whether a child is staring out the window because of ADHD, a seizure, or willful disregard for the teacher's instructions. So how do you do that? How do you find out why a child is acting a certain way? You conduct a "functional behavioral analysis," or FBA.

CONDUCTING FUNCTIONAL BEHAVIOR ANALYSES

Doing a functional behavioral analysis is much like being a detective who is trying to solve a crime or a mystery. There is no one correct way of doing it. Moreover, much of what you do will depend upon your instincts and intuition. However, there are some general steps that will help you determine why your child acts the way that he does.

Step #1: Define the Behavior

The first thing that you have to do is identify *exactly* what behavior you are trying to analyze. You must be specific. You can't merely say, "I want to figure out why he acts like he does," or, "I want to find out why he is so annoying!" You have to narrow your scope down to something that is observable and measurable (e.g., doing household chores, talking with peers, hitting).

Also, you can't focus on several different behaviors at the same time. You can only investigate one.

Which behavior should you explore? That is up to you and your particular situation, but maybe I can help you decide.

Take a few moments and brainstorm a list of your child's behaviors that are problematic for his future. For instance, maybe he is aggressive and hits people. Maybe he hits himself. Maybe he runs away from home or school. Or maybe he has a fascination with putting things in electrical outlets. Just write down any specific behaviors that you think need to be changed.

Now look over your list. Do you see any behaviors that are really critical? Are there any that affect your child's immediate health or safety? If so, perhaps that is the behavior with which you should start.

Or maybe you see a behavior that seems to be the root cause of many of the other behaviors on your list. For example, maybe he doesn't let anybody get within three feet of him. As a result, it is very difficult to get him dressed in the morning, help him with homework, or even play with him. If you could just get him to let others within arm's length, he would be able to learn better at school, make more friends, and be more pleasant to be around.

At any rate, before you can move on to the next step, you will need to select one behavior that you want to focus upon. Remember, the behavior must be observable and measurable. So don't pick something that is within your child, such as "self-esteem" or "negative thoughts."

Step #2: Identifying the End Result

By now you should have selected a behavior that you want to change. The next step is to ask yourself, "How do I want my child to act?"

For example, maybe you have identified a behavior that you want your child to perform more often, such as cleaning his room or studying or being socially adept. In which case, you will need to develop a way to promote the behavior.

Or maybe you have identified a behavior that you want to reduce or stop altogether, such as harming the self or setting fires. In these situations you should replace the behavior with one that gets your child what he wants, but in a more appropriate way.

For instance, suppose that your child is banging his head against the wall to get your attention. Rather than just trying to stop the behavior, try to teach him how to get your attention in a less harmful manner.

Before I go on to the next step in the behavior modification process, I want to talk about a few things. Some of them might sound a bit mean or negative. Still, I think that they are important concepts to consider.

For starters, please don't expect your child to change overnight or to be "perfect." Remember, your child has autism. I am not saying this is good or bad. I am simply reminding you that people with autism have certain needs and characteristics. Expecting them to act exactly like everybody else is probably unrealistic.

Instead, concentrate on making incremental, positive changes in your child's life. Rather than making him act like a social butterfly, which is very difficult for kids with autism, focus on having him make one good friend or increasing the number of times he says hello to his teachers and classmates. In other words, try to make small changes in an effort to reach a larger goal.

Finally, work on behaviors that will actually help your child's future. Why spend nine months trying to teach him how to tie his shoes when you can have him wear penny loafers or shoes with Velcro straps?

Step #3: Developing a Hypothesis

Okay, so you have identified a behavior that you want to change and have a good idea of how you want your child to eventually act. Now you need to figure out why your child is acting the way that he does. This will take a lot of work, reflection, and data collection, but it is an essential step in the process.

I suggest using a method this is often referred to as ABC, which stands for "antecedent," "behavior," and "consequence." Basically, you need to consider what happens before and after the behavior in an effort to figure out what is going on and why.

Let me ask you a few questions to get the ball rolling. Write down any ideas that come to you. Remember, you are brainstorming, so write down anything you like, even though you think it might not be useful.

When does your child's behavior tend to occur? This is a very important question, so take your time and really think about your answer. Is there a specific time when the behavior is particularly prevalent? For example, is it mostly in the morning? Afternoon? Evening?

Does the behavior tend to happen after a certain event? For example, does he start screaming or hitting after you tell him to do something, such as "go to bed?" Or does his behavior happen after somebody he doesn't know speaks to him?

Does the behavior tend to happen at a specific place? If so, try to pinpoint what makes that location different from all of the other locations where the behavior doesn't occur. For instance, is it hotter? Noisier? More crowded? Brighter? Darker? Are there any smells?

Okay, hopefully that gets you thinking about what happens before the behavior occurs. Now consider what happens after the behavior occurs.

How do you react? Do you get angry? Do you yell? Do you give him attention when you weren't giving him any attention before the behavior? Do you take away things or put him in "time out"?

How do other people react to your child's behavior? Do they laugh? Do they give him something?

When does the behavior stop? When somebody leaves the room? When he gets something? When something is taken away?

What does your child do after the behavior? Does he leave the environment? If so, where does he tend to go?

Now take a look at all of the notes that you jotted down. Do you see a pattern? Are you starting to come up with an idea as to what your child might be trying to accomplish (consciously or unconsciously) with his behavior? Ask other people what their thoughts are. Maybe they see something that you have missed.

Again, the idea is to step back and take a good hard look at what is going on. When does the behavior occur? Where? Who is around? What is happening? What could be triggering the behavior? What is the end result of the behavior? Is the child getting something as a result of the behavior? Is he getting away from or avoiding something?

Once you are able to answer these questions, you can proceed to the next step of the behavior modification process.

Step #4: Collect Data on the Behavior

Now that you have defined the behavior and have a working hypothesis as to why it might be occurring, you will need to collect some data. If you don't have a working hypothesis as to why your child is acting the way that he is, collecting data might open your eyes and give you some new insight.

How you collect data depends largely on the type of behavior you are addressing and what you want to do to it. For example, let's suppose

Robert Evert Cimera

that you are trying to increase the number of times your child does his weekly chores or homework assignments. In these situations, you will need to simply count the number of times he does what he is supposed to do. This is called "frequency recording," or "event recording."

However, let's suppose that you don't care how often a behavior occurs. Maybe you want to alter its duration. For instance, maybe you want to increase the amount of time that your child socializes with other kids. Or maybe you want to decrease how long his temper tantrums last. In such cases, you would want to record the time that a behavior starts and when it ends. This is often called "duration recording."

Or perhaps your child does everything that you ask, but not when you tell him to do it. For example, suppose in the morning, you instruct your child to clean his room; however, he doesn't start until after dinner. In such a situation, you might measure the time between when you tell him to do something and when he actually starts. This is called "latency recording."

The idea is that you have to collect data so that you can determine whether the behavior is changing. For example, maybe you want to reduce the number of times your child is aggressive towards other people (or maybe you want to stop the behavior altogether). So you count each time your child tries to hit, bite, kick, grab, or otherwise touch others inappropriately. Maybe you even put this data on a graph.

After investigating for a few weeks, you find out that on average, your child engages in six aggressive acts towards other people every day. Further, you realize that he hits more on weekends when he isn't in school and adhering to a schedule! Now you have an idea of how often the behavior occurs and why.

Next you have to figure out how to change your child's behavior to something more desirable. Perhaps you want to decrease his aggressive acts to two a day, and then to once a week, and then to no aggressive behaviors at all. But how do you do this? Great question! Let's go on to the next step!

Step #5: Developing Strategies to Change the Target Behavior

There are many strategies that you can employ to change your child's behaviors. For example, you can use rewards and punishments. Rewards are things that will encourage or increase a desired behavior. Punishments, on the other hand, discourage or decrease an undesirable behavior. However, there is far more to these strategies than that!

First of all, what you think of as a reward might actually be a punishment to your child. For example, when I was a teenager, my mother would make a big fuss if I did well on a test or class project. She would act all excited and say in a high-pitched squeal, "Oh! I am sooo proud of you! I knew that you could do it!"

I am sure she meant this to be reinforcing. She was praising me in an attempt to encourage future hard work. But I was a teenager. I just wanted to be left alone. Plus, to me, my mother's comments sounded as if she were saying, "I told you so!" In other words, her praise was actually a punishment. If I got a good grade, I didn't tell her. I didn't want her to gush all over me.

You can apply the same concept to children with autism. Imagine that you want to reward your child with a big tight bear hug and a kiss on the forehead. Well, to a lot of kids with autism, such contact isn't appreciated! So what you end up doing is inadvertently responding to the desired behavior by punishing him!

Robert Evert Cimera

Let me put it another way. Imagine that your boss said, "Hey, if you meet your goals for the week, I'll give you brussels sprouts and Spam!" Well, if you don't like brussels sprouts and Spam, are you going to work hard to accomplish your goals? Probably not.

In other words, it is *very* important that you develop reinforcers and punishers with your child specifically in mind. So before you begin, I want you to take a break and generate a list of things that your child likes and dislikes. Maybe your child likes to play computer games or ride his bike around the block or sit in his room. Maybe your child doesn't like to go to bed at nine o'clock or eat vegetables or rake the leaves. Write down whatever comes to mind.

Once you have some ideas as to what your child likes and dislikes, you need to figure out a way to use this knowledge to change his behavior. As I said before, there are several methods of doing this. Let me start with ways of increasing behavior, which as I said, involves rewards, and then I'll move on to strategies for decreasing behavior, which involves punishments.

Positive reinforcement. One way to increase your child's behavior is by utilizing "positive reinforcement," or "classical reinforcement." You probably already know what this is. It involves giving your child something that he wants if he performs the appropriate behavior. For instance, if he gets an A on his spelling test, or says hello to his teacher in the morning, he gets something that he likes, such as an hour of free time or ice cream after dinner. Pretty straightforward, right?

Negative reinforcement. Negative reinforcement involves taking away something that your child does not like if he performs the desired behavior. This is a bit tricky, so let me explain.

Imagine that your child makes his bed or puts away his toys. As a reward for his good behavior, he doesn't have to go to bed at nine o'clock. Of course, I am assuming that he doesn't want to go to bed

Making Autism a Gift

that early. Otherwise, staying up later wouldn't be very motivating. Let me give you a couple more examples.

When I was a kid, my class had two spelling tests each week, a pre-test on Monday and a post-test on Friday. If the students got an A on the pre-test, they didn't have to take the post-test. In effect, the teacher took away something that the students didn't like doing (i.e., taking the Friday spelling test) if they did a desired behavior (i.e., performed well on the pre-test).

My father used to make me do various weekly jobs around the house. I had to take the trash cans to the curb on garbage day, bring the trash cans back behind the house, wash dishes after dinner, clean my room, and pick up dog poop in the yard. However, if I got all A's on my report card, I didn't have to do any of this for the entire summer!

I didn't like doing these tasks, so getting out of my weekly chores was something that I wanted. Unfortunately, I was a C-minus student. I never got close to getting all A's. Consequently, I had to take the garbage out, wash dishes, clean my room, and pick up dog poop every week.

This leads me to an important topic. In order to be effective, you have to make the goals match your child's abilities. You see, I was never very good at school. I tried to do well, but I was never very smart. So my father could have offered me a billion dollars and I still wouldn't have been able to get all A's. It was completely beyond my intellectual abilities. A much more reasonable goal would have been for me to get all B's, or one A and no D's, or something along these lines.

Also, you have to consider the power of the reinforcer. It has to exceed the pain of changing the behavior. For example, imagine if my father said, "If you get all A's this school year, you can have a candy bar!" Well, first of all, I could have a candy bar any time that I wanted. I could go down to the grocery store and buy one with my allowance. Second, getting one stinking candy bar for a year of hard work just wasn't worth it! Why bother?

This brings me to yet another vital topic regarding reinforcement: how often you should reward your child. You want to reward your child frequently enough so that he understands that there is a connection between his behavior and the reward. For young children as well as those with mental retardation, you may have to reinforce the behavior each and every time that it occurs. However, there is a problem with this.

Imagine that your teacher gave you a piece of chocolate every time you raised your hand before speaking in class. Let's also suppose that you really love chocolate and would work extremely hard to earn it. In other words, to you, chocolate is a reinforcer—at least initially.

After a while, all of that chocolate would start to make you sick! That is to say, given too frequently, reinforcers can lose their power to motivate. Toward the end of the day, your teacher could offer you ten pieces of chocolate and you probably wouldn't raise your hand. You would be sick of chocolate!

Consequently, you may want to give rewards intermittently rather than after every single time your child does what he is supposed to. For example, maybe he has to do the behavior five or ten times. Or maybe he has to go for an entire day or week of doing the behavior before he gets the reward.

You can also change the reinforcement schedule as you go along. For example, maybe you initially reward your child every single time he responds verbally to you. Then the next week, you reward him for every two times that he responds verbally to you. Then if he reaches that goal, you reward him every five times.

Making Autism a Gift

By moving the reward farther and farther into the future, you create behavior that is less bound to the reward. In essence, your child ends up working harder for the same outcome. However, don't delay gratification too much! You don't want your child to give up!

Presentation punishment. In addition to rewarding appropriate behavior, you can also develop strategies for punishing inappropriate behavior. One method of doing this is called "presentation punishment," or "classical punishment."

Presentation punishment involves exposing your child to something that he doesn't like if he does what you don't want him to do. For example, when I was a kid, my father wouldn't let me run around the house. If I ran, he would make me walk very, very, *very* slowly up and down the stairs. My feet had to be on the step for at least five seconds! It was excruciating for a hyperactive kid like me.

If that didn't work, my father would spank me, which is another type of presentation punishment. As a result, I didn't run in the house. At least, not when he was around!

Again, the idea here is if your child does something he shouldn't, something happens that he doesn't like. You could send him to his room. You could make him sit in a "time-out" chair. You could lecture him or make him do push-ups until he collapses! But whatever it is, it has to be something that he doesn't like; otherwise, his inappropriate behavior will continue.

Response-Cost. Another way to decrease undesirable behavior is to take away things that your child likes. This is usually called "response-cost." Let me give you an example.

Suppose that you want your child to stop throwing things. So every time he throws something, he loses a toy for a week. It is a pretty simple strategy to implement. You could even combine it with a positive reward system where your child can "earn" back the toys he lost.

Extinction. Extinction is a process by which a behavior is no longer reinforced. It, therefore, dies out on its own.

Many actors who have to say funny lines with straight faces often use extinction. For example, in the movie *Airplane*, actor Leslie Nielsen apparently kept cracking up when he tried to say his famous line, "I am not joking . . . and don't call me Shirley." In order to break the cycle of his behavior, he kept saying the line over and over and over until it was no longer funny. Eventually, he could then say the line with a blank expression.

I frequently used extinction when I taught junior high students. For example, once, a student kept making farting noises with his armpit. All the students laughed and laughed, making it almost impossible for me to get them back on topic. Guessing that their laughter was reinforcing his behavior, I made the student stand in front of the class and make farting noises for five minutes.

At first, everybody laughed and thought it was funny. The student flapped his arm with a big smile on his face, eager to get the attention. But by the second minute, his peers weren't laughing any more. They became bored and just sat there staring at him.

By the third minute, the student wanted to stop. He wasn't getting the reaction that he wanted, so his behavior wasn't reinforcing anymore. But I made him continue for the remainder of the five minutes.

Nobody ever made farting noises in my class again.

Promoting incompatible behaviors. The final strategy that I want to discuss involves promoting appropriate behaviors that make it difficult for your child to misbehave. For example, suppose that your child rocks in his chair at school, distracting the students who sit near him. If you have him work standing up, maybe using a podium or a drafting table in the back of the room, he won't bother anybody else.

Making Autism a Gift

Here's another example. Suppose that you have a child who always throws things. If you have him using his hands for something that he likes to do, such as drawing or playing a game, he can't do what he wants to do and throw things at the same time.

Okay, there you have several very general ideas for increasing or reducing behaviors. Remember, you know your child better than anybody. So think about the behavior that you want to change. Think about what seems to motivate him. And then develop some sort of plan of action that will help accomplish your goal.

Be creative! If your child is able to, have him participate in the plan's formation. Tell him what you want him to do and ask, "If you do what I expect, what do you think is a fair consequence?" Studies have found that behavioral interventions are far more effective when children are involved in their creation.

Many parents even draw up "behavioral contracts" with their children. They go though a big formal process of negotiating what is to happen if such and such behavior occurs. They type up a document outlining the agreement, sign it, and then post it somewhere where everybody can see. That way, it serves as a constant reminder of what is expected.

Step #6: Testing Your Hypothesis

At this point, you should have selected one specific and measurable behavior that you want to change. You have collected data and come up with an idea as to why the behavior is occurring. You have also developed a plan for either increasing or decreasing the behavior's frequency, duration, or latency. Now what?

Implement your strategy and test your hypothesis. At the same time, continue collecting data to see if you are making any difference. Did the behavior change?

It could be that the behavior improved, but not enough. For instance, maybe your child is self-abusing half as much as he did before, but that is still not appropriate! Or maybe the behavior changed, but in the wrong direction! Maybe now your child is self-abusing even more! In either case, you would need to go to the next step.

Step#7: Revise Your Plan or Pick Another Behavior

Okay, you have intervened and the behavior is still not where you want it to be. What do you do? Well, the first thing you should do is try to figure out why your intervention didn't work. Was it that your child didn't understand the link between the behavior and the consequences? If so, you might want to continue with the intervention and try to have the consequences fall immediately after the behavior occurs.

Maybe you weren't consistent enough. Many times behavior modification programs don't work well because people don't implement them consistently. This is very important! You have to address the behavior the same way all of the time or else your child might get confused.

Picture it from the child's perspective. Sometimes when he throws a fit, he gets what he wants. Other times he doesn't. Since he doesn't know a better way to get what he wants, he might as well keep throwing fits. After all, it works some of the time. That is better than not at all!

In addition to lack of consistency, maybe your plan didn't work because the reward or punishment wasn't powerful enough. That is to say, your child might realize that he will be sent to the time-out chair if he throws a fit, but being sent to the time-out chair doesn't bother him. So it has no effect on changing his behavior.

If you think that the consequences that you selected were not strong enough, consider changing or adding other consequences to them. For example, maybe instead of five minutes in the time-out chair, you increase the time to fifteen minutes. Or move the chair to a less desirable location. Or you could add the consequence that your child has to clean up the mess that he made during the fit after he is finished with his time out.

On this note, I would like to add that it is always better to reward appropriate behavior and punish inappropriate behavior than to just pay attention to one or the other. So rather than just punishing your child for throwing a temper tantrum, try to also reward him for behaving himself.

It could also be that your child didn't change his behavior because you misunderstood why the behavior was occurring. For instance, maybe your child isn't throwing temper tantrums. Maybe he is in pain and trying to get your attention. Perhaps he has frequent ear infections or migraines and his fits are the result of a physiological problem and not necessarily a willful disregard for your authority. In which case, your intervention of sending him to the time-out chair wouldn't be effective no matter how long or consistently you kept it up!

So take time to reflect on what you have learned about your child. Reevaluate all of your data and assumptions. It could be that if you reexamine when, where, and with whom the behavior occurs, you will come to a different conclusion as to why the behavior is occurring!

Finally, your behavior modification program might not be working because your child simply cannot help himself. The behavior is part of who he is! Imagine expecting a blind person to "watch" where she is going or to make "eye contact"! It may be that the behavior you are addressing is not going to go away no matter what you try. For example, a child with mental retardation by definition will always have sub-average intelligence. This doesn't mean that you

Robert Evert Cimera

can't teach him skills that will help him in his life. It just means that you won't be able to make your child a genius!

But please don't jump to this last conclusion too quickly. If you give up trying to change your child's behavior too soon, then you will never really know if it is something that you can change. And if you don't change the behavior, your child's future may be limited.

FINAL ISSUES TO CONSIDER WHEN TRYING TO MODIFY BEHAVIOR

Before I move on to the next topic, I think that I should cover a few more things. For example, I want you to seriously consider why you want to change your child's behavior. Are you changing it because it annoys you? If so, maybe you should worry about changing your attitude toward the behavior rather than changing the behavior itself.

Change your child's behavior because the end result will help your child succeed in life. Focus on teaching your child new, more appropriate behaviors rather than merely taking away the behaviors that are mildly bothersome.

Also, whenever possible, try to give your child what he wants when he acts in an appropriate way. For example, if your child wants attention and is smashing things to get it, try to give him attention for good behavior. In other words, make the behavior modification process a "win-win" situation. Your child gets what he wants (attention from you); you get what you want (appropriate behavior).

Another issue to think about is whether your child can really change. I know this sounds negative, but not everybody can bench-press three hundred pounds! Not everybody can sit in a seat for an hour straight! Not everybody can be a social butterfly! So ask yourself whether your child can really do the things that you are expecting. After all, you can't stop a kid from having seizures by establishing a reward system!

Making Autism a Gift

Also ask yourself, "Is the desired behavior really what I want?" For instance, I have had students with mental retardation who used to show their "private parts" to anybody who was interested. So their parents and teachers developed intervention plans and really worked on eliminating this behavior.

Unfortunately, the desired behavior (i.e., students not showing their private parts) was overlearned. Many of my students ended up not showing their privates to anybody, including their doctors!

The same is true for issues involving lying or tattling. Imagine telling your child not to lie and he ends up telling everybody the unabashed truth all of the time! Or imagine if your child never tattled, even when he was being sexually molested. Again, the issue here is to really contemplate what you want your child to be like.

SUMMARY

Behavior modification is the foundation of all education. Whether you have a child with or without a disability, teaching him how to act "appropriately" is a critical role for both parents and educators. So how do you do this?

As I discussed in this chapter, you have to figure out why the unacceptable behavior is occurring and then attempt to replace it with something that is more beneficial. This can be accomplished in a number of ways, including (but not limited to) using punishers and reinforcers.

If you would like more detailed information about how to develop behavior modification programs, consider reading *Enhancing Your Child's Behavior: A Guide For Parents and Teachers*, or consult the resources listed in the back of this book.

SIX

"Why Is Everything That I Like to Do Wrong?"*: Strategies for Addressing Self-Stimulation

In the last chapter, I talked about some basic principles of behavior modification. Hopefully, by now you have an idea of how to look at a behavior, determine why it might be occurring, and develop a strategy for either reducing or increasing it.

In the next few chapters, I want to start addressing more specific difficulties that you are likely facing. For example, in this chapter I am going to focus on self-stimulation. In later chapters, I will talk about aggression, social and communication skills, and fears and fixations.

---

* Very early in my career, I was working with an adolescent who had autism. Brian had a tendency to spin things, flick his fingers, and tap himself on the chin. Once, as I was trying to get him to stop these activities, he screamed, "Why is everything that I like to do wrong?!" It was a fair question. After all, his self-stimulating behaviors weren't hurting anybody. In fact, they were only mildly annoying at most. After some reflection and discussion with his parents, we decided to focus on other, more critical, issues, such as teaching Brian self-help skills so that he could someday live independently within the community.

Before you try to eliminate your child's self-stimming behaviors, ask yourself if they really need to be addressed. The answer might be no.

Making Autism a Gift

WHAT IS SELF-STIMULATION?

Let me start by asking the question, "What is self-stimulation?" To many people, "self-stimulation" sounds . . . well . . . sexual, and it certainly can be. I have had many students with autism who would gratify themselves in my classroom or in public. However, self-stimulation can be *any* repetitive behavior that heightens the child's senses. Children may spin things like tops, wring their hands (as if they were washing them), rock back and forth, flick their fingers, flap their hands in front of their eyes, rub themselves, tap their temples, and engage in a million and one other behaviors.

WHEN IS SELF-STIMMING A PROBLEM?

Whenever I conduct a workshop on autism, somebody inevitably brings up self-stimming behaviors and how to eliminate them. The first thing that I always ask is, "Why is self-stimming a problem?" We all do it to some degree. For example, I have a student in one of my classes who constantly clicks her pen on and off. Others crack their knuckles over and over again or twirl their hair. My wonderful wife clinches and unclinches her toes. I tend to bounce my knees. So what is the big deal about self-stimming behavior?

After some discussion, most parents and teachers tell me that self-stimming behaviors "bother them." They find it unnerving to be around people who are rocking or flicking or spinning. It somehow makes them feel uncomfortable.

When this is the case, I suggest that parents and teachers focus on changing some other behavior that really matters, such as improving the child's reading ability or communication skills. After all, you only have so much time to teach your child. Make each lesson count! Don't waste time changing behavior that is mildly annoying.

Robert Evert Cimera

But this is not to say that all self-stimming behavior should be overlooked or ignored. I am not saying that at all! In fact, I believe that self-stimulation should be addressed in three situations.

One is when it interferes with learning. Many times students with autism will rock back and forth, flapping their hands in an attempt to block "outside" stimuli. They don't want to hear or see or sense the presence of other people. In such circumstances, it is very difficult to teach these students. And if they don't learn, their futures are not going to be very promising.

I would also try to change self-stimming behaviors that are dangerous to the child or somebody else. For example, I would intervene if a child habitually picks at his skin so that he causes open sores, or if he hits himself in the head.

Finally, I would alter a child's self-stimming behavior if it were an attempt to communicate. As I will discuss in a few pages, individuals with autism often self-stim when they are nervous or anxious or in pain. In such situations, I wouldn't try to eliminate the self-stimming just for the sake of eliminating it. Instead, I would attempt to replace it with a more effective method of communicating.

So before you try to reduce or eliminate your child's self-stimming behavior, ask yourself why you are doing it. If the behavior is just mildly annoying or if it creeps you out, then leave it alone and focus on something else. If, however, the self-stimming behavior impacts your child's learning, is dangerous, or is an ineffective method of communicating, then try to replace it with more functional behaviors. How? First you have to figure out what is causing your child's particular behavior!

COMMON CAUSES OF SELF-STIMMING

As I have been hinting at, there are many different reasons why your child might be self-stimming. One is that he is anxious or stressed because he has too many demands being placed on him. Maybe you or his teachers are pushing him too hard. Or maybe he is stressed because of recent changes in his environment. Perhaps something has been moved or there is a new person around.

Another potential cause of self-stimming is that he has excess energy. I am sure you know how that is! You have been sitting all day at your desk at work or in a car on a long trip or trapped on a plane, and you have this overwhelming desire to move! You start bouncing your leg or tapping your finger or shifting in your seat simply because your body needs to do something other than sit! Perhaps that is why your child is rocking back and forth, tapping his finger, or whatever he does!

Or your child could be sensation seeking. That is, he self-stims because it feels good!

Another possibility is that your child is trying to communicate. As I discussed earlier, maybe he isn't feeling well or he is excited or he wants something.

Finally, it could be that your child is self-stimming because it is a habit. For example, a coworker of mine picks at the back of his head. Another strokes his beard. Maybe your child is doing the same thing over and over again not because of any hidden meaning or purpose, but because it is an ingrained behavior.

So how do you tell what is causing self-stimulation?

You have to collect data. You have to see when the behavior occurs, with whom, where, and so forth. You have to look at what happens before and after the behavior. You have to examine all of the evidence that you can gather and be a detective! You have to figure out what it all means.

For example, let's suppose that your initial hypothesis is that your child is rocking because you are asking him to do things that he doesn't want to do. In effect, he is showing his displeasure and his behavior is a way to avoid unwanted activity.

However, after observing for awhile, you realize that the behavior occurs when no demands are being placed on him. In fact, once in awhile, he seems to rock back and forth for no reason. Sometimes he rocks when he is watching television or sitting quietly in his room.

Clearly, this behavior isn't being caused by frustration or his desire to show his displeasure. So, you have rethink everything. Maybe there is something in the environment that is bothering him or he isn't feeling well or he is bored. You have to keep going through the analytical process outlined in the previous chapter until your hypothesis fits.

STRATEGIES FOR REDUCING OR ELIMINATING SELF-STIMMING

Now that you have a solid theory as to why your child self-stimulates, let me talk about what to do about it. As always, remember that not every strategy works with every child. So you may have to modify what I discuss to suit your child and his situation.

Let's begin by assuming that your child is self-stimming because he is stressed or anxious about something. There are two things that you should do. The first is to figure out what is bothering him.

Is there something in the environment causing the anxiety, such as noise or a certain color? If so, maybe you could remove the offending stimuli. Or perhaps you can gradually reintroduce your child to that environment so that he becomes more comfortable.

Is he stressed because of the tasks that you are asking him to do, such as academic work or household chores? If so, maybe you should try some different, less intensive teaching strategies. Or perhaps you could break the tasks down into smaller units. Or maybe the tasks are too difficult and they need to be modified.

Is he stressed because of tension within the family? As we explored in the third chapter, having a child with a disability is very challenging. Consequently, many families with children who have autism experience times of stress and dysfunction. Even though your child might have profound mental retardation and be non-verbal, it is likely that he will pick up on this tension and feel anxious himself. Remember, just because your child is autistic doesn't mean that your child is stupid! You can't hide your family's problems from your child!

If you think that family issues are contributing to your child's behaviors, then you need to fix the underlying cause. Get counseling. Talk to somebody. Do whatever you can to strengthen your family's relationships. Without a healthy family supporting him, your child won't make the progress that he is capable of.

To recap, if you believe that your child is self-stimming because he is stressed or anxious, you must address the stressor. This isn't always easy. Often it is very difficult to remove everything that bothers your child. For example, you can't stop trucks from blowing their horns or planes from flying overhead.

The next thing that you should do is give your child the skills he needs to deal with stressful situations. If you can do this, you will help him immeasurably! But what skills should you teach? Try anything that works for you!

For example, I sit in the hot tub at the YMCA. The hot water really helps my muscles untighten and my body to relax. A good massage also works wonders. However, these ideas might not be appropriate for individuals with autism who don't like to be touched or to sit in hot water. The point is, try some of the things that work for you and then model that behavior.

You also might want to create environments in which your child can relax. For instance, my classroom had "quiet" areas where students would go if they were feeling anxious. These areas were partitioned from the rest of the room, forming little cubbies. There were also beanbag chairs and CDs of soft music or nature sounds, such as falling rain and waves hitting the beach. Other teachers had "lava lamps," chairs that vibrated, and heavy blankets with which their students could wrap themselves.

It is important to customize the quiet area to match the unique needs of your child. So try different lighting. Try different colored walls or pictures. Maybe even try different scents, such as ones from candles or perfume. Again, the idea is to create a soothing environment in which your child can relax.

If you believe that your child is self-stimming out of a need to feel sensations, you might want to utilize interventions such as "brushing." Brushing is a technique where individuals with autism are stroked with a specially designed brush. It is often used in conjunction with techniques called "compression" and "wrapping."

Compression is where joints, such as the elbow and shoulder, are pushed firmly together. It sounds horribly painful, but apparently it isn't. From what I understand, many massage therapists use similar techniques.

Wrapping, on the other hand, involves placing the child in a weighted blanket, kind of like the lead vests that you wear when you get x-rays taken at the dentist's office. These heavy blankets will "stimulate" the child all over his body. It is kind of like receiving a big firm hug.

Such techniques are often collectively known as "sensory integration therapy" or just "SI." I should note that there is presently very little research that indicates sensory integration therapy is effective. However, several of my former students' parents swear by the techniques. They indicate that not only do their children with autism self-stim less, but they also are more willing to be touched and held.

Still, there are people who are very skeptical of such practices. There have even been reports of kids being harmed. For instance, in my home state of Wisconsin, a little boy was smothered to death by somebody trying to perform the wrapping therapy.

I don't want to give the impression that I am against such practices. I am not. They might be of tremendous help to your child. However, I believe that people should understand both the benefits and the risks of everything that they do for their kids—whether that involves knowing the side effects of medications or the potential dangers of interventions.

If you are going to utilize sensory integration therapy or similar strategies, please get trained in a reliable program! Further, practice your skills often and get recertified every year. The last thing you want to do is hurt your child!

Another way to reduce your child's self-stimming behavior is to get him physically active. Several studies have found that self-stimming behavior decreases if children exercise regularly. This makes sense. After all, physical activity can reduce stress and burn off excess energy, both of which can cause self-stimulating behaviors! However, please have your child see a physician prior to beginning any strenuous workout program. Better to be safe than sorry!

The same precaution should be taken for using medications. Some are very effective at minimizing self-stimming behavior. However, all medications have potentially dangerous side effects. So please consult with your doctor and make sure you make an informed decision.

Of course, the best way to reduce or eliminate self-stimming behaviors is to replace them with more appropriate behaviors that accomplish the same goal. For example, if your child is self-stimming because he is trying to communicate, then teach him how to indicate what he wants. I am going to be talking about how to teach communication skills in chapter eight.

There is one final issue that I want to cover regarding this topic. Many parents and teachers with whom I have worked try to reduce

Robert Evert Cimera

or eliminate self-stimming behavior overnight and that simply can't be done—at least not ethically.

Yes, some people use highly aversive techniques, such as shock therapy, to bring self-stimulating behaviors to an abrupt end. But these procedures are no longer thought to be morally appropriate.

So, when trying to change any of your child's behaviors, be patient. It takes time. It also takes a great deal of thought and consistency.

Further, maybe you don't even need to eliminate the self-stimming behavior completely. Maybe you just want to reduce it or redirect it so that it only occurs in certain environments, such as your child's bedroom. In which case, you could set up reinforcement programs that encourage your child not to self-stim in public. For example, if your child doesn't flap his fingers at school, he gets to have something that he likes, such as watching television for an hour. He can still flap at home so that his "need" to perform the behavior is satisfied, but you can just regulate where the behavior transpires.

SUMMARY

As I discussed in the first few chapters, one of the defining characteristics of autism involves repetitious behaviors. Some people with autism rock back and forth, others twirl things, and still others flap their fingers in front of their face or stroke their arms. Most of the time, these behaviors can be ignored. However, sometimes they need to be reduced or eliminated altogether, such as when they interfere with the child's ability to learn or are physically dangerous.

In this chapter, I talked about how to minimize self-stimming behaviors. Keep in mind that many of these behaviors serve an important function, such as helping the child cope with anxiety or communicate his needs. In these cases, you should teach your child how to accomplish his goals in more appropriate ways.

SEVEN

"Attack Me with This Banana!"*: Strategies for Addressing Temper Tantrums and Aggression

In addition to self-stimming, many individuals with autism display aggressive behaviors. For instance, as I mentioned in the first chapter, a student of mine put his aide in a coma by bashing her skull against the pavement in the teachers' parking lot. Now that is certainly an extreme example; however, each semester, several of my student teachers are injured by children with autism. In fact, not too long ago, one of my students had her eyeball scratched. Another had her finger broken. Others have ended up with various bumps, bruises, and cuts, not to mention patches of their hair pulled out.

Most of these injuries occurred because my student teachers didn't understand autism. They treated a child with autism as they

---

* Monty Python had a funny skit where a drill sergeant (played by John Cleese) is training his troops how to defend themselves in case they have to fight a fruit-wielding maniac. In the skit, the drill sergeant gives one of his men a banana and tells the soldier to attack him with it. When the soldier does, the drill sergeant pulls out a gun and shoots the soldier dead. Turning casually to the rest of his men, he then says, "And THAT'S how you defend yourself against a banana!"

I teach a course on crisis management. In it, I go over a ton of topics regarding how to deal with violent students, such as how to deescalate behavior before it turns aggressive and how to restrain students safely. When I get to the session where I discuss disarming students who have potential weapons (e.g., scissors, sharpened pencils, etc.), I show a video of the skit. It is a good tension breaker during a very serious class!

would have treated any other child, which sounds nice, but is often not the wisest move. For example, some of my student teachers tried to reward their pupils with hugs and other physical contact, not realizing that individuals with autism often respond negatively to such stimuli.

In addition to being aggressive towards other people, individuals with autism may abuse themselves. This is usually called "self-injurious behavior," or SIB. I told the story earlier of the little boy who killed himself by running headfirst into walls. That is an example of SIB.

While my students' SIBs were never *that* severe, I worked with many children who would certainly hurt themselves if they had a chance. For instance, one of my students would pinch himself so hard that he would leave large purple bruises all over his arm. He had to wear oversized gloves that looked like oven mitts. Another of my students would give himself black eyes by slapping and hitting himself. He wore a helmet with a face guard much like what football players wear.

But it isn't as if people with autism are monsters who go around attacking themselves or the unwary! Generally speaking, most of my students left everybody alone. Still, there were numerous times when my classroom aides and I were in significant jeopardy of getting hurt. It got so bad with one student that I had to wear an athletic cup and his aide had to wear a chest protector. I can laugh about it now, but back then, it almost made me quit teaching. This leads me to another important point.

The effects of aggressive behavior go way beyond the physical. It was an incredible mental and emotional drain to work with some of my students. Not to sound melodramatic or anything, but I literally went home some days and cried for no reason.

Making Autism a Gift

Also, working with my aggressive students was physically exhausting. I got home around 4:30 and was in bed by 7:00. Every day felt like I had run a marathon.

And that is just me as a teacher! I only had to work five or six hours a day with these children and I had the luxury of summers off. I can only imagine what it is like to be a parent or a sibling of an aggressive child with autism!

In this chapter, I want to briefly discuss the many potential causes of aggression and how to calm your child down or prevent future outbursts. If your child is a serious danger to himself or others, please contact your child's psychologist immediately. He or she may know of in-home programs or medications that may help.

WHY DO INDIVIDUALS WITH AUTISM BEHAVE AGGRESSIVELY?

Before you can change aggressive behavior, you must first understand why it is occurring. After all, if you understand what children are trying to get or avoid by acting aggressively, you can give them what they want if they act more appropriately. So why do people with autism hurt themselves and other people?

Well, as with everything that I am discussing, it really depends upon the individual. Please don't think that all people with autism are the same. They aren't.

Yet, statistically speaking, aggressive behaviors are five to ten times more likely if the individual is non-verbal. Why?

Think about it. You are upset, angry, hungry, or in pain, and you can't tell people. What do you do?

If you are like a lot of my non-verbal students, you get people's attention by grabbing or touching them. And if they don't understand, you grab or touch harder. Further, the more aggressive your actions, the more likely they will pay attention to you. In other words, violence is a very effective way of communicating that you are unhappy or that you want something.

As you can imagine, anxiety and frustration can also cause aggression. Sometimes I pushed my students too far, too fast academically. I gave them tasks that I knew would be a challenge to them. Sometimes they rose to the occasion and they learned. Other times they would react negatively.

Finally, aggressive behavior can be the result of physiological problems. For example, one of my female students with autism had a yeast infection and she kept throwing temper tantrums for no apparent reason. Another one of my students needed a root canal. He kept falling to the ground, rolling back and forth, slapping his face, and kicking and screaming. In both cases, my students must have experienced considerable amounts of pain before somebody realized what was going on.

For this reason, I strongly recommend that you get annual physicals for your child. Also, if your child suddenly starts to exhibit violent or aggressive behavior, assume that there is something physically wrong. Once you are able to rule out a physical cause for the behavior, you can begin trying to change the behavior through behavior modification.

HOW TO REDUCE AGGRESSIVE BEHAVIORS

So how do you go about reducing or eliminating aggressive behaviors? The first step is to always try to figure out why behaviors are occurring. So take a few moments and, using what I discussed in chapter five, try to figure out what your child is trying to get or avoid or communicate. Then, try to teach your child more appropriate behaviors for accomplishing those goals.

Making Autism a Gift

However, that is easier said than done! Plus, what are you supposed to do in the meantime? You can't just let the temper tantrums go on and on, nor can you let your child hurt himself or others. So what do you do?

The first thing you should do is get a handle on the sequence of your child's behavior. Chances are your child doesn't just suddenly erupt into some sort of violent fit, although it may seem that way at times. Once you can figure out the sequence of your child's behavior, you can often stop it before it becomes a full-blown tantrum of biblical proportions. Let me tell you a story that illustrates this.

I had a student with autism named Ron. Ron, if you remember, was the student who grabbed my testicles and squeezed as hard as he could. Needless to say, I was very motivated to figure out what was going on with him. If his violent outbursts didn't stop, I was going to quit my job and become a forest ranger somewhere.

As required by Ron's IEP (I'll talk about what an IEP is later), I had to collect all kinds of data. I collected data on how many times he hit himself or others, how long he worked, when and how often he went to the bathroom, what and how much he ate, and so forth. I literally kept pages and pages of data on him every day.

So, in an effort to record everything that I needed to, I videotaped him. I then sat down in the evening, watched the tapes a couple of times, and recorded what I saw. It was a very long process, and it took a great deal of my time, but what I learned was critically important to my future and Ron's.

As I sat in my living room watching the tapes, I realized that Ron kept repeating the same behaviors in roughly the same sequence over and over and over again. Moreover, the sequence always seemed to end with the same result: he either hurt me or himself.

At first, Ron would clap his hands and wiggle his body. I always thought that he was excited to get to work (I was teaching him to wash dishes at a restaurant). But as I later learned, he wasn't happy at all.

After Ron clapped and wiggled for a minute or two, he began to stomp one foot and shake his head. Then he would poke his temple with his right index finger with increasing vigor. Soon, his finger would turn into a fist. At this point, I started coding his behavior as an SIB and I had to count how many times he hit himself, where, and so forth.

From here, Ron's behavior quickly escalated. He would hit himself in his right temple, scream, and begin grabbing anything or anybody that he could get his hands on, often with painful results. He would throw himself on the floor and bite his hand, frequently drawing blood. At this point, he had to be restrained.

When I realized that Ron followed the same sequence of behaviors before he exploded into his fits, everything became much easier. Not only was I able to prevent him from becoming abusive but I was also able to spend more time teaching him things that he needed to know.

In other words, understanding what leads up to your child's tantrums can be just as important as knowing what is causing them. So let me talk about the typical sequence that aggressive behavior tends to follow and help you figure out what to do at each stage.

Stages of Behavior

Stage #1: Normal
In the first stage, your child is going to exhibit whatever behavior is normal for him. This, of course, will vary from person to person and situation to situation. Maybe your child typically sits in the corner and rocks back and forth. Or maybe he likes to run around outside or watch television. The point is, this is how your child usually is. Anything different from this is atypical.

This stage is important because it gives you valuable information about your child and how to handle his outbursts. At this time, you should keep an eye out for things that your child really likes. This could be specific items (e.g., a toy or favorite object), or activities (e.g., swinging on a swing or playing a video game), or topics of conversations (e.g., airplanes). Keep a list of such things and add to it as often as possible. What you are doing is developing an arsenal of powerful distracters or reinforcers that will make your life much, MUCH easier.

Also keep an eye out for factors—such as times of day, environments, people, and activities—that seem to be less associated with tantrums than other factors. In other words, if you discover that your child rarely has outbursts in church, figure out why. What is it about that environment that is different than environments in which he frequently goes ballistic? Maybe it is the smell of the candles or the organ music or the singing. If so, you can introduce those variables into other environments, thus reducing his tantrums in those places as well.

Stage #2: Irritation

Okay, so your child is in his normal state—whatever that means. Then something happens. It could be anything. There is a loud noise, or somebody new walks into the room, or you used a new deodorant and it smells different than what you normally wear, or you change his routine. It could be anything! These are called "triggers."

Whenever you find a trigger, write it down! You need to keep a running log with "triggers" on one side of the paper and "resulting behaviors" on the other side. For example, you might have something like this:

Trigger	Resulting Behaviors
1. Somebody touches him	Grunting, turning away, slow rocking
2. Loud noise	Screaming, hand flapping, fast rocking
3. Change in routine	Echolalia (says "un naw" for "oh no")

Update your log as frequently as possible. Moreover, share it with your child's teachers! Having such information will be a godsend for them! In essence, it will help them "translate" your child's behavior into something that they can understand.

"How do I know when a trigger occurs?" you might be wondering. Well, your child's behavior will begin to change. He goes from normal to a state of irritation.

How your child behaves when he is irritated depends upon your child. Ron, for example, clapped his hands and wiggled his body back and forth. That was his way of saying, "Things aren't right and I don't like it!"

Your child may do something else. Maybe he tries to leave the room or he starts talking to himself. Maybe he repeats what other people have just said. Whatever he does, remember to write it down!

So your child was fine, and then something happens. A trigger occurs. Now what?

First, don't do anything that will escalate the behavior. Remain calm. Don't talk in a louder or exaggerated voice or touch him unless he likes to be touched.

Individuals with autism tend to "feed" off of other people's emotions. They seem to sense other people's anxieties and frustration, which in turn seems to make them more anxious and frustrated. Relax and try to be reassuring.

Remove the trigger as quickly as possible. If it is a new person, calmly explain what is going on and ask him or her to step into another room while you prepare your child for a visitor. If the trigger is a scent, such as the smell from magic markers or burnt popcorn, open a window.

If you can't remove the trigger, try to relocate the child. Get him to someplace calming. Have a special room in your house and in the school where the child can go and regroup. I mentioned in the previous chapter that my classroom had a little cubicle with a beanbag chair and soft music. Develop someplace like that where your child can relax.

Further, encourage your child to go there on his own whenever he feels anxious or out of control. Remember, your goal is always to teach your child the skills that he will need to succeed in life. Learning how to monitor and de-escalate his own behaviors will be a tremendous help!

In addition to removing the trigger and relocating your child, you might also want to try to redirect your child's attention. This is where the list that you developed during the normal stage becomes worth its weight in gold.

Imagine that something just happened, and you can see that your child is starting to become irritated. You can't remove the trigger. You can't move your child away from the trigger. So try to distract your child from being aware that the trigger exists.

Pick something that you know will get your child's attention in a good way. For example, if he likes to talk about trains or baseball, bring that topic up. But be careful not to go to the same attention-getter too much or it might cease to be a good distractor.

Or maybe your child likes to do something, such as play one of those handheld computer games that all the kids seem to have these days. Give the game to him under the guise of rewarding appropriate behavior. For example, you might say, "Hey, you are really doing a good job being patient! You aren't making any noise, so I am going to let you play your favorite game!"

This does two things. One, it rewards a behavior that you are trying to reinforce. And two, it gets your child's attention away from whatever is causing the anxiety.

I also recommend that you give your child choices. For instance, you might say, "Which would you like to do? Play with this game or look at this book?" Giving your child a selection of distracters makes him stop and think, which, in effect, pulls his mind away from the trigger and focuses his attention upon the options that you provided. It also increases your chances of having one distracter being reinforcing enough for you to prevent an escalation of behavior.

Stage #3: Escalation

Let's suppose that you tried your best, but you were not able to distract your child or relocate him or remove the trigger. Moreover, the behavior keeps escalating. Soon it will be a full-fledged tantrum! What should you do?

The first thing that you should do is start thinking about your safety and the safety of your child, valuable objects, and anybody else in the immediate area. Look around. Where are the exits? You don't want your child running away in his present state of mind. Mentally note where the exits are and be prepared to step in between them and your child. Moreover, if things get very bad, you might have to run and get help. So don't let your child get between you and the door.

Are there any other children in the room? If so, you might want to start getting them all either out of the room or to a part of the room that is away from your child. This was particularly important for me when I had several students with autism in the same class. When one threw a tantrum, they all did! So I really had to be proactive and get the other students out of the room before the first volcano erupted.

Are there any potential weapons nearby? And when I say "weapons," I don't necessarily mean guns, knives, or chainsaws, although I would certainly remove any of these if they were present! By weapon, I mean anything that can be used to injure somebody. For example, I was stabbed between the eyes with a sharpened pencil. I have had desks and chairs thrown at me. One student broke a wooden yardstick over my head. Hopefully, you get the idea.

Nearly everything can be a weapon to a hysterical, out-of-control child. So before your child begins to go crazy, take a quick look around for anything that can hurt you or him. If you can't remove those items, such as a bookshelf that can be pulled down, then try to guide the child away from them.

Are there things that you don't want broken or damaged? Maybe a high-definition–big-screen television set? Or perhaps you have a nice painting or something that is within the child's reach. Again, either try to remove these items or guide the child away from them.

Keep in mind that you probably don't have much time, so you have to quickly look around for exits, weapons, other children, or valuables. Moreover, as you are trying to make everybody safe, keep trying to deescalate your child's behavior.

Keep talking to him. Use calming tones and gestures. Don't point! That is often perceived as being aggressive. Also, don't stand directly in front of your child with your shoulders square. That can also be interpreted as confrontational.

Finally, don't stand within arm's reach! This is important for two reasons. First, if you are within arm's length, your child can hit or grab you. If you put a little distance between you and your child, you will be safer.

Second, keeping your distance is critical because people have a sense of "personal space." If you violate that space, that is, if you get too close, you risk increasing their anxiety and escalating the behavior rather than calming them down.

I know what you are probably thinking. You are thinking, "But this is my child and I just want to let him know that I love him!" You probably believe that leaning really close and whispering some soothing words in his ears will help calm him. But it probably won't.

Robert Evert Cimera

People with autism are very sensitive to changes in their environment, including the space immediately around them. Even under ideal situations, individuals with autism are likely to back up when somebody gets too close, even when it is somebody who loves them. Moreover, they tend to be very sensitive to sounds. So having something whispered in their ears, no matter how lovingly it is uttered, will probably have disastrous repercussions.

Still don't believe me? Try this. Ask a friend to stand really close to you. I mean, really close! Have him or her get within an inch of your nose and then just stand there. Notice anything about your body? Can you feel it shrink back just a little bit? How about your heart? Feel it quicken ever so slightly? That is your body reacting to anxiety. You are able to control it pretty well. How do you think that your child will respond?

Now I am not saying that you should be across the room from your child. That wouldn't do at all, especially if he has a tendency to hurt himself or run off. Try to be between four and six feet away. That would give you plenty of time to react if he runs at you with a flaming chainsaw but also close enough so that you could grab him if you absolutely had to.

Stage #4: The Eruption
You can see it coming, but there is nothing that you can do about it. It is like a train going full throttle towards a brick wall. Your child's self-destructive sequence is locked in and the timer has just reached zero. Your wonderful little son disappears behind a glow of a red face and a whirlwind of kicking, screaming, and potentially very violent behavior. What do you do?

As always, remain calm. Panicking isn't going to help. It might actually get you or your child hurt. So keep your head and breathe.

Making Autism a Gift

The first thing that you have to decide is, do you really have to intervene? Just because your child has blown a gasket doesn't mean that you have to do anything about it right now. Kicking and screaming and carrying on are obviously annoying to say the least, but that doesn't mean you have to jump in and try to stop the tantrum.

Sometimes letting a child carry on with a temper tantrum is *exactly* what you should do, especially if your child is throwing a fit to get your attention! You don't want to reinforce the inappropriate behavior by dropping everything and fussing over him. That will just promote more tirades. Sometimes ignoring the behavior and letting it die out is the best course of action.

However, there are times when you *must* intervene! When? Well, ask yourself these questions:

Is he about to hurt somebody, including you?
Is he about to hurt himself?
Is he about to cause damage to something that you don't want damaged?
Are you in a position to do anything about the behavior?

Let me talk about these questions for a moment. Obviously, if your child is about to hurt somebody or himself, you want to do something. You can't just stand there letting him pound somebody's skull into the concrete or gouge his eyes out. That is a no-brainer.

But what if he is throwing a plastic chair or a toy around the room? Yes, he might break the chair or the toy. He might even mark up the walls or floors. Does this merit you intervening? Do you think that the objects in question are worth the risks of doing something?

Keep in mind that if you attempt to restrain your child, there is a possibility that you or he might get hurt. You might also escalate the behavior even more. Think before you jump in and try to wrap him in a bear hug!

The final situation that I mentioned above probably needs some explaining. You will probably find yourself in situations where your child is throwing a temper tantrum, and there is just nothing that you can do to stop it even if you wanted to. Let me give you an example.

A friend of a friend has a young child with autism. I believe that Evan is about three or four years old. Anyway, one day, without thinking, Evan's father drove through an automatic car wash with Evan in the backseat. When the water and brushes began pounding the car, Evan apparently flipped out, as you probably can imagine.

Again, the father simply wasn't thinking. The noise, the vibrations, and the car being covered in white foam were completely unexpected, and Evan reacted like most kids with autism would. He began thrashing around screaming bloody murder! Fortunately, he was strapped into his car seat, so he couldn't go anywhere (which brings up another ancillary point: always have your child safety locks on your car doors and windows! I have heard of kids trying to get out of cars as they were speeding down the highway!).

Anyway, there was nothing that Evan's father could do other than to sit behind the wheel hoping that the car wash would soon be over. He couldn't stop the tantrum so he had to endure it. Unfortunately, he had paid for the "deluxe" car wash, which lasted a lot longer than the basic car wash. Needless to say, he didn't stop under the car dryer!

Notice that I didn't mention anything about restraining your child in a public place. That is because I don't think that you necessarily have to restrain a child who is throwing a tantrum in public. I know that everybody else in the restaurant or theater or some other public place will disagree with me. However, I am very reluctant to

Making Autism a Gift

try to restrain any child who is out of control. There are simply too many risks, as I'll talk about in a little bit.

Yes, I know that it is no picnic being in a public with a child who is raising holy hell, but he is probably doing it to get out of that environment. If you remove him because he is throwing a fit, you are effectively rewarding the behavior and it will continue. But again, this is just me. I would rather buy everybody a round of drinks and apologize than create a child who is going to blow up every time I take him somewhere. You might have a different take on such situations and that's okay.

Restraining Your Child

Let's suppose that you absolutely must restrain your child during a tantrum. He is in danger of hurting you, himself, or somebody else. Maybe he is likely to run out into a busy street or punch a hole in the Mona Lisa. For whatever reason, you feel that you have to restrain him. How do you do it?

First and foremost, before you ever attempt to restrain your child, I *STRONGLY* suggest that you get properly trained. There are several programs that teach parents how to safely restrain children. For example, I was trained by a company called Crisis Prevention Intervention. It provides workshops all over the country. You might want to investigate the website at http://www.crisisprevention.com.

Also, you might want to check with your local schools and police stations. They often have programs or self-defense classes that are helpful. However, make sure that you go to trainings that only use non-violent restraints. You don't want to take a karate or kickboxing class and then use what you learn on your child!

The idea should always be to restrain your child in a safe manner, not to beat him up! The right kind of professional training is a must for parents and teachers who have potentially aggressive children.

Robert Evert Cimera

Although I can't teach you how to restrain your child in these pages (you will need lots of hands-on practice), I can give you a few tips that will make your life a little easier. For instance, don't take your child's behavior personally. Even if he says very nasty and hate-filled things or he tries to take your head off with a weedwacker, he really doesn't mean it. Just picture him when he was a newborn or when he is sleeping. Try to put an angelic face on the crazy person who is throwing the fit.

If you take it personally, you will likely lose your cool and do something that you will regret. Also, you can damage the relationship that you have with your child. So just keep telling yourself that you are restraining your child because you love him and don't want him hurt.

Next, I need to talk about what you should wear. Believe it or not, your safety and your ability to restrain your child will often depend a lot on your sense of fashion! Let me explain.

The last thing that you want to have happen is to have your hair pulled, especially from behind. As anybody who has gotten into even a minor car accident will tell you, your neck is a very sensitive part of your body. Having your head pulled suddenly to one side can frequently result in a long-term painful injury. Moreover, there is very little that doctors can do to fix a neck that has been damaged. So you need to take great care and make sure that you don't hurt it.

One way to minimize neck injuries is to prevent your hair from being pulled during a restraint. Now, I am not suggesting that you go and get all of your hair shaved, but shorter hair is better than longer hair, at least in terms of safety. However, if you have long hair, you might want to put it in a ponytail when you see that your child's behavior is beginning to escalate.

Ponytails will lessen the chances of your child being able to grab your hair. Plus, they keep your hair out of your eyes during any struggle in which you might find yourself. Many of my colleagues used to keep a rubber band or one of those scrunchy hair things around their wrists so that when a child began to get agitated, they were able to put their hair in a ponytail within a moment's notice.

Hats are also very effective for minimizing the risk of getting your hair pulled. Again, it doesn't have to be a "specially designed" hat. Just a regular baseball cap will do the trick.

In addition to thinking about your hair, think about the jewelry that you are wearing. Do you have any rings on? Do they have any high stone settings? If so, this could be very dangerous.

One of my colleagues had to restrain an aggressive student a few years back. Unfortunately, she was wearing an engagement ring that had a large diamond in a high setting. As she struggled to get the student under control, the ring got turned around so that the stone was facing the palm of her hand. When she went to grab the student, she accidentally cut him across the stomach.

The wound wasn't severe. It wasn't like his guts were falling out onto the floor or anything like that! Still, it was painful and it drew blood. The child began to panic and fought "for his life." Other students saw the blood and started freaking out. Soon, fourteen kids with mental retardation and autism were running around the room screaming.

When the aggressive child went home that afternoon, his parents saw the cut and were understandably upset. They called the superintendent and complained. I think that they even got a lawyer. In the end, my teacher friend was suspended for a while, pending an investigation. Fortunately, the child healed fine and there weren't any scars, physical or emotional.

So, the moral here is if you have a ring with a large stone or a high setting, you might want to consider taking it off when you see that your child's behavior is escalating. Just put it in your pocket or set it off to the side where you won't forget it. If you don't want to take the ring off, then be very conscious of where it is. Keep the stone facing away from the child's body at all times!

Also be cognizant of the earrings, nose rings, or other such piercings that you are wearing. Studs or things that don't hang down from your earlobes are fine. But you probably shouldn't wear any hoops or things that dangle down. Why?

Earlobes aren't attached very securely to your head. They are just pieces of flesh that can easily be torn. I know many teachers who have had parts of their earlobes severed during restraints.

Seriously! I am not making this up or trying to scare you. One of my friends wasn't even trying to restrain a student. She was playing with a toddler who accidentally got his finger caught in her hoop earring. When she pulled away, the earring sliced through her earlobe; now there is a small chunk missing. It looks like her earlobe is forked.

So consider your earrings, nose rings, eyebrow rings, and so forth. If you must wear them, try to wear studs or something difficult to grab. If you have to wear hoops and the like, think about taking the backs off of them so that if they do get pulled, they will come out of the ear naturally.

Okay, now look at your watch. Does it have one of those expandable metal bands? If so, it is likely to grab your child's hair or scrape his skin. You might want to either take it off when the occasion arises or wear a watch with a leather or plastic band.

What else? Oh, yes! Don't forget about necklaces and ties. When I was a rookie teacher, I used to wear ties to school, at least until another teacher approached me in the hallway.

"Let me teach you an important lesson," he said as he grabbed the knot of my tie and twisted it. "Try to get free."

Immediately I began to panic. The air had only been cut off for a fraction of a second, but I still had this tremendous urge to start thrashing around. At the other teacher's urging, I tried to get free. I pulled. I hit his hand. I tried to pry it off. But nothing that I tried worked. Thankfully, the teacher let go. I never wore ties to class again.

If you have to wear a tie, wear ones that are attached by clips or Velcro. That is what police officers wear. If somebody tries to grab their ties, the ties come right off.

The same is true for necklaces. First of all, you shouldn't wear necklaces that you wouldn't want broken. So keep the family pearls locked up until you really need them.

Second, wear only necklaces that will break if pulled hard. Thin metal necklaces are usually fine. However, the rope necklaces with the beads that used to be really popular are probably a bad idea.

Okay, now let me talk about some of the basics about how to deal with violent children. As I discussed earlier, keep at least an arm's length away from children who are violent. This will give you some time to react to whatever they do.

If somebody tries to hit or kick you, in which direction should you move? Now think about this for a moment. Picture yourself standing in front of your child. You are about four to six feet away and you are attempting to talk him down. You see him clinch his fist and pull it back. His right foot is lifting and coming toward you. In which direction should you go?

The answer will often depend on your surroundings. You don't want to move into a corner or any place where you will be in greater danger than you already are. Still, all things being equal, you want to move to the side, rather than backward or forward.

If somebody is trying to hit you in the face, for example, you need to only move a few inches to one side for the person to miss. However, if you move a few inches backward, the person will still probably hit you. And if you move forward, the person will definitely hit you! So it is safer to move from side to side than backward or forward.

Think of it this way. Imagine that your child is trying to kick you. His left leg steps forward, his right leg swings back, and his weight begins to shift. Even if you back up several feet, out of the way of his initial kick, he could easily kick again. He, in effect, could do the goose-step or act like a Rockette and keep forcing you to back up.

But, if you move to one side, he has to stop kicking and pivot around to where you are. As he does this, you can continue moving around him, turning him in a complete circle.

Also, if you move to the side and your child misses you or gives you a glancing blow, you will be in a better position to grab and restrain him. You could put him into a bear hug or perform something called a "basket weave," which is a type of hold you should learn when you get trained to restrain children.

Now, let's suppose that you can't move out of the way quickly enough and somebody grabs you. Perhaps he grabs your wrist or your arm. No matter how big and strong the person is, you should be able to get free fairly easily. Let me show you how.

Grab one of your arms. Look at the hand with which you are grabbing. Notice where the thumb and fingers point at each other? Even if your fingers overlap the thumb, this is the weak part of the grip.

When somebody grabs you, you don't want to pull away. Even if you are successful, you are likely to pull the person on top of you—which would be bad. Further, if the person is stronger than you are, you probably won't be able to pull away.

Instead, you should break through the weak part of the person's grip where the fingers and thumb meet. You can do this by merely twisting and pulling in a very sudden movement. Again, this isn't a feat of strength. You don't want to outmuscle the person or pull the person toward you. Just twist and move.

Making Autism a Gift

You'll need to practice on somebody. Have a friend grab your arm and then practice twisting and pulling away. If you do it correctly, you will be able to get out of anybody's grip. Even if your friend uses two hands, you can break free where the thumbs meet.

"But what if the person grabs my hair or clothing?" you might be thinking. "What do I do then? I can't twist and pull."

True. If somebody grabs you by the hair or clothes, what you want to do is first secure the hand. For instance, if somebody were to grab your hair, you want to take one of your hands and push the person's hand against your own head. Then with your other hand, dig a thumb or a finger in the space between the person's knuckles. This should loosen the person's grip enough for you to pull free.

Again, I can't teach you all of this through a book. You really need to experience how it all works. So go to a workshop or seminar where the teacher demonstrates these maneuvers.

Finally, let's pretend that you have been bitten. For example, let's suppose that your child just affixed his teeth to your forearm and he is clearly hungry. What do you do?

What you should NOT do is pull away! Why? Well, this is going to sound a bit disgusting, but bear with me.

Have you ever bitten into a cooked chicken or turkey leg? What happens if you pull away without biting completely through the meat? More than likely, all of the meat will come right off the bone.

Something very similar could happen if somebody bit you and you pulled away. You could rip your ligaments and cause some serious damage.

What you SHOULD do if somebody bites you is push into the person's mouth. People have very sensitive gag reflexes. The attacker's mouth will open if you put more into it than the person was expecting. You can also do this and squeeze the nostrils shut so that the person can't breath.

Stage #4: The Cooldown

Although they may seem to go on forever, tantrums can only go on for so long. They take a lot of energy to sustain. Eventually your child will run out of steam and stop. But your job isn't finished when the tears have dried. I think, in many respects, it has just started.

At some point, your child is going to have to learn how to behave appropriately. Otherwise you and everybody around him will have to endure his tantrums for the rest of his life. And I am sure that you don't want that!

Seriously, so much of your child's life will be dictated by how well he can behave. Imagine your child at fifty years old still pitching hissy fits that shatter windows miles away every time he is upset. Can you imagine how his life would turn out? Where would he live? With whom? Would he work? Have friends? Have any kind of social life? Imagine his run-ins with the law!

Perhaps more than any academic skill, teaching your child how to control his outbursts will be most critical thing that you can do. But how do you do this?

You need to eventually figure out why the behaviors are occurring. If you think that your child is using his tantrums to communicate something, then teach him more appropriate communication skills and the behavior should go away.

If you think that your child is having tantrums because of environmental factors, such as noise, bright light, or things that are out of place, you need to systematically reduce his sensitivity to these things. Or you develop adaptive behavior, such as wearing sunglasses and earplugs.

Teaching children right after they have had a tantrum is often the ideal time. They are tired and more likely to be compliant than at other times. Don't wait until they recharge their batteries! Make every moment a teachable moment!

Making Autism a Gift

Other Tips and Information

Before you move on to the next chapter, I have a few more topics to cover regarding dealing with aggressive behavior. Consider these "bonus tips" that might help your situation!

Develop A Unified Front

Consistency is *extremely* important when working with children who have autism. If you want to change your child's behavior, you have to make sure that the people working with him are all doing the same thing. You can't hope to extinguish a behavior when you are doing one thing at home and your child's teachers are doing something completely different at school!

So work with your child's teachers. Talk about why you all think the behaviors are occurring. Develop a plan of attack based upon your conclusions. Then implement the plan to the letter everywhere your child is; that means at home, at school, and in the community!

Put a BIP in the IEP

In order to ensure that your child's behaviors are being addressed consistently, you should consider putting a BIP in his IEP. A BIP is a "behavior intervention plan." An IEP stands for "individualized education plan." I'll talk more about these concepts in chapter eleven; however, I want to bring them up very briefly here as well.

BIPs outline how certain behaviors are going to be handled by school officials. For example, maybe certain behaviors, such as rocking or spinning, are going to be ignored, while other behaviors, such as hitting and biting, are going to be addressed with a time-out or response-cost program.

If a BIP becomes part of the student's IEP, the school must adhere to it. It is like having a contract between you and the school. It should help guarantee that everybody is on the same page and doing the same thing.

Take Notes!

Take notes after every temper tantrum and behavioral outburst! I know that you are exhausted after restraining your child, but you have to figure out why the behavior is occurring. You can't do that without data. So immediately after everything calms down, jot down some of your thoughts. Go back to chapter five where I talked about behavior modification and answer some of the questions that I covered. For example, what happened right before the behavior? What was different about that environment than other places where he hasn't had a tantrum?

Again, I know that you are tired and overworked as it is. But you need information to solve the mystery of your child's actions. Keep a little notebook and pencil in your back pocket and write down everything that occurs to you. Or, have a little tape recorder into which you can dictate your thoughts and observations. If you wait until well after the incident, you will probably forget important details and lose your opportunity to help reduce your child's aggressive behavior. So please take notes and keep them organized. Think of it as a "behavioral diary" and add to it whenever possible.

To Spank or Not to Spank?

I grew up in the late 1960s and early 1970s. Back then, spanking unruly children was far more acceptable than it is now. Even though it is no longer in fashion, I think that it is important that I discuss it for a moment.

After trying everything else, some parents spank their misbehaving child out of sheer frustration. However, studies have found that physical punishments only increase aggression. Think about it this way.

Making Autism a Gift

Your child doesn't know how to behave. So you spank him for misbehaving. He then models that kind of behavior. Again, why wouldn't he think that hitting is acceptable? After all, you do it! Why shouldn't he?

Whether you spank your child or not is completely up to you. However, please realize that children might not understand that you are allowed to do things that they can't. So if you run in the house, they will run in the house. If you act aggressively, they will act aggressively.

Be Proactive! Not Reactive!!

This next point is extremely important. If you have a pen or a pencil handy, highlight it and put little stars in the margin. When addressing your child's aggressive behaviors, you have to be proactive. You have to anticipate them happening before they occur. Try to break the cycle of escalation and teach appropriate behavior. If you are only going to be reactive, you will merely be putting out fires your entire life.

Lovaas

Finally, I want to discuss Lovaas. Lovaas is a behavioral intervention that is frequently used with individuals with autism. Also called "discrete trial training," Lovaas uses the principles of applied behavioral analysis and operant conditioning by breaking down tasks into a series of very small, measurable steps. The student practices each step over and over again in rapid sequence with various levels of support from the teacher. These levels of support are then faded until the individual can perform the steps independently.

For example, suppose that a teacher is trying to get the student to learn how to use a fork. The teacher might begin by placing her hand over the student's and manually making the student use the fork. Gradually, the teacher will remove her hand and reduce the amount of intervention offered until the child is independent. Immediately after each successful attempt, the child is rewarded.

There is some controversy among some people regarding the Lovaas approach. It tends to be very physical, especially initially, and the instructor may force the student to do things against the student's will. Consequently, the procedures appear very aggressive and violent. However, research has found it to be an effective method for teaching students with autism.

If you are interested in using Lovaas, make sure that you are trained by a certified instructor. Don't just start forcing your child to do things that he doesn't want to do!

SUMMARY

In this chapter, I talked about the aggressive behaviors that many individuals with autism display, both toward themselves and other people. I discussed some of the likely causes of such behavior and how to deescalate it before it erupts into violence. I also covered some very basic information about what to do during and after a violent temper tantrum.

If your child is aggressive, please get trained in how to use nonviolent restraints. Consider contacting the Crisis Prevention Institute (or similar programs). There are probably workshops available in your state.

Finally, do what you can to reduce the stress resulting from having an aggressive child. Spend time with yourself and other adults. Exercise. Talk to people about things other than autism and disabilities. Remember, the effects of aggression aren't just measured in bumps and bruises!

EIGHT

*"What We Have Here Is a Failure to Communicate . . ."**: *Strategies for Addressing Social and Communication Skills*

Probably more than anything else, having poor social and communication skills can really limit your child's future. Think about it! Imagine that you couldn't communicate your thoughts, wants, or needs very effectively! What would you do? Either your needs would go unmet or, as I discussed previously, you would use inappropriate behaviors, such as violence, to get what you wanted.

Further, think about what your life would be like if you didn't have any real friends or if everybody made constant fun of you! How would you feel about yourself?

People frequently forget how social humans are. Try going a week without talking to anybody and you will begin to see what I mean. Without some sort of social interaction, most people become very

---

* One of my students, Richard, was a BIG movie fan. He would watch movies all day long and remember every scene by heart. One day, as some students were working in a small group on a social skills lesson, I was becoming frustrated by my students' inability to master some particular skill. When I leaned back and took a deep breath, Richard put his elbows squarely on the table and said in a fair imitation of Paul Newman, "What we have here is a failure to communicate!" Evidently, Richard had watched *Cool Hand Luke* the night before.

Please remember, sometimes your child's lack of learning is because of the teacher's failure to communicate effectively, not your child's ability to learn!

lonely, anxious, or depressed. Some even become suicidal or mentally unbalanced.

If your child lacks effective social and communication skills, nearly every aspect of his life is going to be rather limited. Education, vocation, recreation, even dating and adult relationships will all be adversely affected if your child cannot interact effectively with others. This is why you and your child's teachers have to really work on these areas! But how do you do this? Good question!

TEACHING APPROPRIATE SOCIAL SKILLS

What Is Appropriate?

Before you can begin teaching your child appropriate social skills, you have to first figure out what "appropriate" social skills are! For example, should your child yell in the house? Yes, if there is a fire or an ax-wielding maniac running around! No, if he is merely yelling for the sake of making noise or if he doesn't want to leave the television to go find you. In other words, the situation in which a behavior occurs will often determine whether it is appropriate or not.

The same thing is true for age. What is appropriate for a four-year-old to do isn't appropriate for a twenty-four-year-old!

The point is, before you start trying to change your child's social behaviors, you have to figure out what you want. How do you want your child to behave? This is a critical step! You have to know what you are going to teach before you teach it!

So how do you figure out what social skills you need to teach your child? First of all, observe some children who are roughly your child's age. It might take a while for your child to master the skills you are going to teach him, so you might want to observe children who are a couple of years older than him. That way, you will be planning for the future rather than always playing catch-up.

Making Autism a Gift

Observe some older children who are genuinely well behaved. You don't want to model your child's behavior after hoodlums! Look at what they are wearing, how they initiate conversations, how they interact with each other. Are they joking around? If so, how? How do they play? Do they take turns or just sit in a sandbox playing independently?

Try to observe many different kids in several different environments. Take notes, but don't look like a stalker!

Generate a list of behaviors that you see other kids using. From this list, select two or three that will help your child interact successfully. Don't select too many! You don't want to overwhelm your child. Keep things simple and try to take baby steps toward a larger goal. In a little bit, I'll share what social skills I used to teach my students. It might help you brainstorm ideas for your child.

What Is Your Child Doing Wrong?

Before you start teaching your child the two or three social skills that you have written down, stop and think, "What is my child doing wrong?" By that I mean, what is it about his behavior that makes it inappropriate for him at his age, the situations in which he finds himself, and so forth? Why do you think that your child is socially awkward?

Don't just shrug and say, "Because he has autism!" That isn't going to help. Try to identify the exact behaviors that your child does that make him socially inept. For example, does he habitually pick his nose? Does he poke people in the chest? Does he dominate conversations? Does he get very anxious around new people? Does he talk about bizarre things, such as dog poop or belly button lint? What does he do that is atypical?

Once you have identified why your child isn't fitting in, figure out why each of those behaviors is occurring. For example, if he is picking his nose all of the time, maybe he is suffering from allergies. Perhaps some medications or allergy shots will help unplug his nose, thereby reducing his need to pick. If he pokes people in the chest in order to get their attention, then teach him a better method of getting attention. If he gets anxious around new people, try to get him used to one new person and then gradually increase his circle of friends. If he talks about dog poop and belly button lint because he doesn't have anything else to talk about, teach him other topics of conversation that his peers might like.

As I discussed in chapter five, behaviors often have a purpose. Figure out why the inappropriate behavior occurs and replace it with suitable behaviors that achieve the same ends!

Some Specific Skills to Teach

Okay, by now you should have a list of social skills that your child could really use! These are skills that, if he masters them, will greatly help him in a variety of facets of life (e.g., job interviewing, dating, making and maintaining friends, etc.). If you haven't generated a list or need additional ideas, don't worry. As I promised, I am going to take a few moments to talk about what I used to teach my students. As always, focus on your child's unique needs. Don't teach him something simply because I think it is important!

With that said, I would guess that the skills that I taught most often involved how to initiate conversations or playing. These behaviors are critical for your child to be socially included with his peers. After all, your child can't just stand in a corner and wait for somebody to interact with him! He will have to start interactions himself!

So how did I teach initiating interactions? I taught students how to ask their classmates things like, "Do you want to play?" "What did you do this weekend?" and "Did you see this movie yet?" Whenever they initiated activities or conversations, my students got a reward.

I also taught many of my students how to take turns. Taking turns affects not only conversations, as I will soon discuss, but also playing. If your child refuses to take turns with other children, pretty soon nobody will play with him.

Of course, learning to follow rules is also critical. If you can teach your child how to follow rules, not only will he be able to play games but he will also do better in structured environments, such as school or work.

Another skill that I used to teach my students was sharing. When you think of sharing, you probably think about two kids playing with the same toy. But sharing isn't just for children! Think of all the things you share with other adults, such as your popcorn at a movie theatre or the sofa at home or your stapler at work. If you can teach your child how to share, he will get along better with his peers, be less rigid in his behaviors, and be more tolerant of others.

Perhaps the hardest social skill that I used to teach my students with autism was joking. Life isn't all work and no play! Joking around, teasing, and kidding are part of being friends, coworkers, and class-mates. However, most of my students with autism simply did not know how to tell jokes or understand humor, especially sarcasm!

For example, one of my non-autistic students used to quote characters from the television show *The Simpsons* all the time. If somebody asked him, "Do you want to play?" He would say something like, "Sure . . . when monkeys fly out of my butt!" (This is a line that Bart Simpson used to say.) This would perplex my students with autism. They didn't understand why their classmate would say sure, which indicated yes, but then not be willing to play.

How to Teach Social Skills

So there are a few of my suggestions. You can certainly focus on other social skills. Again, you should keep your child's individual needs in mind.

But how do you teach a child with autism social skills? According to most definitions of autism, social interaction isn't exactly easy for these kids. So how do you improve their abilities in these areas? Here are some ideas.

Most people learn social skills by observing others. For example, if you go into a new restaurant and don't know whether to seat yourself or wait for a hostess, you probably watch the people in front of you. Or if you are at a party and you don't know how to address somebody (e.g., by Dr., Mrs., Miss, or by the person's first name), you might wait to see what other people say.

However, people with autism don't learn very effectively in this manner. They often don't pick up on the subtle nature of social interaction. For instance, they might see that people extend hands and shake when they meet, but they might not take into consideration which hand to extend, or how hard to grip, or how aggressively they should shake, or for how long.

Because of this difficulty, you have to be very overt when teaching students with autism. You can't just say, "Watch me and do what I do." You have to explain *exactly* what you want them to notice and then demonstrate the behavior.

"See which hand I am extending?" you might say. "Further, I am not squeezing too tightly, just a little firmly. And I am not shaking the other person's hand up and down fast or hard. I am being gentle. Just move your hand up and down a couple of times, then let go."

So the first necessity for teaching kids with autism is to be very clear and obvious. Explain *everything*. Don't be subtle!

The next is to give concrete examples and cues. Don't be abstract. For example, suppose that you want to teach your child how to read people's body language so that he can determine if somebody is bored with a conversation. You might want to give your child a checklist of observable behaviors that often mean that somebody is losing interest in what is being said. "Is the person frequently looking at his watch? Is he looking away from you a lot? Is he tapping his foot or finger?"

Also, consider role-playing with your child. Act out the social situations and skills that you are trying to teach. Using videos that show social interactions has been particularly effective, especially if you discuss them with your child. For example, you might say, "Look at his face. See how he is smiling and looking at the other person in the eye? He is happy and interested in what she is saying. Now this person is angry. See how her eyebrows are pointing down and her face is kind of puckered?"

There are tapes of social situations that are specially designed for this kind of instruction. However, many teachers and parents whom I know simply watch the television with the sound off. They watch scenes from *Friends* or whatever show they like and then discuss how to interpret body language and facial expressions.

Another key to teaching appropriate social skills is to create numerous and meaningful opportunities for your child to interact with somebody. For example, if your child enjoys playing video games, only let him play if he is playing with another person. Or, create team activities that your child would like. Or, if your child has certain topics that he loves or obsesses about, such as Harry Potter or Pokemon or birds, find other children with the same interests! Do whatever you can to foster social interactions that aren't forced or contrived.

Additionally, make sure that your child has plenty of opportunities to practice the skills you are teaching him. Practice! Practice! Practice! You simply can't have enough of it! Unlike his peers, your child will need a great deal of repetition before he masters certain situations, so try to give him opportunities to employ his new skills several times per day every day!

Finally, reward all social activity! In chapter five, I had you write down some of the things that your child likes, whether it is M&M's or time alone or swinging. Whenever your child interacts, reward him, even if he doesn't interact particularly skillfully. Keep rewarding him until he begins to get the hang of the skill you are teaching. Then gradually only reward more appropriate behavior. Eventually, when your child is interacting willingly, fade the rewards out altogether.

Other Tips and Strategies

Before we move on, I want to give you a few more tips that might be of help. The first is not to expect sudden changes in your child's behavior. Remember, your child has autism. By definition, he is going to have abnormal social skills. That is part of the condition. However, this doesn't mean that your child can't improve his skills! He can, but he will probably never be like everybody else in every way. I am sorry. I hope that didn't sound negative. It is just that you can't "cure" autism nor can you teach autism "out" of your child. So try for small, incremental changes, not dramatic turnarounds.

Also, when you are instructing your child on social skills, don't talk in absolutes. Don't say things like, "You should *always* do that." Kids with autism tend to latch on to such things. So when you tell them to never talk to strangers, they may never speak to anybody other than you and immediate family members, including the police or teachers.

When teaching your child anything, whether it is social skills or math, try to use multiple approaches. Don't just show him flash cards or have him watch videos. Try several different techniques in multiple environments. This will help your child generalize and master the information.

Help your child broaden his interests. Don't try to force his interests in a completely new direction, but try to expand them a little bit. For example, if he has read all of the Harry Potter books 203 times, suggest that he read *The Lord of the Rings* or *The Chronicles of Narnia*. Or if your child likes dinosaurs, bring him to a museum and see if anything else catches his eye! The greater the variety of interests that your child has, the more he will have in common with potential friends and classmates.

If you want other people to interact with your child, you may have to educate them about what autism is. They might not have been exposed to autism before. Or, they might have heard misinformation, such as "autistic people are crazy and dangerous!"

So in addition to preparing your child, you may have to prepare your child's peers, classmates, and teachers! Give them some information about what autism is and why your child acts the way that he does. Talk to them about his triggers or interests. The more willing they are to interact with your child, the more success your child will experience.

This last suggestion is going to sound trivial, but it really isn't. If you want your child to be accepted by his peers, he has to dress the part! I know that is incredibly shallow, but kids *are* incredibly shallow! Chances are they will pick on your child not because he has a disability, but because he isn't wearing the latest "must have" designer jeans or tennis shoes!

Look around! Kids with disabilities stand out in a crowd not because of their behavior or their disabilities but because they often dress as if they were . . . well, "nerds"! They wear clothes that are too small or big for them, or their siblings' hand-me-downs that went out of style a decade earlier. They have haircuts or wear glasses that are unflattering. Or—my favorite one—they have school supplies that are not age appropriate, such as Hello Kitty lunch boxes in high school! What high schooler would want to interact with a kid who has a Hello Kitty lunch box?!

If you don't know what the latest fashions are, just go to your local mall and look around. Or look as some catalogs or magazines. You can even have the teenie bopper next door take your child shopping! This would not only help you figure out what is in style, but it might build a friendship!

TEACHING EFFECTIVE COMMUNICATION SKILLS

I just talked about teaching appropriate social skills. Now let me shift to teaching effective communication skills. Don't picture these as unrelated or separate topics. They aren't. They overlap considerably. Clearly, it is difficult to have good social skills without effective communication skills. The two go hand-in-hand, so much of what I discussed earlier will apply here as well.

Typical Communication Issues with Individuals Who Have Autism

Before I begin talking about strategies to improve your child's communication skills, you first must understand some of the problems that your child may be experiencing. Then you might be able to figure out how to address these particular issues.

For example, as I discussed in the first chapter, one of the defining characteristics of an autistic person is delayed language ability. For this reason, it is very important that children with autism be identified early and be given access to speech and language services as soon as possible.

In addition to delayed language acquisition, individuals with autism frequently exhibit periods of echolalia. If you don't remember, echolalia is when people repeat things over and over again.

There are two types of echolalia: delayed and mitigated. Delayed is when people repeat something that they heard an hour or day or even several weeks in the past. For example, they might suddenly just start blurting out lines from a movie that they saw a month ago.

Mitigated echolalia involves more immediate repetition. For instance, you might say, "Boy, it is a nice day!" and your child repeats, "Nice day. Nice day. Nice day. Nice day."

Generally speaking, there appear to be three "functions" of echolalia. One is that it comforts the person. Repeating the same thing over and over again is much like a chanting a mantra. So it could be that your child is being echolalic because he is anxious or stressed. If this is the case, you will need to reduce his anxiety by either removing whatever is causing it or teaching your child how to cope with whatever is bothering him.

The second function of echolalia is to communicate some sort of need or idea. For example, you might ask your child, "Do you want anything to drink?" And he replies, "Want anything to drink. Want anything to drink." It is his way of saying, "Why yes, mother. I would indeed like to have a drink. Thank you very much!"

In these situations, you can simply translate the echolalia in your head. When he repeats what you said, he is trying to tell you something. You can also try to reinforce proper sentence structure. You might only give him a drink if he says, "May I have a drink?" or "Yes. I would like a drink." However, this depends largely on your child's abilities. You, after all, don't want him to become dehydrated!

The final reason why many people with autism often repeat things is simply because it is a habit. It is much like how some non-autistic people talk out loud to themselves or say "ummm" while they are thinking. They do it because they have always done it. Behavioral interventions, such as self-monitoring and reinforcements, are often effective at addressing such situations.

Another characteristic that individuals with autism often display is called "autistic leading." Autistic leading is when children with autism rely on physical prompts to communicate what they want. For instance, your child might walk up to you, take your hand, and guide you to the cookie jar. He might even open the cookie jar and put your hand in it, indicating that he wants you to give him a cookie.

The problem with autistic leading is that it often inhibits children from developing more age-appropriate verbal skills. Indeed, why should they speak when they can get what they want by gesturing or manipulating your hand? If your child does this, you might want to try to replace his behavior with another type of communication, something more effective and acceptable.

In addition to expressing themselves, many individuals with autism also have difficulties with receptive language. For instance, they might take everything that they hear as being the literal truth. So if you were to say, "Boy! It is raining cats and dogs out there!" they might actually expect to see Persians and Pomeranians falling from the sky!

Moreover, they have a tendency to overgeneralize comments. Let me give you an example.

A friend of mine lives next door to a boy with autism. One rainy morning, she noticed that her neighbor was standing by the curb waiting for the school bus to come. He was simply standing there with no umbrella or raincoat, as if it were a bright, sunny day.

The boy was soaked to the bone. So my friend told him that he could wait for the bus inside her garage, where it was dry and warm.

Months later, my friend had to get to work early. She went into her garage and found this boy standing there in the dark. Apparently, he had been waiting for the bus in her garage every morning since the rainstorm.

He didn't understand why he was told to stand in the garage. He didn't comprehend the fact that it was raining and that my friend wanted him to be dry. She said to "wait in the garage," and he did—every day until he was told to stop.

In these situations, it is often very valuable to teach your child how to rationally analyze what people tell him. Many of my students were very good at this once they realized it was something that they should do.

How did I teach them to consider the underlying meanings and purposes of what people told them? Basically, my students played a game where I would say something and my students would have to determine whether I was telling the truth or lying. Sometimes I would use figures of speech and ask my students what I meant by them. They might even work on identifying sarcasm.

It was a fun game and my students tended to continue "playing" it even at home, which was my goal. For example, if their parents said something like, "You just can't beat this heat!" my students would look at them and say, "You mean that it is hot." Or if somebody said, "This traffic is a bear!" my students would respond, "No, it isn't. You are using a metaphor." Again, the idea is to get your child to realize that what people say isn't always what they mean.

The final point that I want to make is even though your child may be non-verbal (i.e., doesn't "talk"), this doesn't mean that he doesn't communicate. He does. However, you might not notice it.

For instance, in a previous chapter, I told you about how I video-taped a student named Ron and learned that he would go through a series of behaviors before becoming very aggressive. Well, those behaviors—swaying his head, stomping his feet, hitting his temple—were all ways that he was communicating. The problem was, until I started analyzing the videotapes, nobody paid attention to him. I thought that he was merely swaying his head, stomping his feet, and hitting his temple. I didn't know that he was telling me that he was unhappy.

It is critically important that you watch your child and attempt to figure out what he is "telling" you. Look for patterns of behaviors.

Maybe one leads to another, such as in Ron's case. See what the behaviors end up producing for your child. You might even want to videotape him and watch for clues. See what your child is gesturing toward or trying to move away from. Again, just because your child doesn't speak, that doesn't mean he isn't communicating!

Strategies for Teaching Effective Communication Skills

Okay, so I have covered a whole bunch of issues related to your child's communication skills. Now you can figure out how to improve the skills that he has as well as teach him ones he doesn't have. Here are a few suggestions.

Many times, the communication delays that kids with autism experience get worse because they aren't "motivated" to speak. Let me explain.

If you were in a foreign country and all you had to do was point at things to get whatever you wanted, how quickly would you learn the foreign language? Probably not very quickly! Why would you? After all, there is no real necessity for you to learn to say things correctly because most of your desires are met when you gesture and grunt.

The same tends to be true for kids with autism. Parents and teachers soon learn what their children are trying to "say" and then respond accordingly. Try to gradually fade away from doing this. Make your child work a little bit for things that motivate him.

For example, give your child something that he really likes to eat, such as ice cream, but only give him a little bit. Then encourage him to say or sign "more" or "may I have more."

I am not encouraging you to starve your child! I am just pointing out that you should use everything in your power to encourage and motivate him to communicate effectively.

Furthermore, you will need to give your child numerous and meaningful opportunities to communicate. Asking for food or toys that he wants is one way. Another is to encourage him to play games that require some sort of interaction, such as "Go Fish!"

Or you can pair your child up with a peer who has similar interests. For example, if your child likes a particular television program, book, or sport, have him talk with other people about that topic. Again, the idea is to get your child to communicate as often as possible.

Finally, when your child does communicate, try to reward him as immediately as possible. Then, as the frequency and duration of interactions increase, you can gradually fade reinforcement.

Alternative Communication Systems

Every few months of so, I get a phone call or an e-mail from parents who want me to teach their non-verbal child to speak. During the course of the intake interview, I always ask the same question: "Why is it so important that your child learn how to talk?"

The parents look at me, rather perplexed, as if the answer were obvious. They then explain in great detail the importance of being able to communicate and how their child's behavior will improve if he could say what is on his mind.

"Yes," I respond, "but why does he need to *talk*?"

The parents typically look at each other and then back at me, as if they were worried about my sanity. Some have even gotten up to leave the meeting.

Parents and teachers often think that speaking is the only effective method of communication. But it isn't! There are many different ways people can communicate. Some of them have been found to be extremely useful for people with autism. Let me talk about a few of these.

Sign Language

The use of sign language in public schools has increased dramatically over the past decade. In fact, nearly all of my colleagues teach their students with autism how to sign at least a handful of words, such as "bathroom," "hungry," "thirsty," and "help." For some reason, using sign language appears to be the desired mode of communication for many kids with autism. Perhaps this is because signing doesn't make noise.

At any rate, there are several types of "sign" languages, such as Signed English, which involves signing, or finger spelling, exactly what somebody says. There is also ASL, or American Sign Language, which is actually modeled after French in terms of its sentence structure.

In ASL, you don't sign every word. For example, instead of literally signing, "I want to go home now," as you would with Signed English, with ASL you might sign, "go home want." The context of the sentence clarifies the message.

Lastly, there is something called "home signs." Home signs are signs that are specific to a certain person or group of people. It isn't a "proper" language in that a stranger could understand and use it to communicate. Maybe I can illustrate this.

One of my students was deaf and had mental retardation. We tried to teach him formal ASL, but he would be very sloppy with his gestures, which changed the meanings of his signs. When he was trying to say "good," he would actually sign "thank you" and so forth.

Finally, we ended up learning *his* language. For instance, rather than finger spelling my name as "R . . . o . . . b," he would point with his index finger to the bridge of his nose between his eyes. That was his sign for me. I have a scar between my eyes. An outsider wouldn't comprehend the meaning of this, but everybody who worked with him did. Once we figured out what signs meant what, we were able to communicate with him far more effectively, which in turn reduced some of his undesirable behaviors.

Making Autism a Gift

Picture Languages

In addition to sign languages, there are also languages that are pictorial in nature. No, I'm not talking about hieroglyphics here, although that is a good example of a "picture language." What I am talking about is a way to communicate by using drawings or photographs.

For example, there is something called PECS, or Picture Exchange Communication System, which is a program that teaches students how to use pictures to express themselves. PECS has over 10,000 images that can be downloaded from a computer and printed on paper. Students communicate by pointing to the pictures. Sometimes the pictures are strung together to form sentences.

Of course, you don't need to buy an official program to get your child to communicate by using pictures. You can simply get a digital or Polaroid camera and take snapshots of various things around the house, such as a toilet, certain foods and drinks, and people. You can then put these images on large sheets of paper or poster boards.

You can also put them in a small booklet that your child can carry around with him. These are often called "communication wallets." If your child wants to talk about his teacher or his best friend, he opens up his wallet and points to the appropriate picture. Such strategies can be very effective.

Writing

Of course, rather than using signs or pictures, you could always teach your child how to write! You could give him a pad of paper and a small golf pencil to keep in his back pocket. He could then write down what he wants to say!

Computers

In addition to "low tech" strategies, such as using communication wallets and writing on a pad of paper, there are also many "high tech" gadgets that can help your child communicate. For example, there are devices where students push a button and a voice from the computer says, "I want to go to the bathroom," or whatever the button is programmed to say. Perhaps you have seen pictures of the world-famous physicist Stephen Hawkings. He has a device like this.

In the past, computerized communication apparatuses were big, bulky, and expensive. Fifteen years ago, one of my students had one attached to his wheelchair. It cost over $15,000 and didn't work very well.

Nowadays, computerized communication devices are much cheaper, more portable, and have many desirable features. For instance, one of my recent students has a system that is a little bigger than a palm pilot and it not only contains thousands of images and voices but also keeps track of the student's schedule and homework. It even beeps when the student needs to take his medication!

I have two suggestions if you choose to purchase a computerized communication system. The first is to insure it, especially if you get an expensive model. The second is to check the battery often. There is nothing more frustrating than to sit down with a student to start a lesson only to find that the battery to his communication device wasn't charged the night before! If you don't charge the battery, the computer becomes nothing more than an expensive paperweight!

Facilitated Communication

The final method of communicating that I want to discuss is called "facilitated communication," or FC. I am a bit reluctant to talk about FC because it has had some bad press over the past couple of years. There have been some incidences where it has been abused and words have been "put into" people's mouths with disastrous results. Still, there are people who swear by it and you are entitled to know about all of the options.

Facilitated communication is a system of communicating where the individual with autism points to letters or types out words with the assistance of a "facilitator." The facilitator might encourage the person or steady his hand or provide whatever assistance the individual may need.

Through such methods, wonderful poems and books have been written. However, critics suggest that it is the facilitator who is actually doing the writing, not the individual with autism. In the end, you have to decide whether FC is right for you. If you would like additional information, I suggest that you consult some of the resources listed in the appendix.

Final Tips and Strategies

Before I conclude this section, I would like to end with some final tips and strategies that might help you teach your child more effective communication skills.

The first is make sure that you continue to build upon the skills that your child already has. Don't work on something for months and then stop working on it once your child has reached mastery. Much like a muscle, your child needs to keep utilizing these skills, otherwise they will disappear from his repertoire.

Second, educate teachers, peers, family members, and other parents about autism. If there are people who interact regularly with your child, make sure that you teach them how your child communicates. Show them the communication wallet or computerized devices. Get them comfortable talking *to* your child rather than *around* him.

Finally, when you are teaching your child how to socialize or communicate, don't insist on perfection. Don't force him to make

Robert Evert Cimera

eye contact or spend too much time working on pitch or tonal qualities of your child's voice. Chances are you and your child will only get frustrated. Focus on the things that you can change. Start small and build steadily on your successes.

SUMMARY

Humans are very social creatures. It is difficult for us to be by ourselves for an extended period of time. Yet, children with autism are frequently by themselves, both physically as well as socially. By teaching your child how to act more socially appropriate, you can really improve the quality of his life.

Unfortunately, one of the key reasons why individuals with autism are so isolated is because they lack effective communication skills. Even when individuals with autism are verbal and can speak, they often don't converse or interact in an age-appropriate manner. Social and communication skills, therefore, go hand-in-hand. You can't improve one without addressing the other.

In this chapter I discussed both of these areas. Further, I identified some explanations as to why your child might have difficulty communicating or interacting. Finally, I discussed several strategies for improving these critical aspects of his life.

NINE

*"Ten Minutes to Wapner!"**: Strategies for Addressing Fears, Fixations, and Routines*

In addition to having poor social and communication skills, people with autism often tend to obsess or fixate on things. For example, many of my students had to perform specific routines. They had to get up at the same time, sit in the same seat, watch the same television shows, eat from left to right on their plates, and so forth.

Other students had fixations on objects, such as pens or lights or a stuffed animal or a toy. They couldn't go anywhere without them. For example, one of my students purchased a "glow stick" at a country fair. When it eventually stopped glowing, he was devastated for weeks! He was simply inconsolable. Another student could only write with a novelty pen. A third had a notebook in which he would draw. He wouldn't go anywhere without it.

*If you want an excellent example of fears, fixations and routines, watch the movie *Rain Man*. In it, Dustin Hoffman does an incredible job depicting an adult with autism named Raymond. For example, Raymond has a routine where he watches *The People's Court* every afternoon. As the show's airtime approaches, Raymond makes repeated announcements, such as, "Ten minutes to Wapner!" I show the film in one of my classes. I pause it frequently and discuss the characteristics of autism that it illustrates. I also talk about how these characteristics affect individuals with autism and how parents and teachers can address them.

Still other students fixated on topics of conversation, such as fire trucks, sports, mathematics, cows, or Pokemon. They talked and talked and talked about the same topics to anybody who would (or wouldn't) listen. Many times they actually knew what they were talking about. For example, one of my students was obsessed with cars and could tell you almost anything about any particular make or model, including its gross weight, fuel economy, rear seat legroom, and engine size. Other students would merely repeat things over and over again about the same topic (e.g., "I saw an airplane today! I like airplanes! I saw one today! I like airplanes! I saw a jet yesterday. A jet is a type of airplane. I like airplanes.").

These fixations can actually be beneficial. For example, a child with autism that I met fixates on music. He plays the piano all day and night. It is part of his routine. He practices so much that he got to be extremely good and is now performing all over the country. He is fantastic!

In other words, "fixation" or "obsession" might sound negative; however, they don't have to be. They simply mean giving sustained attention to something. If that something is productive, then what is the harm? For instance, I certainly "fixated" on my studies when I was in my doctoral program! If I didn't, I wouldn't have ever earned my PhD!

However, many of the fixations that people with autism have aren't positive at all. In fact, they can be extremely harmful or dangerous. For instance, many of my students had fixations with fire and would like to watch things burn. One boy accidentally burned his grandmother's house down!

Other negative fixations can develop into all-consuming fears. For example, after hearing about somebody dying in a nearby lake, one of my students became obsessed about people drowning. This later turned into a profound fear of water, all water! Eventually, my student refused to bathe, then to shower, and then to get wet at all!

So what did I do? How do you handle such fears and fixations? Fortunately, that is the topic of this chapter!

FINDING THE PURPOSE

As I discussed in earlier chapters, many behaviors have certain purposes. For instance, an individual might adhere to routines in an order to feel comfortable with his surroundings or to ward off anxiety. Others might simply do what they do out of force of habit. Or the behavior might be the result of "superstitious learning," where the person believes that if he wears his lucky shirt, he will have a good day.

As I will discuss momentarily, how you address fixations will depend largely on why you think the behavior is taking place. So how do you determine why your child fixates on things? The same way you would with aggression or any other behavior. You have to collect data, look for patterns, and figure out when and in what situations the fixations occur and don't occur.

Once you determine the behavior's function, you can then replace it with a more appropriate manner of achieving the same outcome. Let me talk about how to do this.

Habits

Many times people perform certain routines and fixate on various objects merely out of habit. We all do this! I, for example, have this compulsion to check my e-mail every few minutes. As I am sitting here writing this chapter, I must have checked my e-mail fifteen to twenty times. Whenever I get stuck on a word or a sentence, I stop and check my e-mail, many times without realizing it.

You probably have similar habits. Maybe you twist your wedding ring. Maybe you twirl your hair. Maybe you drive to work the exact same way even though there is a quicker or better route.

Humans are creatures of habits. For whatever reason, if we do something and it works for us, we keep doing it. So what do you do if your child displays certain habits? How do you change them?

First ask yourself why they need to be changed. As I discussed above, most habits are completely harmless or even beneficial. Maybe your child's hair twirling bothers you, but that doesn't mean you have to stop it. Chances are there are far more pressing things on which to focus.

But let's suppose your child has a certain non-purposeful behavior that is interfering with his life. Take, for example, one of my students named Ravi. Ravi used to go to his locker after every class period. Further, Ravi used to take a certain route each time. He would go up the blue stairway, across the glass-enclosed walkway, and up the red stairway to his locker, and then he would go to his next class.

Ravi used to perform this behavior in ninth grade. However, back then his classes were closer to his locker so he could complete his route and be where he needed to be on time. That is to say, there was no harm in his behavior. Actually, I encouraged it. I thought his little walks got him physically integrated with his peers, who tended to socialize in the hallways during passing periods.

But when tenth grade came around, Ravi was habitually late for his classes, which were now spread throughout the building. We had to get him to stop his habit. We had to break his pattern.

The first thing that we did was talk with Ravi. We explained why his "route" was problematic and why he needed to change. He understood, but that didn't really help us. Whenever he "wasn't thinking," he would walk his old familiar path, making him late for his next class.

So we tried to do two things. One was to get him "hooked" on a new route that was quicker and more direct. Second, we introduced a self-management strategy that got him to overtly think about where he was going. Let me explain how we did this.

Ravi liked maps. So we sat down with him and showed him a map of the school. We then had him find each of his classes and then plot the fastest course to each room. He enjoyed this.

With the new routes identified, we had to get him used to taking them. For about two weeks, as Ravi was leaving a classroom, each teacher reminded him to "take the new route." This worked fine. However, I didn't want to have Ravi relying on the verbal reminders from his teachers. After all, they have other things to worry about!

So we incorporated a "self-management" strategy where Ravi would remind himself. We already had Ravi using checklists to remember what assignments were due and when, what homework and materials he had to bring home, and so forth. Before he left each class, he would write down all of the things that he had to remember. At the bottom of the list, he would write "use my new route." He never was late to class again.

There are a few things to consider in this example. The first is we got Ravi involved in the situation. We told him what we were doing and why. We even got him involved in finding an alternative behavior (i.e., taking a new route). I believe that this is important not only on an ethical level but also with regard to the plan's efficacy. Students adjust better to behavior modification plans when they participate in developing the plans.

Also, we kept the plan simple. We didn't develop rewards or punishments or paint a line on the hallway floor that Ravi had to follow. We went with the easiest solution first. If it didn't work, then we could have included other features, such as detentions for being late and praise for being on time. But fortunately, we didn't have to embellish too much. We kept things as close as possible to what we would have done for a regular education student.

Robert Evert Cimera

Finally, note that in the end, Ravi was acting independently. We could have had teachers remind him to take his new route each and every day for the remainder of his high school career, but that wouldn't have taught him anything. Essentially, it would have made him more dependent on other people than he already was. Plus, I was very mindful of the fact that teachers are very busy people. Ravi was one of twenty-something students in their classes. The less work they had to do, the better!

Superstitious Learning

Just to remind you, superstitious learning is when people associate variables with unrelated outcomes. Please don't think that this is something that only people who are ignorant or uneducated or autistic do. Everyone does this to some degree. For example, when I was in high school, I used to wear my "best" outfit and my "favorite" cologne on every first date. It was my little ritual.

Somehow, I associated the clothes and the cologne with making a good first impression, which usually led to a fun first date. Deep down, I know that it wasn't the clothes or the cologne that made things go well, but I had to have them to feel comfortable. Let me give you another example to help illustrate this concept of mistaken associations between unrelated causes and effects.

When I began teaching at my current university, I had a couple of very bad classes. I mean, they were horrible! My students were unruly and obnoxious! They hated me. They hated the subject that I was teaching. They hated everything. Every class period was like slow death. I really struggled as a teacher during those classes.

Oddly, these classes were all in the same room. As a result, I developed a very strong aversion to teaching there. Even now, years later, my heart quickens whenever I walk past it.

Making Autism a Gift

The point is, just like Pavlov's dogs, humans tend to develop associations between unrelated variables (e.g., "bad classes" and a "room"). Consequently, your child might develop a certain routine or fixation or fear based upon this erroneous relationship. He might think, "if this happens, then that will happen," even though "this" and "that" are not connected at all! Let me give you another example about one of my autistic students.

Tom was a very smart kid who had to do all of his assignments using the same pen; it had a cute little fuzzy face on it, kind of like the pens you would buy at a novelty store. At any rate, he believed that he got good grades because of this special pen. If he had to take a test or do something for a grade, he had to have the pen. If he didn't, he would get very anxious and self-stim, and his behavior would quickly escalate to where he was irrational and potentially aggressive.

We wanted Tom to be more flexible. After all, he was eventually going to lose the pen or it would get broken or run out of ink or something. Moreover, his parents were afraid that the obsession with the pen was going to grow and he would eventually have to have the pen with him all of the time.

So what did we do?

We attempted to show Tom that his academic success wasn't because of the pen that he used. Of course, we tried explaining this to him logically, but that didn't work. He didn't buy it. After all, all evidence supported his belief. When he used the pen, he did well!

Since reasoning with him didn't work, we tried something else. We had to break the association between using the pen and academic success. We did this by giving Tom activities that didn't require writing. For example, we would quiz him about his math facts verbally. As always, he did well.

Then we gave him some "fun" written activities that weren't going to be graded. These he had to do without his pen. For example, there were coloring assignments that were like the old "paint by numbers" kits. Each portion of the picture contained a math problem. He would answer the problem and then color that section a certain color depending upon the answer he calculated (e.g., sections with an answer of "three" were supposed to be colored green; sections with the answer of "five" would be colored blue).

Again, there was no pressure to do well on these tasks since he was doing them for fun. Plus, they required different colors, which his pen couldn't provide.

Then we started using non-graded "pre-tests." He would practice for upcoming exams by reviewing study guides and completing sample problems. Initially, he was reluctant to do these without his pen, but we kept reminding him that they were just for fun and that he wouldn't be graded. Most of the time, he would acquiesce. Eventually, we made up a rule that the pre-test had to be done in pencil (we told him this was to "save" his special pen for the real tests!).

Finally, when he was successfully doing the pre-tests without the pen, we told him, "Hey! You got an A on this pre-test, so you don't have to do the real test!" That made him very happy.

Well, to make a very long story short, we finally got Tom to do graded activities without his fuzzy-faced pen. Further, he came to realize that his success wasn't caused by the writing implement that he used.

This strategy worked for Tom for a couple of different reasons. One, we took things *extremely* slowly. We didn't steal his pen and make him go cold turkey (as his regular education teacher wanted us to do). We took our time and gradually had him perform activities without the pen.

Making Autism a Gift

Additionally, the activities without the pen became more academic in nature over time. So, as we were weaning him off the pen for free-time activities, we were also making his free-time activities more academic in nature. This was critical because he was doing things that he enjoyed without the pen. In essence, we were breaking the negative association that he had with using pencils and other writing implements.

Overcoming Fears

Humans all have certain irrational fears. I think that is just part of being human. For example, my wife is afraid of mice. She realizes that mice are generally harmless. I mean, even if they bit you, it isn't as if they could take off your entire arm or rip out your spleen! Yet, she is terrified of them.

One of my coworkers is tremendously afraid of clowns! Another is afraid to try on shoes that other people might have already worn, such as the ones at bowling alleys or at shoe stores. Many of my friends are afraid of using public restrooms. I am afraid of heights. I could be on top of a building that has stood for hundreds of years, but I still get worried that it is going to collapse! And so it goes. We all have illogical fears.

So what should you do if your child with autism has an irrational fear? Well, the first thing that I would ask is, "Does it impact his life?" If it doesn't, then don't worry too much. Just try to avoid those kinds of situations! Stay away from mice, clowns, used shoes, or the tops of tall buildings!

But let's suppose that you can't avoid what is causing the fear or that the fear does affect your child's life. What then? What can you do to minimize or overcome it? Let me tell you what we did with one of my students whom I mentioned earlier.

Derek was one of my middle school students with autism. He had heard that somebody drowned in a lake or pond by his house and as a result, he developed a profound fear of water. It was so bad that he refused to bathe! He wouldn't even take a sponge bath! As you can imagine, this was very problematic, especially since he was becoming an adolescent and the hormones that make teenagers stink were beginning to kick in.

Now, we could have tried to force Derek into a shower or we could have just hosed him down periodically. But that wouldn't have solved the problem. Further, he was a big boy and we would have had a nasty fight on our hands. So, like with Tom, we decided to take things extremely slowly.

In addition to being afraid of water, Derek was a video game junkie. He loved to play his games! So they were powerful motivators for him. In fact, prior to developing his fear of water, Derek, his parents, and I developed a behavior modification program where Derek could only play his video games if he performed certain activities. For example, he had to have a "good behavior day" at school and finish his household chores without being told. If he adhered to the requirements, he could have an hour of game time. So, with this knowledge, we began to add to Derek's behavioral contract.

At first, we tried to get Derek in the shower. We promised him new video games and an extra hour of playing time. We even told him that if he took a shower once per week, he could have all day Saturday to play his games, but he wasn't buying it. That is how strong his fear was! He would rather go without playing his precious video games than jump into a shower for five minutes every week.

This is an important concept. Derek's fear of water was more powerful than his desire to play video games. We could have promised him a thousand hours of gaming and he would never have agreed to take a shower! We had to try something different.

Instead of making Derek take a shower in order to earn his gaming time, we decided to start small. We first made him wipe himself down with "baby wipes." Derek thought that these had "cleaning solution" on them and not water, so he wasn't too resistant. If he wiped himself down each night, he could play his games.

Then we started making Derek use the baby wipes and a slightly moistened towel. This wasn't too bad either. In all honesty, you could barely tell that the towel was damp.

Gradually, we made Derek use more and more water. Eventually, he went from washing in the sink to standing in the shower under a very light trickle. After two months or so, Derek was able to take showers with the water on full blast.

We never got him to take baths or go swimming, but that was okay. We succeeded in correcting the main hygiene issue.

As with Tom, we were successful with Derek because we took baby steps. We didn't go too fast or expect him to do more than he could handle. We focused on one small goal at a time and got him closer to where we wanted him to be. This is often called "systematic desensitizing."

Further, we knew what he liked and was willing to work for. Had we not known about his love of video games, I would imagine that Derek would have been a very stinky boy for a very long time.

Learned Behavior

Finally, it could very well be that your child has certain routines, fixations, and fears because he *learned* to act that way! Let me give you a few examples.

My brother has a young son, Carson. When Carson entered his terrible twos, he began hitting himself on the head. He would take a book or a magazine or something like that and keep hitting himself over and over again. Of course, my brother and his wife were mortified and would run to stop him.

As you might imagine, Carson kept hitting himself and it embarrassed my brother and his wife no end. They would be in the store or out in public and little Carson would start whacking away. Eventually they asked for my help.

The first thing that we did was figure out where he was seeing this behavior. That was actually pretty easy. He loved to watch cartoons and, wouldn't you know it, in almost every episode, somebody was getting hit on the head! Somebody would step on a rake, and it would come up and bonk them in the face. Something would fall from a tall building and land on somebody. So we took away the bad influence (i.e., violent cartoons).

Secondly, it was very plain to me that Carson was being rewarded for his behavior. Every time he hit himself, his parents gave him attention, which was exactly what he wanted! So we began ignoring Carson when he hit himself and giving him more attention when he was behaving appropriately.

Now, I should point out that Carson wasn't in any danger of actually hurting himself! He usually hit himself with pretty soft things. So please don't think that we were letting him self-abuse!

I did something very similar with one of my students with autism who used to tell the same "joke" over and over and over again!

"What did one flea say to the other flea?" Jamie would ask everybody five or six times a day. "Shall we walk or take the dog?"

It was kind of cute at first. He was trying to fit in and he had figured out that people tell jokes to be socially included. But after several months, his joke was like nails scratching a chalkboard. Other students stayed away from him.

So we (i.e., his teachers, parents, and classmates) had a meeting and we decided that we weren't going look at or respond to Jamie whenever he told that joke. We would just walk away. However, if he told a *new* joke, we would laugh and praise him.

Further, every day as part of his reading program, we would read a book entitled *1001 Jokes!* For a half hour, we'd practice reading and he would learn fresh material in the process.

Sure enough, Jamie made an effort to go around telling his new jokes to his family and classmates. He never had a very good delivery, mind you. For example, he would say, "Knock! Knock! Who's there?" But many of the jokes he learned became a big hit with his peers and he benefited socially as a result.

SUMMARY

Individuals with autism often have various routines, fixations, and fears. Sometimes these behaviors are actually beneficial. For example, if your child obsesses about music or physics, perhaps he will become a famous musician or scientist! If he is afraid of guns, he will be less likely to accidentally shoot himself. However, if your child's behavior adversely affects his life, you will need to change it.

In this chapter, I discussed several ways for reducing or eliminating problematic routines, fixations, and fears. I talked about not rewarding inappropriate behaviors, replacing them with appropriate ones, breaking cycles of behavior, and systematically desensitizing your child.

In the next chapter I will move away from addressing specific issues, such as fears and fixations, and begin looking at general strategies and philosophies that will assist you in teaching your child many academic and life skills.

TEN

"One Must Be a Student Before One Can Be a Teacher"*: General Strategies and Philosophies for Teaching Your Child

Thus far, I have talked a great deal about what autism is, how it is diagnosed, some of the characteristics that people with autism often display, and how to address certain problematic issues that you and your child are likely to face. In this chapter, I want to discuss less specific topics. That is to say, rather than telling you how you can address fears or model social skills, I want to outline some basic techniques that you could use to teach a wide variety of skills, behaviors, and knowledge.

Many of the strategies that I will discuss will have to be modified to match your child's needs. For instance, if your child is tactilely sensitive (i.e., doesn't like to be touched), then you might have to alter how you do "hand-over-hand" instruction. So please feel free to use what I am about to cover in whatever way that suits your situation.

---

*This is an ancient Chinese proverb. It is probably self-explanatory, but its meaning is paramount to your child's future. If you want to successfully teach your child, you'll have to become a successful student of your child's behavior. You'll have to watch and study your child in order to determine where and how he learns best!

Making Autism a Gift

DEVELOPING APPROPRIATE
LEARNING ENVIRONMENTS

The first topic involves where your child learns. I can't stress this enough. Your child's environment is *the most* critical aspect of his learning! You could be the best teacher in the world. Your child could be extremely motivated to learn. You could have computer programs and high-tech games and fun learning activities and everything that is trendy. However, if your child cannot concentrate, he will not learn effectively! It is as simple as that.

I have already talked about how various environmental factors can influence your child's behaviors. For instance, many of my students had very negative reactions to loud noises or changes in where they sat or how things smelled. Clearly, if these things bother the child to such a degree that he had to act out or start self-stimming, they will also affect the child's ability to concentrate and acquire new information.

So before you begin teaching your child how to do math or how to make a peanut butter and jelly sandwich or how to sing the alphabet, you need to first think about what environmental variables affect your child. Ask yourself, "What tends to set my child off? Where does he tend to act out the most, and what is common among these environments?" Consider such things as noise level and pitch, smells, lighting, space (e.g., big and roomy versus small and cozy), and colors. Much of this you probably have already thought about when trying to deal with his inappropriate behaviors.

But also consider where your child is able to sit down and concentrate for an extended period of time. Ask yourself, "When my child has free time, where does he go? What is that environment like? Where does he seem to behave himself the most?"

The idea here is to identify stimuli that can affect your child, both in good and bad ways. Once you know how certain environmental factors affect your child, you can develop a study area that can opti-mize his learning. Let me give you a few examples.

Many of my students were sensitive to loud sounds and bright lights, especially fluorescent lights. So, in my classrooms, I used only floor lamps that had full-spectrum bulbs (full-spectrum light bulbs have a very soft light that is often used to treat those with depression and children with ADHD).

I also played subtle background music to drown out noises from the hallway and playground. For example, I had CDs of gentle jazz and nature sounds, such as ocean waves, which would play all day long. I highly recommend this kind of "mood music." It really seemed to calm my students down and help them concentrate.

Moreover, many of my students like the environmental pre-dictability that the music offered. For instance, when they worked on math, I played a classical CD. When they worked on writing, I played piano jazz. When it was time to transition from one subject to another or from one place to another, the music stopped. It was their cue that things were about to change. It was very effective.

Many of my students had certain issues with where they sat. For instance, a few of my students couldn't sit at desks that had attached chairs. They evidently felt smothered or confined. Other students didn't like wooden seats because they were too hard.

So I had students sit in whatever chairs that they liked. Some students had pillows on which they sat. Others enjoyed beanbag chairs. Others had stools and worked at long tables where they could spread their things out.

As I said before, you have to know your child. Once you figure out what affects him, customize an environment in your home where he can feel comfortable and learn. You'll have to be creative. Nobody can say what works best for all kids. For example, some of

Making Autism a Gift

my students loved wearing earphones to block out noise. Other students absolutely hated having things over their ears!

Finally, make sure your child's teachers know what you are doing. Maybe they can use similar strategies at school. Remember, you might not be a teacher, but you know your child better than anybody. Share your expertise!

MULTIMODALITY TEACHING

In order to be an effective educator, you have to make sure that your pupil can retain information. One way to increase your chances of doing this is to use a variety of modalities. For instance, I could *tell* you that 2+2=4. I could *show* you that 2+2=4. I can have you *say* that 2+2=4. These examples all illustrate different modalities of learning—hearing, seeing, and speaking.

Although some people learn better using one modality over another, there is one "truism" for all students; that is, the more senses that a person uses to process information, the more likely the person will retain it. So rather than just telling your child something or showing him something, try to have him see, hear, feel, and say what you are trying to teach him.

Let's go back to teaching 2+2=4. Can you think of ways of teaching this while using several different learning modalities all at the same time?

Here is a suggestion. Give your child two blocks and have him count out loud as he touches each of them. Then add two more blocks and again have him count and touch. When he is done, have him say, "two plus two equals four!" This way, not only does he get to see and feel two objects being added to two other objects but he also hears himself counting and saying the final answer.

Multimodality teaching is one of the reasons why educational computer programs are so successful. Think about it! There is plenty to look at! There is a computerized voice telling you stuff. And you are actively doing something (e.g., manipulating whatever the game entails). Plus, they are just plain fun! So if you are trying to teach your child academic skills, such as reading or math, go to your local computer store and see if it has any games that your child might like, such as "Reader Rabbit" or "Mathblaster." My students loved them!

TASK ANALYSES

Another cornerstone of teaching in special education is the "task analysis." Task analyses are step-by-step breakdowns of whatever it is that you are trying to teach. For example, in one of my college courses, I make my students write the steps to making a peanut butter and jelly sandwich. They might write

1. *Get the ingredients and supplies from the cabinet and refrigerator.*
2. *Open the jars and bread bag.*
3. *With a butter knife, scoop out a lump of peanut butter.*
4. *Spread the peanut butter so that it covers one side of one piece of bread.*
5. *With a butter knife, scoop out a lump of jelly.*
6. *Spread the jelly so that it covers one side of the other piece of bread.*
7. *Put the two pieces of bread together so that the peanut butter and jelly are touching.*
8. *Put all ingredients away and the dirty butter knife in the sink.*
9. *Eat the sandwich!*

Making Autism a Gift

The degree of specificity in a task analysis depends upon the needs of the student. For instance, if a student had difficulty identifying the difference between peanut butter and ketchup, you might add several steps to help him overcome this obstacle.

Task analyses do two things. First, they force teachers to think of lengthy tasks in smaller, more manageable steps. This increases the effectiveness of a teacher's instructions.

Second, task analyses enable teachers to collect data on each step of the process and then focus on those that are problematic. For instance, suppose that your child can perform all of the steps to making a peanut butter and jelly sandwich except for opening up the jars. Maybe his hands are just too small or weak. Realizing this, you could buy peanut butter and jelly in squeezable plastic bottles.

Again, the idea is that task analyses allow teachers to identify the exact areas with which students struggle. So rather than reteaching the entire sandwich making process, you can focus on modifying only one or two steps.

SYSTEM OF LEAST RESTRICTIVE PROMPTS

Task analyses become even more powerful when coupled with "systems of least restrictive prompts." System of least restrictive prompts is a method for systematically reducing the amount of support a student requires to perform a task. Let me give you an example to illustrate this.

Let's suppose that I am trying to teach you how to make a peanut butter and jelly sandwich using the task analysis above. I can do this a number of ways. I can take you literally by the hand, lead you to the cabinet, make you open up the door, and put your hand directly on the jar of peanut butter. This is called "hand-over-hand," since my hand will be placed on top of your hand.

I could also tell you what to do. I can say, "Get everything that you need." This is called a "direct verbal cue," since I am telling you exactly what to do.

Moreover, I could give you a verbal hint. I could say something like, "What do you think is your first step?" This is called an "indirect verbal cue."

I could use gestures to prompt you to go to the cabinet (i.e., "gesture prompts"). Or I could use a combination of all of these techniques, such as pointing to the cabinet, guiding you to the peanut butter, and saying, "Now get what you need."

Keep in mind that I want to use as little support as you need to complete the step. After all, my end goal is to have you make a peanut butter and jelly sandwich independently. So even if I begin teaching you using hand-over-hand, I will eventually try to fade away all help.

Now, let's apply this teaching strategy to task analyses. Imagine that I am still teaching you how to make a peanut butter and jelly sandwich. Moreover, as I am teaching you, I am also recording the level of support that you require to complete every step of the process. Over time, I might generate a table like the one presented below (see table 10.1).

By examining the data presented in the table, I can learn a great deal about you. For instance, the first thing that I notice is that you are improving very quickly with nearly every step. However, you continue to require somebody to physically help you open the jars. Now I have to figure out why.

As I mentioned before, it could be that you have small or weak hands. Perhaps you need occupational therapy. Perhaps you just need jars that have flip-top lids.

Do you see how using task analyses and a system of least restrictive prompts can help you not only teach your child but also evalu-

Table 10.1. Task Analysis for Making a Peanut Butter and Jelly Sandwich

Step	Try #1	Try #2	Try #3	Try #4
1. Get the ingredients and supplies	H	V	V	I
2. Open the jars and bag of bread	H	H	H	H
3. With a butter knife, scoop out a lump of peanut butter	H	V	I	I
4. Spread the peanut butter over one side of one piece of bread	H	H	I	I
5. With a butter knife, scoop out a lump of jelly	H	I	I	I
6. Spread the jelly	H	I	I	I
7. Put the two pieces of bread together	H	I	I	I
8. Put all ingredients away and the dirty butter knife in the sink	H	H	V	V
9. Eat the sandwich!	I	I	I	I

Note: "H" indicates that the child was able to perform this step with hand-over-hand. "V" indicates that the child was able to perform the step with a verbal prompt. "I" indicates that the child was able to perform this step independently (i.e., without any clues or prompts).

ate his abilities? Used together, they can really enhance your child's learning and your teaching!

CHAINING

"Chaining" is another popular and effective way for teaching individuals with and without disabilities. There are two kinds of chains: forward and backward.

Forward chaining is when you teach the first step of a task, followed by the second, and third, and so on. You are, in effect, teaching tasks in their natural order.

Backward chaining is when you teach the last step first. Once the student masters the last step, you teach him the second to last, then third to last, and so on until the entire sequence is completed.

Why would you teach things in reverse order? Let me see if I can explain using the peanut butter and jelly sandwich example again.

Let's suppose that you want to teach your child how to make food for himself. You could start from the beginning of the task analysis (i.e., getting the ingredients); however, your child doesn't understand why he needs to get the peanut butter and jelly out of the cabinet. After all, to him, they are just glass jars and they have nothing to do with curing his hunger. You try to put your hand over his, but he fights you. Again, he doesn't see why he should cooperate.

By using backward chaining, you can get to the rewarding outcome right away. In other words, you start by letting your child eat a peanut butter and jelly sandwich. Then the next time you are making a peanut butter and jelly sandwich, you have him perform the second to last step (i.e., putting everything away) before he can eat. Then the next time you make a peanut butter and jelly sandwich, your child has to put the two pieces of bread together, put everything away, and then be rewarded by eating the sandwich.

Can you see the benefits to this method? It allows some students to understand the connection between the work (i.e., performing each step in the task analysis) and the outcome (i.e., being able to eat the peanut butter and jelly sandwich). This can make them more motivated to complete each step independently.

DIRECT INSTRUCTION

The term "direct instruction" is very popular and contentious in the field of special education. I think that I would be remiss if I didn't discuss it, at least in passing. However, be aware that there are entire books on this topic alone and that I can't do it complete justice in just a few paragraphs.

Direct instruction (also called DI) is a teaching strategy or philosophy that incorporates teacher-led, repetitious activities that are followed by immediate feedback. For instance, perhaps you have seen teachers standing in front of a chalkboard pointing at math problems as the entire class repeats what the teacher says.

"Two plus two equals four," the teacher says as she points to 2+2 on the board. "What is it?"

"Two plus two equals four," the students chant back as the teacher points to the two, the plus sign, the two, the equals sign, and the four.

The teacher and students might go over the same material several times. If a student struggles or gets the wrong answer, he or she is immediately corrected.

Direction instruction has been found to be very successful for teaching students basic math facts, reading, and spelling. However, critics often call it "drill and kill." They suggest that DI focuses too much on memorization and not enough on creative problem-solving.

This is my two cents for what it is worth. I personally believe that some kids learn very well using direct instruction and other kids need a different approach. It is up to teachers and parents to figure out what is best for each child.

Moreover, I think that all children should be taught via different strategies. I believe that this promotes better learning outcomes and cognitive flexibility. Besides, who wants to spend an entire day doing the same thing? But this is just my opinion. You'll have to form your own.

NATURAL CONSEQUENCES

As with direct instruction, the concept of "natural consequences" is often the center of heated debates. Essentially, natural consequences means that students are allowed to experience the negative outcomes that arise from their actions. For instance, if a student forgets to bring her parental permission slip home, she can't go on the fun field trip. Or if a student wastes all of his class time goofing around, he has to do his assignment after school or during recess. Or if your child breaks all of his toys during a temper tantrum, he doesn't have any toys with which to play.

The idea is that natural outcomes are often the most effective teachers. Moreover, When students with autism are allowed to experience natural consequences, they are being treated like other children who don't have disabilities.

However, I am not saying that this strategy is appropriate in every situation! For example, what if your child doesn't draw a connection between his behavior and the natural consequences? Suppose that he never does any work in school and just assumes that everybody has homework every night.

Or imagine a behavior that is so dangerous that its natural consequence is unacceptable! A student attempts to run across a busy street. Should the teacher let her get hit by a car? After all, that probably would teach her a valuable lesson. No, of course not! Still, there are times when the natural outcomes of behaviors convey important lessons. So don't be afraid to use them when appropriate.

DIGNITY OF RISK

The underlying concept behind natural consequences is closely linked to the next topic, the "dignity of risk." There is an old story that I tell my students to illustrate this philosophy. It goes something like this:

Two couples are sitting in the kitchen talking. One couple is Caucasian, the other is Native American. As they talk, the young child of the Native American couple is trying to open up a cabinet door. But he is standing directly in front of the door so that every time he opens it, it bangs him on the head and closes.

This happens several times. The toddler grabs the handle and pulls the door open, but the door bonks him and then closes.

Finally, the wife from the Caucasian couple gets up and tries to show the child how to open the door while standing to one side so that the door doesn't hit him. But the Native American parents ask her to stop and let the child figure it out for himself. Eventually, after a few more bonks to the head, the child learns how to open the door by himself without being hit.

I first heard that story in a class that I took on multiculturalism. It is meant to illustrate how different cultures view learning, but I think that it also illustrates the concept of the dignity of risk.

Dignity of risk means that there is inherent value in letting a child try and fail. Failure, after all, can be very motivating. Further, by helping students too much, a teacher often teaches them how to be helpless.

However, as with the natural consequences technique, you have to be selective as to when you let your child fail. Failing an assignment might prompt your child to study more. Failing to cook food thoroughly might result in a serious illness!

PREMACK PRINCIPLE

Finally, I want to talk about the "Premack principle." Basically, this is a strategy that makes students do required, less desirable behaviors before they indulge in activities that they want to do. For example, they have to finish their math before they can go to recess. Or, they have to eat dinner before they can have dessert.

This is also called a "contingency program." Students get to do something they like if they adequately perform what they are supposed to do. If you recall my discussion about positive reinforcement back in chapter five, then this concept should ring a bell. It can be very effective if the "desired" activity outweighs the pain of performing the "undesired" activity.

SUMMARY

In previous chapters, I talked about strategies for addressing specific behaviors, such as aggression, communication, or social skills. In this chapter, I discussed several strategies and philosophies that can be applied to many different content areas (e.g., math, writing, science, etc.) and life tasks (e.g., self-care, cooking, cleaning, etc.). Please keep in mind that you can modify these suggestions to suit the unique needs of your child. No one strategy works for everybody in every situation!

ELEVEN

"Okay! I Am the Quarterback!": Working Collaboratively with Special Educators*

Well, here we are, closing in on the final chapter. Our time together is almost over. By now, you should have a good grasp about what autism is, how it is diagnosed, and some basic strategies for addressing many of its defining characteristics.

The theme of this chapter involves special education programs and the educators who run them. Of everything that I have discussed thus far, these topics will probably be the most important to you and your child. Why?

Well, I believe that in order for your child to reach his full potential, you have to do several things. First, you have to understand

---

*As a teacher, I made it a policy to invite all of my students to their IEP meetings, whether the student would understand what was going on or not. I liked having students there because they kept everybody focused on our goal (i.e., helping the child)! Anyway, one day, I was trying to explain to a young man with Down's syndrome what the IEP team was. "We are like a football team and helping you do well in school is like winning the Super Bowl!" I said in my overly enthusiastic teacher voice. "Okay!" my student said equally enthusiastic, "I am the quarterback!" If we had had a ball, he would have run out to the playground right then and there!

While special education teachers usually run IEP meetings, it is important to remember that everybody is on a team. Further, even though each participant has different areas of expertise and training, everybody should be a valued member!

what autism is, which hopefully you now do. Without understanding autism, you will be constantly reacting to bizarre behaviors without a clue as to why they are occurring or how to change them.

Second, you should get your child enrolled in as many educational programs as possible and as early as possible. Numerous research studies have found that early intervention is critical to the long-term success of individuals with autism.

Finally, in order to maximize the effectiveness of these educational programs, you must work collaboratively with the people who run them. Look, by and large, the special educators and therapists who will be working with your child are wonderful people. They have spent years of their lives getting their degrees and have committed themselves to assisting people with disabilities and their families. They have good hearts and are skillful practitioners.

However, they don't know your child as well as you do! So, you have to get involved and educate them just as much as they educate you. Share your notes, data, and thoughts with them. The more that you can teach them, the more they can teach your child.

Further, in order for your child to succeed, everybody has to be on the same page. If you are dealing with your child's behavior in one way and his teachers are dealing with it another way, very little progress is going to be made. Consistency is the key for helping kids with autism!!

I guess what I am trying to say is that teaching is a team effort. If you and your child's service providers don't collaborate effectively, your child's future will suffer. So how can you become a valuable team member?

You'll first have to understand the nature of the programs that are providing services to your child. You need to understand the scope, goals, and limitations of these programs as well as the perspectives of the personnel who run them. Finally, you will need to know your rights as a parent of a child with a disability and how to tactfully advocate for him. There is a lot to cover here, so let's get started!

EARLY INTERVENTION PROGRAMS

Early intervention programs, often referred to as EI, are services and supports that are provided to you and your child. Note that I said "*you* and your child." This is very important!

The goal of early intervention programs isn't just to help your child but to help the entire family. The idea is to teach family members what they need to know so that any developmental delays or difficulties that a child may have will either be eliminated or minimized.

EI services can be provided in a number of different environments. For example, you might bring your child to a center, or therapists might come directly to your home. It depends upon the needs of your child and family.

The services furnished by EI programs vary considerably from family to family as well as from state to state. So you'll need to consult with local agencies in order to see what is available to you.

The assistance that you and your child receive will be outlined in what is called an IFSP, or "individualized family service plan." An IFSP is a document developed and agreed upon by you and the agencies providing the services. It also denotes specific goals that your child will be attempting to attain.

As the I in IFSP indicates, the services that are provided are based upon your unique situation and needs. So don't be surprised or upset if somebody you know gets occupational therapy and your child doesn't, or if your child is working on speech and somebody else's child isn't. Everything is individualized.

Eligibility for early intervention programs differs from state to state. However, generally speaking, children must experience delayed progress in their development or be at risk of experiencing developmental delays. So, if your child has autism, he most likely qualifies regardless of where you live. For more information, contact your state's public health department.

SPECIAL EDUCATION

When most people hear the term "special education," they tend to think of people with "mental retardation" or kids who are "stupid." First of all, special education has nothing to do with intelligence. Only about 11 percent of special education students have mental retardation. Further, there are more kids who are gifted in special education (about 3–4 percent) than there are in the general population (about 2 percent). So students in special education do not have to have mental retardation, nor are they "stupid."

"So what is special education?" you might be asking yourself.

Special education is a federally mandated entitlement program that provides individualized education to qualifying students. There is a lot to digest in that last sentence, so let me go over some of the key phrases.

Federally Mandated

Special education is mandated by federal law. Specifically, the Individuals with Disabilities Education Act (IDEA) requires that all public schools and private schools receiving federal funds provide special education to qualifying students. I'll talk about who qualifies in a few moments.

Making Autism a Gift

Entitlement Program

Special education is an entitlement program. That means that if your child qualifies, he is guaranteed access to special education. Your child cannot be denied for any reason, including lack of school funds or the severity of your child's disability.

Qualifying Students

In order to qualify for special education, your child must have one of the following disabilities:

> *Specific Learning Disabilities*
> *Speech or Language Impairments*
> *Mental Retardation*
> *Emotional Disturbances*
> *Hearing Impairments*
> *Orthopedic Impairments*
> *Other Health Impairments (OHI)*
> *Visual Impairments*
> *Autism*
> *Traumatic Brain Injury (TBI)*
> *Developmental Delay*
> *Deaf-Blindness*

In addition to having one or more of these disabilities, the child must be between three and twenty-one years old. Lastly, the disability must be so severe that it adversely affects the child's ability to receive an "appropriate" public education.

THE IDEAS BEHIND IDEA

There are six core concepts that constitute the federal law IDEA. These include

1. *Zero Reject*
2. *Nondiscriminatory Evaluation*
3. *Free and Appropriate Public Education (FAPE)*
4. *Least Restrictive Environment (LRE)*
5. *Procedural Due Process*
6. *Parent and Student Participation*

Let me talk about each of these in turn.

Zero Reject

I talked about this earlier, but it is important enough to repeat. "Zero reject" means that if your child qualifies for special education, he cannot be denied services for any reason. So even if your child has profound mental retardation and a number of significant needs, or he has very aggressive behaviors or an infectious disease, he is still entitled to special education.

This isn't to say that your child has to be served in your neighborhood schools. He doesn't. As I will talk about in the next few pages, your child can be in special education but be placed in a separate school or facility. However, regardless of where he is taught, he *must* be provided the services that he needs to get an "appropriate" education (I will be talking about what an appropriate education is shortly!).

Nondiscriminatory Evaluation

The second component of IDEA involves nondiscriminatory evaluation. As this applies, your child must be evaluated in a fair and non-

Making Autism a Gift

biased manner. But there is more! If you do not agree with the school's assessment of your child, you can request another independent evaluation. In most cases, the school will have to pay for this.

So, let's suppose that you think that your child has autism and you request that the school do a formal evaluation. The school psychologist administers some tests and concludes that nothing is wrong.

"Your child is fine. He is just a bit slow," the school psychologist says.

You disagree. According to this part of IDEA, you have the right for another evaluation that is completed by somebody not associated with the school.

However, let's suppose that you don't like what the second evaluator thinks. Can you have a third independent evaluation? Sure! You can get as many evaluations as you like. But the school doesn't have to pay for them. The school is only required to provide you with one additional opinion.

Free and Appropriate Public Education (FAPE)

This section might confuse you a bit, or at least get you a little annoyed. So just relax and go with the flow here.

According to IDEA, students with disabilities are guaranteed a free and appropriate public education. This is usually referred to as FAPE. Now, the "free" part probably makes sense. Education up until twelfth grade in the United States is free. This isn't to say that you won't have to pay for certain things, such as art supplies or the occasional field trip. It just means that the school can't charge you for its services.

The "public" part is also pretty clear. Everybody is entitled to a public education. This isn't to say that you can't send your child to a private school. You can. But you will have to pay for it.

Robert Evert Cimera

The part that seems to throw a lot of people is the word "appropriate." According to federal law, your child is entitled to an "appropriate" education, not the "best" education. Let me give you some examples to help you process this.

Let's suppose that your child is in regular education earning mostly A's and maybe a B here or there. One day, you find out that he has autism (remember, just because he has autism, that doesn't mean he can't be excelling in school!). So you refer him to special education thinking, "Hey, if I get my kid more support, he could be on the honor roll and get into a top-notch college!"

However, when you approach the school, the principal denies your kid access to special education services. "That's not fair," you tell the principal. "IDEA says that you can't deny qualifying students special education services!"

"That's true," the principal replies, "but special education is only meant to provide students with an *appropriate* education, which your child is already getting. So, technically, your child isn't entitled to special education." And the principal is correct.

The key here is that the end goal of special education is to provide a certain level of instruction. If your child is already getting the maximum benefit at that level, he is not entitled to special education even though he has a disability (e.g., autism) that is listed in IDEA.

Now, here comes the problematic part. You are probably sitting there wondering what an appropriate education is. Unfortunately, I can't tell you. It is treated much like "pornography" or "indecency": judges know what it is when they see it. In other words, one person might think an appropriate education is anything that is passing; so earning a D minus indicates that your child is getting an appropriate education. Other people use more qualitative indicators, such as, is the child progressing at a reasonable rate without special education? or, is the child benefiting from instruction without special education?

The main point is that special education doesn't provide the best education possible. IDEA only mandates that special education students get a suitable or appropriate education, whatever that means!

Least Restrictive Environment (LRE)

People seem to misunderstand the concept of LRE, or "least restrictive environment," more than any other aspect of IDEA. IDEA mandates that students who are enrolled in special education be taught alongside their peers as much as is appropriate, taking into consideration the needs of the student and the student's effect on those around him. This does not, I repeat, *not*, mean that ALL students with disabilities have to be taught in regular education classrooms every moment of every day!

Don't think of LRE as a specific place, such as the regular education classroom or a pull-out classroom or residential facility. Think of LRE as a continuum of environments where your child could be given special education services. IDEA mandates that your child be placed in the environment in which your child can receive a free and appropriate public education (FAPE) that is as integrated with non-disabled students as possible.

How is a child's LRE determined?

Usually this is what happens. The IEP team (which I will discuss later) gets together and starts at the top of the LRE continuum (i.e., putting your child in the regular education classroom all day with minimal help). They then decide whether your child can get an appropriate education in that manner. If the answer is yes, that is where your child's LRE probably is. If it is no, they will consider a slightly less inclusive option, such as having your child in the regular education classroom all day, but with a full-time one-on-one aide.

The IEP team will continue to look at various environments and levels of support until they find a place where your child can get an appropriate education. They might decide that your child needs to be in a separate classroom for kids with autism or even a special residential school or even a residential lock-down facility. Again, the decision is based mostly on the educational needs of your child.

Notice that I said based "mostly" on your child's educational needs. There are a few other issues that might influence your child's LRE. For example, suppose that your student was so incredibly violent that putting him in the regular education classroom could result in the other students getting seriously hurt. In such extreme cases, your child's LRE might be in a self-contained classroom even though he could do the work of a regular education student.

I'll give you an example from my own life. I used to work at a lock-down facility for "juvenile delinquents." These were kids with disabilities (usually mental illnesses) who had committed serious crimes, including murder, rape, and arson. Many of my students were brilliant. I mean that. They were geniuses! But they were also immensely troubled. One student killed his sister and mother with a hatchet. Even though he could learn effectively in a regular education classroom, his LRE was in my facility.

You are going to be exposed to a great variety of opinions regarding this topic. Some people are going to be "pro-inclusion" and will push you to have your child in the regular education classroom every waking moment. They will tell you that the regular education classroom is the only place where your child can learn appropriate social skills.

Other people are going to tell you that "those kids" (meaning children who have disabilities) don't "belong" in regular education and that their presence is going to be disruptive. They may also insist that the teacher spend the majority of the time helping the one or two special education students, while the other children are neglected.

Making Autism a Gift

In the end, you will have to decide where your child should be taught. If you want my personal opinion, I am neither for one way nor the other. I believe that it depends on the specific situation and the unique needs of the child.

If you are interested, here is where students with autism are served throughout the country:

Regular Classroom Only—20%
Regular Classroom and Resource Room—14.5%
Separate Classroom in Regular School—49.5%
Separate School—13.3%
Residential Facility—1.3%
Home School or Hospital—0.4%
Other Environments—1%

Keep in mind that just because the majority of students have LREs outside of the regular education classroom, that doesn't mean your child shouldn't be placed in regular education full time! Again, where your child's LRE is depends upon your child's needs and circumstances.

Parent and Student Participation

The fifth component of IDEA involves parent and student participation. IDEA mandates that parents and students be allowed to participate in the development of educational plans. Not only are parents and students "allowed" to participate, but schools must also document how they have "encouraged" their involvement.

For example, as a teacher, I had to document how I solicited the opinions and feedback of my students and their parents. I had worksheets and checklists that I would send home every month asking questions like, "Are you happy with the progress your child is making?" "Would you like the school to be doing anything different than what it is doing now?" "What other goals would you like your child to be working on?"

In other words, your child's teacher should not only be inviting you to meetings and scheduling them at times when you can come, but the teacher should also be actively asking for your thoughts and ideas. As I will talk about a little later, there is even a place in IEPs where the concerns of parents are specifically noted! So get involved and make sure your input is heard!

Procedural Due Process

The final component of IDEA is "procedural due process." This means that, as a parent of a child in special education, you not only have the right to be involved in your child's education, but you also have the ability to seek formal conflict resolution should problems arise.

For example, suppose that you are meeting with your kid's teachers, school officials, and the rest of the IEP team. They all want your child to be put in a self-contained classroom, but you disagree. You want your child to spend at least some time with his non-disabled peers. What do you do?

If you and the school can't come to an agreement, IDEA outlines policies and procedures that you can take to rectify the impasse. The specific procedures for initiating due process should be provided to you annually at your child's IEP meeting. They will probably be listed on a form or a pamphlet. If you don't receive such information, then ask for it! You need to know who to contact and what papers to fill out should you disagree with the school!

So that was IDEA in a very basic nutshell. There is obviously much more to it. After all, it is a very important piece of federal leg-

Making Autism a Gift

islation. If you want more detailed information, consult the resources listed at the back of the book. There are many books, websites, and organizations that can give you updated information about IDEA, state laws, court rulings, and the like.

THE SPECIAL EDUCATION PROCESS

Now let me talk about the special education process. How do kids get enrolled in special education? What happens once they get there? These are some of the questions that I will tackle next.

Step #1: Somebody Notices a Problem

The first step in the special education process obviously is that somebody notices that there is a problem. Who this is and when it occurs will depend largely on the situation. If a child is born without functioning legs, the doctor will probably notice the problem right away. Or, if the child has Down's syndrome, the doctor might know well before the child is born.

Generally speaking, the more severe disabilities are, the earlier they are diagnosed. With regard to autism, I have known parents who knew that their child was "different" as soon as they held him for the first time. I have also known parents who didn't find out that their child was autistic until well into adulthood. It all depends on how well informed parents are and how the autism manifests itself with the specific child.

Let's assume here that you have a child who is in school, perhaps in kindergarten, or first or second grade. Chances are the regular education teacher will notice that your child isn't interacting with other peers in an age-appropriate manner, or that your child is self-stimming or displaying repetitious behavior, or is otherwise not "typical." What happens next?

Step #2: Pre-Referral Strategies

The next thing that happens is that the regular education teacher will contact the special education teacher and explain what is going on. The regular education teacher might express his concerns and explain what he has done to try to rectify the situation. Hopefully, at this point, the regular education teacher will also contact you to see if you have identified similar issues at home and in the community.

The special education teacher will then observe the classes in which your child is having difficulty. The focus at this stage is not on the child. Instead, the special education teacher will attempt to find things in the environment or how the regular educator is teaching that might be causing the problem. Nobody should be thinking of a "disability" at this point. They are trying to rule out all other possibilities, such as external distractions.

Step #3: Nondiscriminatory Evaluation

Now let's suppose that the regular and special education teachers get together, discuss what is going on, try new teaching strategies and so forth, but nothing changes. Your child still seems "different" and nobody really knows why.

At this stage, somebody from the school has to contact you. It will probably be the special education teacher or director of pupil services or principal. The official might call you, have you come in for a parent-teacher meeting, or send you a letter. Regardless of the modality, the official will explain the regular educator's concerns and what has been done to correct them.

The official will also ask you to sign a consent form enabling the school to formally evaluate your child. It should outline specifically what the evaluation will entail, including what tests will be administered, by whom, and when the evaluation will be complete. The school must also inform you that you have the right to stop the evaluation at anytime.

If you sign the consent form, the school will then begin collecting data in an attempt to determine what is going on. The staff should collect data from a wide variety of sources. For example, they should give your child several different standardized tests, conduct observations in multiple environments, and even interview you and your child.

Step #4: Enrollment into Special Education and Development of an IEP

After getting your permission, the school conducts a formal, in-depth evaluation. Shortly thereafter, you and various school officials should get together to discuss and interpret the results. Keep in mind that the diagnosis of "autism" is often pretty subjective, so there might be some disagreement as to what is going on. But for our purposes, let's go with the idea that everybody is in agreement. The data collected clearly indicates that your child has autism and that he qualifies for special education. Now you have to decide whether or not to enroll him in special education.

As with any important decision, there are positives and negatives. The positive is that your child will hopefully get the help that he needs to succeed. The only negative that I can think of is that there is often a stigma to being in special education.

In the end, you have to make the call. If you decline to enter your child into special education, the process stops here. If you agree to enroll him, you and the rest of the team develop what is called an IEP, or "individualized education plan."

As I mentioned earlier, an IEP is a legally-binding document between you and the school. It outlines the goals that your child will be working on as well as the services that he will receive. I'll go over IEPs in greater detail in the subsequent pages.

Step #5: Implementation of the IEP

So you and the rest of the team (which usually includes your child's teachers, the director of special education, the principal, and anybody else who is involved with your child) develop a great IEP that is really going to help your child. Now what?

Now the IEP gets implemented. This means that the school begins providing the services that were promised and the teachers begin working on the goals that everybody agreed upon. At the same time, somebody (usually the special education teacher or case worker assigned to your child) will begin gathering data on the child's performance toward achievingthe IEP goals.

You should be collecting data as well. Do you see an improvement in your child's behavior or academic abilities? Do you see any areas in which your child needs to improve? Your observations are going to be critical for the next step in the special education process.

Step #6: Revision of the IEP

IEPs are good for one calendar year, so they must be revised at least every twelve months. They, however, can be revised anytime before this. For example, maybe something has changed in your child's life or you just don't think that the present IEP is appropriate. Regardless of the situation, if you want the IEP revised or updated, contact your child's special education teacher and have the IEP team reconvene.

I have had several parents who wanted to revise the IEPs every few weeks. As a teacher, that drove me crazy! There is, after all, *a lot* of paperwork to complete with IEPs. But they were within their rights to ask for revisions!

Making Autism a Gift

Step #7: Re-Evaluation of the Student

At least every year, your child's IEP has to be updated. At least every three years, your child has to be reevaluated. This is to determine whether he still qualifies for special education.

Keep in mind that the school officials aren't expecting your child to suddenly be "cured" of autism! They aren't thinking that at all. They simply want to make sure that your child still requires special education services in order to receive an appropriate education.

WHAT IS AN IEP?

Okay, so you should have a good idea of what special education is and the basic process. Now let me tackle the cornerstone of special education—the IEP! As with special education law in general, talking about IEPs could fill entire books!! But I am only going to discuss them briefly here. If you require more information, please consult some of the resources listed in the appendix.

As I have mentioned before, an IEP is a legally-binding document that delineates what services the school is going to provide to the student and what goals the student is going to work on for that year. There are eight components to most IEPs. They are

1. *Present Level of Performance (PLOP)*
2. *Annual Goals*
3. *Special Education and Related Services*
4. *Projected Dates, Frequency, Location, and Duration of Services*
5. *Statement of Least Restrictive Environment*
6. *Modifications Needed for State and District-Wide Assessments*

Robert Evert Cimera

7. Transition Plan

8. Parental Notification and Involvement

Present Level of Performance (PLOP)

The PLOP, or "present level of performance" (also called the PLEP, or "present level of educational performance"), often starts the IEP. In this section, the child's current behaviors, skills, and strengths are discussed. It should include test scores from the latest evaluation, comments from teachers, and an explanation as to how the child's disability adversely affects his ability to receive an appropriate education. It must also include a statement from you regarding any concerns that you might have. If you don't have any concerns, the PLOP should have a statement saying something like, "Susie's parents do not have any concerns at this time."

The PLOP is probably the most important part of an IEP. Think of it as a snap-shot of your child right as the IEP is about to take effect. Without an accurate picture of your child, you won't be able to tell whether the services and strategies that are being utilized are actually working. So make sure that the data in the PLOP is very specific and up-to-date!

Annual Goals

Annual goals are brief, very specific one-sentence statements that indicate what your child is going to be working on while the IEP is in effect. For example, one goal might be

> *"Billie will increase his reading comprehension from a 2.3 grade level to a 3.5 grade level as measured by the results of weekly reading comprehension tests."*

Notice how the goal is very precise. You know where the child is performing right now (at the 2.3 grade level) and where the IEP is hoping to get him by the end of the year (3.5 grade level). Moreover,

Making Autism a Gift

the goal indicates exactly how progress is going to be measured (by weekly reading comprehension tests).

You can always tell the quality of a special education program by how the goals are written in the IEPs. Really bad special education programs have vague IEP goals like, "Krissy will improve her reading." or negative IEP goals like, "Rob will stop acting like he is stupid." (I actually saw this one in a child's IEP! Seriously! Apparently the student would walk around the classroom saying "Duh! I am stupid! Duh! I am stupid!" and the teacher wanted him to stop.)

Make sure your child's goals are not only measurable but useful and based upon his unique needs! One of my students had an IEP goal of learning to tie his shoes. After six or seven years of having this same goal, his mother eventually got him all penny loafers and tennis shoes with Velcro straps!

Remember, IEP goals should attend to the main issues that your child is facing. So if he is have temper tantrums because he can't communicate effectively, one of his goals should obviously involve teaching him communication skills. If your child is self-stimming all of the time because he is anxious, then a goal should focus on teaching him to lessen his anxiety. In other words, whatever a student learns through his goals should help him have a better life!

Now, before we move on, I want you to understand that just because something isn't written into the annual goal statement, that doesn't mean your child won't be learning it. For example, let's suppose that your child is in first grade and his class is working on coloring maps, but there are no goals in your child's IEP mentioning coloring maps. Your child can still work on these classroom activities; it is just that the teachers are really going to focus on the areas mentioned in the goals.

In other words, think of IEP goals as your opportunity to customize your child's curriculum. Goals list the areas that your child needs to work on in addition to the material already being taught.

Special Education and Related Services

So the PLOP sets the stage by describing how your child is doing when the IEP was written. The annual goals state specifically what your child is going to be working on over the year. The special education and related services section of the IEP lists all of the services that your child needs to complete the annual goals and achieve an appropriate education.

If the IEP says that your child is supposed to get X, Y, and Z services, then the school *must* furnish them. However, if services aren't listed in an IEP, the school could provide them, but there is no guarantee that it will.

Projected Dates, Frequency, Location, and Duration of Services

In addition to listing what services your child is guaranteed, IEPs must also indicate projected dates, frequency, location, and duration of those services.

Note that I said "projected." Basically, this is to give you a fairly firm idea of how many minutes a week your child will get a specific service, such as speech therapy. However, the school can deviate slightly from this from time to time.

For example, let's suppose that your child has been promised physical therapy twice a week for twenty minutes each time. Yet one week, a session was cut short by ten minutes because there was a fire drill or something. That is okay as long as your child's services aren't "cut short" every week! Again, the IEP lists the projected times and durations for services; some fluctuations are to be expected.

Statement of Least Restrictive Environment

Somewhere in your child's IEP, there should be an indication of where your child's LRE is. This usually takes the form of a chart indicating where your child will be taught during each class period. For example, your child's IEP might have something like that shown in table 11.1.

However, it can also be a blanket statement such as, "Mary will be taught in a self-contained classroom 100 percent of the school day with the exception of recess and lunch, during which times she will be with her non-disabled peers."

If your child isn't taught alongside his non-disabled peers 100 percent of the time (i.e., "fully included"), the IEP must have an explanation as to why. The explanation doesn't have to be long. I used to write: "Samantha will not be fully included with her peers because the IEP team determined that such a placement would not meet her needs. She will be receiving physical therapy while her peers have physical education."

This statement does three things. First, it shows that the team considered putting Samantha in the regular education classroom full time. Second, it documents that the entire team made the decision not to fully include her in regular education. Finally, it indicates that the decision was based upon Samantha's need to have physical therapy.

Table 11.1

Period	Subject	Teacher	Location
1	Math	Mr. Blyth	Room 213
2	Social Studies	Ms. Hendricks	Room 127
3	English	Dr. Cimera	Resource Room
4	Lunch	Staff	Lunch Room
5	Gym	Mr. McGee	West Gym
6	Science	Mrs. Baggins	Room 233
7	Study Hall	Dr. Cimera	Resource Room

Modifications Needed for State and District-Wide Assessments

Nowadays, with school accountability such a hot topic, most states mandate that all students take various tests at certain times. For example, in my home state, students have to take a basic reading test in fourth grade, a comprehension test in fifth grade, and a general knowledge test in seventh grade. There might also be a test on the U.S. Constitution in eleventh grade. Plus, each school district can require other exams, such as the California Achievement Tests (CAT) or the Iowa Basics Exams.

What makes these assessments so important is the fact that the school's cumulative scores are available to the public. So, if you were moving into a new neighborhood and wanted to check out how good the schools are, you could look at how they did on each of these tests. This might not sound important to you, but it scares the crap out of principals! After all, they are being judged by how well all of their students do!

About ten years ago, many principals started to exclude certain students (e.g., students in special education) from taking these tests in an effort to increase their schools' scores. Legislators caught on. Now every child is supposed to be assessed in some way or another. Which brings us to this part of the IEP.

Somewhere in your child's IEP, there needs to be some discussion about what tests the state and district are requiring. Moreover, if there are required tests scheduled for that school year, there should be a list of accommodations that your child will need to take the tests. For example, you might request that your child be given the test orally in a separate room and without a time limit.

Now, if your child has profound mental retardation or is nonverbal, you are probably sitting there thinking, "Giving a test to my child is pointless! He would just sit there! It would be a waste of time!"

In such cases, the IEP team could give an "alternative assessment" instead of whatever assessment is being required. For example, let's suppose that your child doesn't read, yet the state and the school district is requiring that all fourth graders be given a reading comprehension test. Rather than having your child take the exam, the IEP team could submit the results from recent evaluations that show your child's reading abilities or lack of reading abilities.

The point is that all of this must be outlined in the IEP. Where it says " fourth-grade reading test," there needs to be some statement regarding your child's needs and modifications. Otherwise, your child will probably end up taking the test without any accommodations.

Transition Plan

By the time your child turns sixteen years old, his IEP must have a transition plan. Notice that I said "by" the time your child turns sixteen. You can include a transition plan at any time! Personally, I believe that every IEP should have a transition plan in place, but that is just me.

What is a "transition plan"?

A transition plan is a written plan that outlines what your child needs to do in order to be prepared for his future. It also documents what services will be required and who will provide them.

For example, let's suppose that your child wants to go to college (and remember, just because your child has autism doesn't mean he's "stupid"! Your child might surprise you and end up going on to obtain a PhD!). In such a situation, your child's IEP might have goals that teach your child how to study effectively, find his way around a large campus, and advocate for himself. You might even have your child take tours of universities and see what it is like. In that case, his IEP will clearly say who is going to take him to the schools and give him the tours.

Transition plans don't have to focus only on post-secondary education. They can also address any aspect of adult life, such as preparing your child for independent living, recreation activities, or whatever you like. Again, the idea is to get the IEP team to think about your child's long-term needs as early as possible.

Parental Notification and Involvement

Finally, IEPs must have some statement as to your involvement as a parent as well as how often and in what manner you want to be notified of your child's progress. For example, you might wish to be contacted in writing every week, so your child's teacher might send a "communication notebook" home with him every Friday. You can read what the teacher wrote and, if you wish, write a note back.

In other words, parents should not only be part of the IEP's creation, but also be well informed as to how the IEP is being implemented and your child's performance towards his goals. By the time you have your next IEP, there shouldn't be any surprises!

HOW TO BE AN EFFECTIVE
IEP TEAM MEMBER

So that is what an IEP is. Now let me talk about how you can help create the best and most productive IEP for your child! As I said earlier, IEPs and related topics could fill an entire book! Here I'm only going to discuss some general ideas. Consult some of the resources listed in the appendix if you need more suggestions.

Preparing for the Meetings

In order for your child to have the very best IEP possible, you have to be prepared. So don't go to the meeting with only a pencil and a blank pad of paper! Go there with your own thoughts and ideas!

A few days before the meeting, review your child's past IEPs, reports, and information that the school has sent home. Also look over the data that you have been collecting. With all of this information in mind, start brainstorming a list of topics that you want to discuss. Maybe generate a handful of ideas for IEP goals.

Keep in mind that other people have things that they want to discuss as well. Further, not everybody wants to stay for hours and hours, so only focus on issues that pertain to the entire IEP team. If you have ancillary concerns that you want to discuss with your child's teacher or therapist, then offer to buy her a cup of coffee and talk about it then. The IEP meeting should address larger issues regarding your child's education and future. Topics of a less significant nature should probably be covered in a phone call or private meeting.

If you think that the meeting is going to be heated or tense, you might want to bring an advocate or a friend to sit with you. A little support can do wonders! You can find experienced advocates though some of the organizations listed in the back of this book.

Finally, get organized before the meeting! I strongly suggest that you buy a large three-ring binder or expandable accordion-style folder where you can keep everything and find it at a moment's notice. You don't want to spend half of the meeting fumbling around trying to find a past assessment report or note from a teacher!

During the Meeting

I think preparing for an IEP meeting is probably easy for most parents. Sitting down and actually participating in IEP meetings, however, is often very difficult. After all, there is typically an army of professionals sitting around the table all talking some strange language. They talk about IEPs, FAPE, LRE, BM (behavior modification) and they use millions of other abbreviations. It is like they have their own little language and it can be very intimidating.

Hopefully, you are starting to get the hang of the special education lingo that is usually spoken at IEP meetings. There is a glossary at the back of this book that might help you decipher it all.

Try not to be nervous. There isn't anything to be nervous about. You might not have a degree in education, but you know your child better than anybody else in that room! In that respect, you are an expert.

Also, when you are in the IEP meeting, try to keep an open mind about what is being said. Yes, you do know your child better than anybody in that room, but some of the other team members might have some valid points too! Listen, don't pre-judge, and consider their point of view. Remember, there is no I in team.

After the Meeting

Okay, so the meeting is over and your child has a new IEP. Now what?

First of all, I recommend that you send a thank you note to everybody who attended. Even if the meeting wasn't especially pleasant, sending a brief letter or card is the polite thing to do. Plus, like mothers and fathers, teachers and other school officials rarely get thanked for doing their jobs, especially if they are good at what they do and really challenge their students. I am a challenging teacher, but nobody ever comes up to me and says, "Hey! Thanks Dr. Cimera for making me work hard and do all of those projects!" So a brief card or a thank you note scribbled on the back of a napkin can do wonders for our egos and build team spirit!

Further, show that you are interested in what is going on. Contact your child's teacher periodically to see how your child is doing and whether there is anything that you could do to help out. Maybe just say hello.

SUMMARY

Education is a team sport and you aren't the only player on the field. In order for your child to learn what he needs to, you have to collaborate with his teachers and service providers. In order to collaborate effectively, you need to understand the purposes of educational programs, the perspectives of service providers, and your rights as a parent.

In this chapter I briefly discussed IDEA, the federal law that governs special education. I also talked about the special education process, IEPs, and how you can be a valuable IEP team member. If you have additional questions regarding these topics, please consult the resources at the back of this book. There are many books and websites dedicated solely to the legalities of special education. I am sure that they could be of help to you.

TWELVE

"Someday You Are Going to Die . . . ": Life After School and You*

Believe it or not, you are going to die someday. That's a pretty grim way of starting a chapter, eh? Well, it is true! Someday your heart will stop pumping, your brain will stop functioning, you won't breathe anymore, and that will be that! My question to you is, "What is going to happen to your child when you are gone?" Now before you get all wigged out, let me explain why I am talking about your pending (although probably very distant) death.

Many people who have children with disabilities only think about the here-and-now or the short-term future. They think about how they are going to get through today or how they are going to help their children get through the school year. But very few of the parents with whom I have worked ever sit down and contemplate what their children's lives are going to be like when the parents are

---

*Every once in a while, somebody will ask me to speak at a workshop or conference. When I presented to parents on topics like preparing children for life after school and similar issues, I used to begin by saying, "Someday you are all going to DIE!" It was a good attention getter. But several people took offense, so I had to change my opening line. Still, it is true. Someday you are going to die! Make sure that you prepare your child for the times when you will no longer be there helping him. After all, promoting greater independence is the purpose of teaching!

Making Autism a Gift

gone. It is almost as if the parents think that they will always be around to help their children, but, of course, they won't.

The purpose of education should be to prepare students for life after school. That is what happens for students without disabilities. They take college-prep classes so that they can get into a good university. Or they take technical classes to prepare them for a career, such as working on cars or being an electrician.

Unfortunately, special education doesn't do a very good job of preparing students with disabilities for adult life. Let me give you some data to illustrate my point.

- 22.4% of special education students drop out of school, compared to 5.3% of regular education students. 36.1% of students with autism drop out before completing high school.
- Two-thirds of adults with disabilities between the ages 16 and 64 are unemployed; 84% indicate that they would like to work.
- Adults with disabilities are nine times more likely to be living in poverty than adults without disabilities.
- Less that 2% of special education students go to a two- or four-year college, compared to 53% of the regular education population.
- Of the special education students who attend a two- or four-year college, 70% will drop out after the first year. Only 13.6% will graduate.
- 15-20% of individuals with disabilities will be sexually assaulted or exploited.
- Two years after exiting high school, 87% of special education students continue to live with their parents. This is compared to 33% of non-special education students.

Robert Evert Cimera

- 33% of adults with disabilities eat out at least once a week, compared to 60% of non-disabled adults.
- Less that 25% of individuals with disabilities have hobbies.
- The life expectancy of an individual with a disability is approximately 63 years. The life expectancy of the population in general is 77 years.

In a nutshell, this is the life of the average special education students: They get done with school, continue to live with their parents, and rarely go into the community. They aren't employed and spend most of their time sitting at home, probably watching television. They don't have many friends and are at risk of being sexually and physically abused. If they do go to college, they will most likely drop out by the end of the first year. Finally, they will die fourteen years before their non-disabled peers.

Is this the kind of life you want your child to have?! If not, you have to begin laying the foundations for your child's future early. You have to teach him vocational and other life skills. You have to expand his interests so that he will do fun things with his free time. You have to teach him how to avoid dangerous situations and advocate for himself. You have to get him ready for the adult world.

In this chapter, I am going to talk about your child's life after school. I am going to discuss special education's adult counterpart— vocational rehabilitation. I am also going to cover various vocational and residential options that are available to your child when he gets older.

As I have stressed in the previous chapter on collaborating with special educators, the importance of these topics cannot be understated. After all, let's suppose that you do everything that I have talked about thus far. You get involved with your child's education, collaborate with his teachers, and develop stellar IEPs! But what then? Your child can stay in special education until he is twenty-one years old, but eventually he will have to leave the structured and safe confines of high school and enter the adult world.

Too many parents and teachers forget about the adult lives of people with disabilities. They don't understand that once special education ends, there are no more entitlement programs. Further, they don't realize that there are often very long waiting lists for what services are available to adults with disabilities. Consequently, once students with autism graduate from high school, they tend to go home and stay there, typically losing many of the skills that their IEP teams tried so hard to teach them.

Preparing your child for adulthood is such a critical issue that I should probably write a book entirely on that subject. But first things first. Let me talk about this topic in general, and if you need further information, consult some of the resources listed in the appendix.

VOCATIONAL REHABILITATION

As I indicated briefly above, individuals with disabilities can stay in special education until they are twenty-one years old. After that, they must leave. Unfortunately, there are very few services for adults with disabilities. Further, none of these are provided by entitlement programs. So, in other words, adults with disabilities are not *guaranteed* anything after they exit school.

There is something called "vocational rehabilitation," but it is quite different from special education. For instance, special education focuses on the student's learning. Specifically, the goal of special education is to ensure that children with disabilities are given an "appropriate" education.

The goal of vocational rehabilitation is to help adults with disabilities get and maintain a job. Part of this process certainly can involve job training; however, vocational rehabilitation counselors are evaluated on how quickly they can get their clients gainfully employed. So it is to their advantage to get your child into a job and to provide as few services as possible.

Moreover, special education programs follow a "zero reject" policy; that is, if people qualify for special education, they can't be denied services. People can be denied services from vocational rehabilitation for several reasons. For instance, if they don't follow through on the things that they are supposed to do (e.g., complete applications, attend interviews, etc.), they can be removed for "failure to comply." Further, many of my former students have been denied services from vocational rehabilitation because the state ran out of money.

Additionally, special education has LRE or "least restrictive environment." So students with disabilities must be placed with their non-disabled peers whenever it is appropriate. Vocational rehabilitation has no such mandate. Your child could be placed in a segregated workshop even if you believe that he could work independently in the community.

Finally, whereas schools are required to allow the parents to participate in their child's education plan, many vocational rehabilitation counselors prefer to develop Individualized Written Rehabilitation Plans (IWRPs) without your involvement. It isn't that they don't like you. It is just that they view your child as an adult and will treat him accordingly. After all, when was the last time your parents attended an important meeting for you?

Like IEPs, IWRPs list various services that an individual may need to reach a specific vocational goal. Unlike IEPs, however, IWRPs are not legally binding. They are merely used to outline the expected path the client will undertake.

So as you can see, special education and vocational rehabilitation are very different programs. You might experience a kind of "culture shock" moving from one to the other. But once you get acclimated to the new "rules of the game," you'll find that vocational rehabilitation counselors can be a big help in getting your child ready for his future.

"How do I get my child involved with vocational rehabilitation," you might be wondering.

Good question! I recommend that you have your child's special education teacher invite a representative from your local vocational rehabilitation office to your child's last IEP meeting. So if your child is going to remain in school until he is twenty-one years old, you should have a vocational rehabilitation counselor attend the IEP meeting when your child is twenty.

If your child is already out of school, you can find your local vocational rehabilitation office in the phone book. Look under the government section under "Department of Vocational Rehabilitation" or "Bureau of Vocational Rehabilitation." It might be called something different in your state. Call the office and make an appointment to talk with somebody about what services are available for your child.

VOCATIONAL OPTIONS

There are many vocational options available to adults with autism. Your child's vocational rehabilitation counselor can tell you more precisely what is available in your county. However, here is a summary of what you can expect.

Sheltered Workshops

Most localities have sheltered workshops, or "segregated" workshops as they are often called. Sheltered workshops are programs where people with disabilities are grouped together to complete various "vocational" tasks.

Robert Evert Cimera

Notice that I put vocational in quotes. There are many professionals who don't believe that workshops provide any kind of vocational training. For example, in many of the workshops that I have visited, workers will sort screws, fold paper, or perform other rather mundane activities. In such situations, workshops are basically daycare for adults with disabilities. However, advocates of workshops say that their programs provide an opportunity for adults with disabilities to learn skills in a safe, highly structured environment.

In the end, you have to decide whether you think workshops are good or bad. If you are thinking of having your child attend a workshop, you might want to do a few things first. For example, tour the facility several times. Look at the "workstations." Are they clean and safe? What kinds of "work" are the individuals performing? Do the employees appear happy? Are they engaged and active, or are they sleeping or staring off into space? Does the work environment seem to fit your child's needs, or does it contain many of your child's triggers? For example, is it too noisy? Too hot? Too active?

Also interview the staff. What kind of training do they have? Do they have degrees that are related to special education, vocational rehabilitation, physical therapy, or any field of study involving individuals with disabilities? What is their philosophy or policy regarding aggressive or self-stimulating behaviors? How do they deal with such behavior?

Ask as many questions as possible. Moreover, talk to administrators as well as supervisors. You would check the credentials of your child's doctors, wouldn't you? So why not check out his other service providers?

Supported Employment

Supported employment programs enable individuals with severe disabilities to work independently within the community. Unlike sheltered employees who work in segregated workshops and typically make only pennies per hour, supported employees generally earn minimum wage or above. Further, they work solely for the businesses that hire them. Sheltered employees, conversely, work for the agency running the workshop.

"How are adults with disabilities provided services through supported employment?" perhaps you are saying to yourself. "What is the process?"

Well, first your child is referred to an agency providing supported employment services. This is usually done through a vocational rehabilitation counselor or special education teacher; however, you or your child can also contact the agency directly.

Once enrolled in supported employment, your child will be evaluated and a job developer will attempt to find a position in the community that matches your child's needs and interests. If a position is located and your child is hired, a job coach will furnish one-on-one support until your child learns all of the essential job functions. Then, gradually, the job coach will fade from the work site as much as possible.

The purpose of supported employment is to promote independence; however, some support might be provided for as long as your child needs it. This is called "follow up" or sometimes "follow along." In such situations, the job coach might come back periodically just to check on how things are going or to "tune up" the supported employee's training.

The advantages of supported employment are that it enables adults with disabilities to work in inclusive environments alongside their non-disabled peers. As mentioned earlier, supported employees are also able to earn far more money and enjoy a higher standard of living than if they were enrolled in sheltered workshops.

The main disadvantage that I have heard about supported employment is that these programs often have very long waiting lists to enter the program. So if this option interests you and your child, you may want to contact the appropriate agency as soon as possible.

I have also heard that some people believe sheltered workshops are safer because they are away from the public and highly supervised. But to tell you the truth, none of my students ever had a problem working in the community. However, as always, you have to decide for yourself which program suits your child's needs.

Work Adjustment

Work adjustment programs provide "fine tuning" for individuals who could obtain and maintain employment if they had certain skills or behaviors. For example, many of my students went into work adjustment programs to teach them how to get along with coworkers or how to interview for jobs. Once they acquired these skills, they were fine.

Unlike supported employment and sheltered workshops, work adjustment programs are time-limited. That is, they only provide services for a brief period, usually 90 to 120 days. After that, services end and the individual is expected to find and maintain a job independently.

Competitive Employment

The final vocational option available to your child is what is available to everybody else; that is, "competitive employment." Basically, under this option, your child would find a job, interview, and then (if he is hired) work. There are no special supports. He is simply a typical person working in the community.

Now, I am guessing that you are thinking, "My child is going to need a lot of help getting and keeping a job on his own! After all, he has autism!"

Making Autism a Gift

But autism doesn't mean that your child has to work in a workshop or that he needs somebody to find him a job. There are many people with autism who work completely independently in the community and don't need any help at all.

For example, one of my high school students (Dylan) wanted a job at a bank. So he typed up a crude resume and letter of introduction and then went to each bank in town. Evidently he just walked up to the tellers, handed them his note, and then ambled out the front doors, leaving the bank personnel rather perplexed.

At one bank, Dylan handed the letter to the manager and began heading for the door. The manager stopped him and asked Dylan if he knew how to use computers, to which Dylan said that he did. To make a long story short, Dylan was hired to enter reports and forms into the bank's database. That was twelve years ago and he is still working there. He sits in a cubicle with earphones on, entering data. According to his mother, Dylan has only missed a combined total of six or seven days of work—all because he had a bad case of the flu. That is less than one absence per year! He is one of the best and most reliable employees that the bank has.

Another one of my students (Jake) was fascinated with baseball. He particularly liked our local minor league baseball team. When he couldn't go and see a game, he would tape the radio broadcasts. He would also compile dozens upon dozens of notebooks on the team. He would record box scores for each game, stats for each player, weather conditions at game time, and so forth. You wouldn't believe the details that he kept! And he knew them all by heart!!

Well, as you might have guessed, Jake became a regular at the ball field and everybody knew him. Players would say hello to him and give him old bats and balls and dirty jerseys. He loved every minute of it.

Eventually people started realizing that Jake had this supernatural memory for stats and a love for the game that surpassed any of the players. To make another long story short, he is currently the Coordinator of Team Stats for the team!

I know that sounds like some sort of made-up or useless position created just to give this kid with autism a job, but it really isn't. Jake actually sits in the dugout with the coaches and keeps track of everything. He tells the coach how a certain batter does with left- or right-handed pitchers, with men in scoring position, with the wind blowing out, and so forth. Based upon what Jake says, the coach makes many decisions, such as who will play and in what positions. Jake even travels with the team! He has his dream job and he doesn't require any supports!

What makes these situations work so well is that the jobs matched the needs and interests of my former students. Further, my students' obsessions (e.g., banks and baseball) actually worked to their advantage.

Moreover, both Jake and Dylan work with people who are extremely supportive. One of the players on the baseball team had a son who was autistic, so he was able to educate the rest of the players and managers. The manager at the bank where Dylan works is a nice guy who wanted all of his employees to be happy and successful. You couldn't have asked for a more flexible and understanding boss.

Finally, the environments in which the jobs were performed were devoid of any stimuli that could trigger unwanted behavior. The bank was cool, quiet, and relaxing—just like Dylan needed. The ballpark was the only place where Jake felt truly comfortable.

There were only two instances that I know of when problems occurred. One was at the bank when some alarm went off. Dylan got very upset and started screaming, but his coworkers understood and were able to handle the situation.

The second was when an opposing team's mascot rode a horse. Jake is immensely afraid of horses and he panicked when it rode by the dugout. But this too was taken care of. Every time Jake's team plays at that particular stadium, the manager asks the mascot not to ride too closely to Jake. The other team is more than willing to comply. After all, who wants to be known for terrifying people with disabilities?

So before you begin thinking, "My kid will never work in the community independently," remember that there are needs in the community of every sort. There are people who spend their entire day digging holes and then filling them back up again. If your child can find the right job in the right environment with the right people, he could be happily employed for the rest of his life! The more environments that your child can tolerate and the more skills and interests that he has, the wider the vocational options that will be available to him. That is why it is so important to begin teaching your child early on the things that he needs to know for his future!

RESIDENTIAL OPTIONS

In addition to preparing your child for his vocational life, you must also consider where he is going to live when he gets older. Whenever I ask parents where they see their child living in ten, fifteen, or twenty years from now, there is usually an uncertain hesitation. They obviously haven't thought about it before.

Then one parent will say very quickly, "Oh, we plan on having him live with us." They indicate that they are going to fix up the basement or garage or someplace so that their child will have an apartment with plenty of privacy.

When I bring up the fact that they are going to get old and die someday, parents look at me rather annoyed.

Robert Evert Cimera

"Where is he going to live then?" I ask.

If the parents have an answer at all, it usually involves the child living with a relative, such as a sibling or a distant cousin. However, when pressed, most parents admit that they have never consulted with this family member nor do they know if the family member would be willing to take in their child with autism (who would then be an adult).

The point of all of this is that most parents seem to be caught completely unaware of the inevitable. Someday they will be too old to take care of their child. What then?

There are many different residential options available to people with disabilities. As with the vocational options that I discussed earlier, you simply have to find one that matches your child's needs.

Group Homes

One residential living option that you might have heard of is a "group home." Group homes are houses, usually owned by some adult service agency, where a small cohort of individuals with disabilities live together. There are supervisors who make sure everything is okay, sometimes twenty-four hours a day, sometimes just at night, depending upon the agency.

There are frequently very long waiting lists for this type of residential program. For example, in my state, there is at least a nine-year wait before placement. So in other words, if you want your child to be in a group home after he graduates from high school, you would have to have him on the waiting list in second or third grade!

As with the vocational programs that I discussed above, you want to check out your child's residential provider thoroughly. For example, tour the facilities. Are they clean? Well maintained? Appropriately decorated?

Interview the staff. What kind of training have they received? Is there a lot of staff turnover? What are their plans for emergencies? How do they handle aggressive behavior? In order to make a well-informed decision, you first need information.

Semi-Independent Living Programs (SILPS)

Many of my students with autism ended up living in what are called "semi-independent living programs," or SILPs. These programs find apartments for adults with disabilities based upon their individual needs (e.g., close to work, the bus line, shopping, etc.) The adults with disabilities rent the apartment just like anybody else would and can live by themselves or with other people.

SILPS also provide additional supports that the tenants may need. For example, a case worker might come in once a week to make sure that the apartment is clean and safe. Or somebody might help the resident budget his money or go grocery shopping. These services are generally limited to a few hours a week, but may continue indefinitely.

Independent Living

Finally, adults with disabilities can live in their own homes without any support whatsoever, just like you and I do. Now, before you start to dismiss this option by saying, "Oh, my child would need so much help! He can't cook or clean or do laundry by himself. He is going to need to be in a more structured environment, like a group home!" you need to keep a few things in mind.

First, there are a lot of people with and without disabilities who can't cook, clean, or do laundry. In fact, just the other day, I was going to make some hardboiled eggs, but I forgot that they were cooking on the stove. The water boiled away and the eggs exploded. They actually launched across the room and splattered on the ceiling!

So I am not a very good cook. Big deal! Nowadays, people can eat very healthy meals by just using a microwave. Further, I am a bit of a slob. So, if I wanted things clean, I could hire somebody to come in and tidy up for me! Moreover, I could bring my clothes to a laundry service.

What I am trying to point out here is that people with disabilities don't always require special services to satisfy their needs! They can utilize services already available in the community! For example, there are maids. There are laundry services. There are "handymen" (handy people) who you can hire to fix nearly everything under the sun! Can't figure out how to ignite your water heater's pilot light? Pick up the phone book and call somebody!

So rather than just assuming that your child is going to have to live in some sort of institution for the rest of his life, maybe you can prepare him to live on his own! Teach him how to operate the microwave and stove safely. Teach him how to call 911 for help if he has an emergency (also teach him what an "emergency" is!). Teach him how to problem solve and to get help when he needs it! If you begin teaching your child these things early on in his life, he will probably be ready to live on his own by the time he becomes an adult! So don't wait! Begin preparing your child for adulthood as soon as possible!

CONTINUING EDUCATION OPTIONS

Okay, so people have to work to make money and to have a purpose in life. They need to have a place to live in comfort and safety. People also must continue developing cognitively. They need to expand their horizons and challenge themselves intellectually. Otherwise, they're lives will be boring and dull!

Making Autism a Gift

So how can your child continue his education after leaving high school? Well, there are lots of ways! Let me discuss a few.

Adult Service Programs

Even though there are no entitlement programs like special education after high school, many towns have numerous programs that provide services specifically for adults with disabilities. For example, there is what used to be called the Association for Retarded Citizens (ARC). It often has workshops and seminars that teach people with mental retardation how to use the computer or access the Internet or cook or many other worthwhile activities. If you ask around your community, you will probably find many such programs where your child can continue learning.

Community Programs

Of course, just because your child has a disability, that doesn't mean he has to access only "special" educational programs. Most communities have a ton of continuing education programs for everybody to use. For example, my local park district and YMCA have catalogs full of tons of courses and activities. They have everything from water painting, to book clubs, to landscaping, to car maintenance! They even have day trips and vacations! My mother just got back from a tour of the Canadian Rockies. She said that it was beautiful. My wife and I are taking dancing classes at the local community college!

Again, the main point here is that people with autism don't always have to attend special programs to suit their needs. There are already many educational opportunities available in the community. All you have to do to find them is look in your local newspaper, go to your town's library, or call the chamber of commerce!

Community and Two-Year Colleges and Universities

Finally, if your child is interested in continuing his education after high school, why not encourage him to go to college? Again, please don't think, "Oh my child has autism, he can't go to college!" Well, maybe college isn't right for everybody. But please don't rule it out just because of your child's disability!

As I mentioned in the first chapter, when I was a professor at the University of Illinois at Chicago, two students with autism were enrolled in programs there. One, I believe, was getting his masters in some sort of technology program. There was even a woman with mental retardation taking classes! She was actually a fairly famous public speaker and advocated for the rights of people with disabilities. She met President Clinton, testified in front of Congress, and has given presentations all over the world! So, again, it is very important that you don't limit your child's future with preconceived notions.

If your child wants to go on to college, there are many options available to him. For example, he could go to a community college, technical college (where they focus on teaching a specific trade such as electrician or mechanic), or a university.

As with everything else that I have been discussing, your child should find the school that matches his needs. Different schools specialize in different programs. Purdue, for example, is really well known for engineering, nursing, and agriculture. Indiana University has a stellar business program. My school produces a lot of teachers. Your child should pick a school that has an area of study that interests him.

Moreover, he should look at the services that the schools have for people with disabilities. For instance, my school has a program called Project Success, which is for students who have learning disabilities. The program provides tutors, note takers, books on tape, and many other services that students with learning challenges require to succeed. So before your child enrolls in any particular school, see if it has services that might help him!

FINANCIAL AND LEGAL CONSIDERATIONS

Well, we are getting to the end of this book and there are still a number of very important topics to cover. For example, you need to understand something about guardianship, powers of attorney, and those kinds of legal things. As always, if you want more information about any of these topics, please consult the resources at the back of the book, or contact a lawyer or financial advisor.

Guardians

This might surprise you, but just because you are your child's parent, you are not necessarily his legal guardian. If your child is eighteen years old or older, he is his own legal guardian regardless of the severity of his disability. That means after age eighteen, he gets to make all the decisions!

Now, this might be fine with you. After all, perhaps your child is fully capable of making well-informed decisions and living without your guidance. However, if your child has profound mental retardation or needs intensive supports, you might want to consider getting legal guardianship.

How do you do this? Basically, you will need to get an attorney who will schedule a hearing with a judge. Your attorney will present a petition for guardianship to the judge who will in turn determine whether to grant it.

There are several different types of guardianship, including regular, limited, and temporary. Let me talk briefly about each.

Robert Evert Cimera

<u>Regular Guardianship.</u> Of the three types of guardianship that I am going to discuss, regular guardianship status grants the most power to the guardian. In these situations, the guardian can make all decisions for the ward, including those involving financial, medical, and residential issues.

However, it isn't as if a regular guardian can simply do anything he or she wants. There are certain checks on the guardian's powers. For instance, the guardian must "care for" and "maintain" the ward. This means that the guardian must make sure that the ward is fed, clothed, housed, and taken care of properly. Further, every two years, the guardian must account for all of the ward's financial assets.

<u>Limited Guardianship.</u> As the name implies, limited guardianship status grants limited power to the guardian. All powers not transferred by the courts to the guardian are retained by the ward. For example, a limited guardian might be given rights to make all financial or medical decisions; however, the ward is free to make decisions in all other aspects of his life, such as where to live.

<u>Temporary Guardianship.</u> Temporary guardianships last for up to sixty days before they must be renewed. Frequently, judges will appoint temporary guardianship of individuals when there is some sort of legal dispute. For example, the parents of one of my students were getting a divorce and both wanted guardianship of their child. The judge appointed a third party to be the temporary guardian of the student until the issue was settled.

Powers of Attorneys

Powers of attorney (POAs) are very much like guardianships in that they give certain rights to other people. However, there are two main differences. Specifically, powers of attorney are legal documents that are agreed upon between the ward and the guardian. Guardianships, on the other hand, are arranged by order of a judge with or without the consent of the ward. Moreover, individuals can always revoke a power of attorney. But only a judge can alter a guardianship.

As with guardianships, powers of attorney can transfer very specific or very broad powers. Somebody might have a financial power of attorney that gives the person's accountants the ability to make monetary decisions. Or another individual might have a full power of attorney that gives away all of that person's rights.

Trusts Funds and Long-Term Financial Planning

One of my roles as a teacher was to prepare my students for adult life. Part of this preparation involved long-term financial planning. Think about it. How is your child going to pay for food, clothes, shelter, and so forth after you are gone? If you are like most of my students' parents, you probably haven't thought about it, or you assume that Supplemental Security Income (SSI) is going to take care of everything, but it probably won't.

I know that many people don't like to discuss financial issues, especially with strangers, but the fact is your child will need money on which to live. If he is going to work for a living, that is great! Then maybe you don't need to worry about it! After all, people with autism can get great jobs and make big bucks! However, if your child is going to work in sheltered workshops or low wage community-based employment, you might want to consider establishing a trust fund.

A trust is a legal entity that holds the ownership of assets for a beneficiary. As with guardianships and powers of attorney, there are many different types of trusts. Further, there are many legal ramifications of setting up one. So before you do, please consult a lawyer who specializes in such matters.

With that said, trusts are often used as a way of making sure that people have money over an extended period of time. For instance, several of my students had trust funds that would begin paying them a monthly "allowance" once they reached a certain age, such as twenty-two or thirty-five or fifty. The trustee, which could be a person or an institution, is responsible for tending to and allocating the funds as prescribed in the trust agreement. In the cases of my students, most of the money was pre-allocated for certain expenditures, such as housing, medical care, and daily living expenses.

Perhaps you are thinking that only really rich people can have trusts for their children. But this isn't true. Anybody can have a trust. Further, a trust can contain any dollar amount.

You might also be thinking that you can't afford to leave your child the money that he will need. However, this might not be the case. Let me explain.

Suppose for a moment that you began putting $100 every month from the time your child was born until he turned twenty-one. Assuming that the money accrued 5 percent interest, your child would have $355,220 by the time he reached sixty-five years old! That could be a big help!

Now let's suppose that you put away $100 a month in the same account for twenty years, but this time you started when the child turned twenty-one. By the time your child turned sixty-five, he would only have $138,237 (see table 12.1).

What I want you to see here is that early planning results in better financial outcomes. The sooner you begin investing for your child's adult life, the more interest will accumulate and the more money your child will be able to live off of when the time comes. In essence, you get more bang for your bucks!

Making Autism a Gift

Table 12.1. The Effects of Long-Term Financial Planning

Age of Child	Cumulative Savings	
	Situation #1	Situation #2
1 year old	$1,200.00	—
5 years old	$6,561.30	—
10 years old	$15,004.82	—
15 years old	$25,781.14	—
20 years old	$39,534.75	—
25 years old	$50,457.47	$6,630.76
30 years old	$64,397.94	$15,093.47
35 years old	$82,189.90	$25,894.28
40 years old	$104,897.46	$39,679.14
45 years old	$133,878.69	$52,100.37
50 years old	$170,866.90	$66,494.74
55 years old	$218,074.28	$84,866.01
60 years old	$278,324.18	$108,312.92
65 years old	$355,220.02	$138,237.79

SUPPLEMENTAL SECURITY INCOME (SSI) AND OTHER GOVERNMENTAL PROGRAMS

Finally, I think that I should talk about various governmental funding programs for which your child might be eligible. Specifically, I want to talk about Supplemental Security Income (SSI), Medicaid, Medicare, and the Children's Health Insurance Program (CHIP). These programs vary greatly from state to state and from year to year, so it will be difficult to discuss them other than in extremely general terms. If you think that your child may be eligible for these programs, please contact your local Social Security office (go to www.socialsecurity.gov or call 1-800-772-1213).

Fundamentally, SSI is a federal program that pays monthly benefits to individuals with various disabilities who demonstrate an economic need. Both children and adults are eligible, although the eligibility of children is affected by the income of their parents. Determination for eligibility often takes up to six months; however, the applications of people with mental retardation, Down's syndrome, and cerebral palsy are often expedited.

Medicaid is a health care program for people who have low incomes. Most of the time, children who qualify for SSI also qualify for Medicaid. However, since Medicaid is heavily influenced by state regulations, you should check with your local Social Security office to see if your child is eligible.

Medicare is a federal health program for people who are sixty-five or older and for people who have been receiving social security disability benefits for more than two years. Because people with mental retardation are not eligible for social security disability benefits until they turn eighteen, children with mental retardation are not eligible for Medicare until they turn twenty.

Finally, the state Children's Health Insurance Program (CHIP) is a program that provides health insurance for children who come from working families that earn too much money to qualify for Medicaid, but cannot afford to purchase private health insurance. CHIP covers prescription drugs, vision, hearing, and mental health services.

SUMMARY

In addition to helping your child through elementary and secondary school, you will also have to prepare him for adult life. Part of adult life involves working and living in the community. In this chapter, I have discussed some of the issues related these topics.

I also talked about various legal and economic considerations that you will have to eventually make. For example, should you set up a trust fund? Should you become your child's guardian? Before making any decisions regarding these questions, please consult legal and economic counselors who are familiar with your situation and goals.

THIRTEEN

Final Thoughts

Well, here we are, at the final chapter! I hope that you have enjoyed our time together and that you have learned something useful. Before we part company, I want to reiterate some of the main points that I have been hitting on throughout this entire book.

GET A SECOND, THIRD, AND FOURTH OPINION

My first tip is if you are ever in doubt about your child's diagnosis, get a second, third, or even fourth opinion. In fact, get a fifth and sixth opinion if you need to. Keep talking to people until everything makes sense!

Now, I am not suggesting that you should keep shopping around until you get a diagnosis that you like. I am not saying that at all. It is just that you know your child and you know what autism is. If a clinician diagnoses your child with OCD and you don't think that sounds correct, get another evaluation. Keep talking to people until all of your questions are answered and all of your fears are addressed.

Robert Evert Cimera

Remember, despite what various professionals may tell you, diagnosing and treating autism isn't an exact science. It is far more of an art than anything else. There is a lot of guesswork and trial and error.

INTERVENE EARLY, INTERVENE OFTEN

My second suggestion is to intervene early and often! Studies have repeatedly found that the sooner you intervene, the better off your child will be. So don't wait! As soon as you learn that your child has autism, enroll him in every reputable program that you can find! You simply cannot "overdo" services, especially when your child is young!

Also, although your occupation might be an accountant or fire fighter or actor, as soon as you have a child with a disability, you also become a teacher. In fact, you become the most important teacher that your child will ever have! So you will have to act like one. You will have to come home from work and, no matter how exhausted you are, teach your child new things as well as reinforce good behaviors and try to minimize bad ones.

PICK YOUR BATTLES

This is a bit of a cliché, but it is very wise advice. Pick your battles! Don't try to change everything about your child. Don't focus on each and every annoying behavior. It will only make both you and him extremely frustrated.

Figure out what the most important areas are to address and then focus on them! Don't get sidetracked by minor annoyances or areas of deficits that don't really matter! Give your child the skills he will need to succeed in life. Everything else can wait.

Making Autism a Gift

GATHER DATA ON EVERYTHING

Collect data on everything! Before you can help your child, you have to first understand him. That requires insightful reflection, but also data! Collect data on good days and bad. Try to figure out what is going on inside of his head. You don't have to be an expert and measure everything exactly. Even a diary where you jot down your thoughts would be helpful. Just make sure that you add to it every day!

MONITOR MEDS

If your child is on medications, monitor them! Find out what the potential side effects are and actively watch for them. Also, use the data that you are gathering to determine whether the medications are actually helping. Report your observations back to your child's doctor.

GET ORGANIZED

As you might have guessed, there is going to be A LOT of paperwork associated with your child. However, I am willing to bet that you have no idea how much! You are probably going to have notebooks full of the data that you will be collecting as well as file folders crammed with assessments, medical reports, and past IEPs. Not to mention stacks of report cards, meeting minutes, and notes that your child's teachers are going to send home!

In order for this information to be useful, it has to be organized! You have to be able to find what you want, when you want it. So get a large filing cabinet and plenty of three-ring binders. Develop some sort of organizational system that makes sense to you. And above all, save everything! You never know when you will need your notes on a phone conversation that you had with your child's principal!

EDUCATION IS A TEAM SPORT

I know that there is often an "us versus them" mentality in education. Parents often feel like they are treated as second-class citizens. Teachers often think that they aren't getting the respect that they deserve. And maybe both are correct. However, one thing is for certain: your child needs you and his teachers to work together. Very little will get done when nobody is collaborating.

Effective collaboration means sharing your data and ideas, but also listening to other people's opinions and keeping an open mind. It also means showing gratitude for the hard work other people do on your child's behalf. Remember, you might not agree with what some teachers or professionals say, but hopefully you can agree that everybody wants the best for your child!

FIGHT FOR YOUR RIGHTS

Just because education is a team process, that doesn't mean you shouldn't fight for your individual rights! If your child's teachers or other members of the IEP team are doing something that you don't agree with, try to mediate the problem yourself. If that doesn't work, then get an advocate and take the school through due process!

Advocates can give you moral support as well as facts, figures, and recent court rulings that may help bolster your argument. Two heads, after all, are better than one! If you need an advocate, contact one of the parent support groups listed in the back of this book.

Making Autism a Gift

TAKE SMALL STEPS . . .

Many parents and teachers with whom I have worked often make the mistake of trying to do too much in too short a period of time. They generate an entire page of goals and quickly find that the child isn't making progress on any of them. The student becomes frustrated. The parents and teachers become frustrated. It is a no-win situation.

The desire to make a huge impact on a child's life is truly admirable. However, rather than trying to make sudden and sweeping changes, try taking small baby steps. Pick one or two skills or behaviors that are almost within your child's reach and work towards those. When success is obtained, pick another one or two areas. It is amazing how far little steps can take you!

BUT WALK TO A BIG GOAL

But don't just take small steps in any old random direction! You need to have an idea of where you want your child to be when he becomes an adult. Where is he going to live? What kind of job is he going to have? What kind of social life do you see him having? What skills is he going to need to be "successful"? Once you are able to answer these questions, you can develop a long-term goal, which will help guide the many small steps that you will be taking with your child throughout his life.

FOCUS ON YOUR CHILD'S SUCCESS

Having a child with autism can often seem as if you are walking in a strong wind, taking two steps forward and one back. If you focus only on the wind, you might soon wonder whether you will get anywhere. But if you focus on the progress you are making, your journey will be a lot easier.

Keep your child's life in perspective. Yes, he might have a lot to learn. Everyone does. But he has probably also learned a lot!

Celebrate every little success and improvement! Keep a "victory list" where you write down all of the things that your child has accomplished! Refer and add to it often! Life becomes a lot easier when you see the fruits of your labors!

KEEP UP WITH DEVELOPMENTS
IN THE FIELD

Autism and special education are constantly changing. Definitions of disorders change. Interpretations of state and federal laws change. Even notions of what are considered the best medications, teaching strategies, and behavioral interventions change. If you are going to be an effective parent, teacher, and advocate for your child, you will need to stay abreast of all the latest developments.

This is often hard to do. Nonetheless, if you join some of the organizations, support groups, and e-communities listed in the back of this book, your task might be a bit easier. Also, you might want to consider going to workshops and seminars. Many of the organizations listed in the appendix have annual conferences with nationally recognized speakers. Some even have informative journals and magazines that could help you.

BE SKEPTICAL, YET OPTIMISTIC

Of course, as you are getting involved with support groups, joining professional organizations, and reading articles, you are going to be bombarded with tons of information, some of which will be useful. Some will be worthless or even counterproductive.

Before trying every new trend and fad, be a bit skeptical. Do some of your own research, and figure out if what you are hearing and reading is really true. Remember, many of the speakers and authors whom you will come across will be trying to sell you something. And while that might not necessarily be a bad thing, many of these "experts" are just con artists. So be optimistic that there is useful information out there, but skeptical that you have actually found it!

GET SUPPORT!

I don't care how emotionally strong you and your family members are. Having a child with autism is going to be a very long, exhausting, and demanding job. So get support! Surround yourself with people who will not only pitch in and help out once in awhile but also keep a positive mental attitude. That is very important. Too many people see only the negative aspects of autism. If that is all you see, your life will be pretty miserable!

So stay positive and take a break once in a while. Pamper yourself. In fact, reward yourself as much as you reward your child. His successes are your successes as well!

In addition to family and friends, you should really consider joining a support group or talking to a therapist just to get out some of the emotions that tend to build up when people are under pressure. Even if you think that you are fine and that you can make it without any help, find out what support is available just in case you need it!

GIVE SUPPORT!

At the same time that you are getting support, you should be giving it! There are many families out there who are going through what you already survived. They don't know what autism is. They think it is a death sentence or that their children are "stupid." They can really benefit from your wisdom and expertise.

So get out there and try to make a difference not only in other people's lives but also in the special education community. Talk to people. Share your experiences. Share resources. If you know of a great babysitter or pediatrician or book, then let others in on the secret!

Consider writing a newsletter or have a website or blog. If there isn't a support group in your community, then form one! Host monthly get-togethers with the parents of your child's classmates. Only by helping each other can we really help ourselves.

DON'T SETTLE FOR A SUB-ADEQUATE FUTURE FOR YOUR CHILD

I think many parents end up settling on sub-adequate futures for their children. Somebody tells them, "Your child has autism and that means he won't be able to do that. He'll have to live in a group home or an institution with constant supervision." And none of this is necessarily the truth.

People with autism can live very rich and rewarding lives. They can live independently, hold important high-paying jobs, and have their own families. But in order to be successful, children with autism have to be given the proper skills and behaviors. That is where you and your child's teachers come in!

Making Autism a Gift

TREAT YOUR CHILD LIKE A NORMAL KID
WHO HAS CERTAIN UNIQUE NEEDS

I realize that this is my own little pet peeve, but I want to share it with you anyway. I hate it when people treat kids with disabilities as if they were freaks from another planet. I hate it when they talk to them with high lilting voices or ignore them altogether.

Again, this is just my philosophy and you certainly don't have to agree with me, but I try to treat people more or less the same—with, of course, modifications for their individual needs. For instance, my grandparents were a bit hard of hearing, so I spoke louder when they were around. I have friends who hate talking about politics or religion, so I don't bring those topics up with them.

My point is, treat your child as if he were like any other kid. Spend time with him. Laugh with him. Play with him. Yell at him if you have had a bad day and then apologize. Treat him just like you would treat anybody else.

But make accommodations for his special needs. Don't touch him if he doesn't like to be touched. Don't expect him to interact or communicate like other kids his age. Give him what he needs, just like you would with everybody else whom you love.

NEVER GIVE UP!

Finally, the very last tip that I can give is never give up! Never stop learning. Never stop fighting. Never stop teaching. Never stop loving your child. Do what you can. Do what you need to. Do your best. That is all that you can do.

Robert Evert Cimera

LAST WORDS

I want to thank you for reading this book. I hope that it has helped in one way or another. Please remember, autism doesn't mean someone is "stupid" or "crazy" or a "failure." It just means he is "different," and that is okay!

Good luck and much happiness.

Glossary

ABC: See "Antecedent, Behavior, and Consequence."

Absence Seizures: Seizures causing a person to stare off into space for several seconds.

Adaptive Skills: The ability to adjust to changing environments and situations.

Age of Onset: The age at which symptoms of a condition first appear.

American Psychiatric Association: The professional organization for mental health professionals that produces the *DSM*.

American Sign Language: A form of sign language that has a grammar that is separate from English grammar.

Annual Goals: The section of the IEP that states what the student is trying to accomplish in the coming year.

Antecedent, Behavior, and Consequence: A way of identifying the function of behavior by investigating what transpired before and after the behavior occurred.

APA: See "American Psychiatric Association."

AS: See "Asperger's Syndrome."

ASD: See "Autism Spectrum Disorder" or "Autism."

ASL: See "American Sign Language."

Asperger's Syndrome: An autistic-like condition characterized by poor social skills and stereotypic patterns of behavior. People with Asperger's do not have delays in language development.

Atonic Seizures: Seizures causing a person to suddenly lose all muscle tone.

Autism: A developmental disability where people display impaired communication skills, poor social skills, and repetitious or stereotypic behaviors.

Autism Spectrum Disorder: See "Autism."

Autistic Leading: The tendency for individuals with autism to physically guide people to what they want. For example, rather than saying that he wants a cookie, a child with autism might take his mother by the hand and lead her to a cookie jar.

Backward Chaining: A method of teaching where the last step in a task analysis is taught first, followed by the second to last step, then the third to last step, and so on until the entire task is mastered.

Basket Weave: A type of restraint where individuals are held from behind with their arms wrapped around themselves.

Behavior Modification: A systematic approach for altering a person's behavior, usually though the use of reinforcers and punishments.

Behavioral Contract: A written statement that contains expectations of conduct and consequences for performing and not performing the desired behavior.

Behavioral Intervention Plan: A formal, written plan for addressing the potentially negative behaviors of students in special education. It is often included as part of the child's individualized education plan.

BIP: See "Behavioral Intervention Plan."

Brushing: A technique often used as part of sensory integration therapy where individuals with autism are stroked with a brush, usually on their backs, arms, or legs. It is thought to reduce self-stimming behavior.

CDD: See "Childhood Disintegrative Disorder."

Chaining: A method of teaching where one step in a task analysis is mastered, then another step.

Childhood Disintegrative Disorder: A degenerative condition where "normal" children develop autistic-like symptoms.

Childhood-Onset Schizophrenia: A form of schizophrenia where symptoms emerge in childhood, usually around age ten.

Children's Health Insurance Program: A program that provides health insurance for children.

CHIP: See "Children's Health Insurance Program."

Classical Autism: See "Autism."

Classical Punishment: See "Presentation Punishment."

Classical Reinforcement: See "Positive Reinforcement."

Communication Wallet: A device that holds pictures so that an individual can communicate.

Competitive Employment: Being employed within the community.

Compression: A technique often used as part of sensory integration therapy where the joints of individuals with autism are pushed firmly together. It is thought to reduce self-stimming behavior.

COS: See "Childhood-Onset Schizophrenia."

Delayed Echolalia: The repetition of what somebody else said hours, or even days later.

Developmental Disability: A disability that manifests itself before the child turns eighteen years old.

DI: See "Direct Instruction."

Diagnostic and Statistical Manual of Mental Disorders: A manual written and published by the American Psychiatric Association that covers diagnostic information and criteria on various mental conditions.

Diagnostic Team: A committee of educators and other school personnel who officially assess students to determine if they qualify for special education.

Dignity of Risk: A philosophy where individuals with disabilities are allowed to fail.

Direct Instruction: A structured method of teaching where students are given frequent opportunities for learning and immediate feedback is provided by the teacher.

Direct Verbal Cue: A method of teaching that is characterized by telling the student what to do.

Disintegrative Psychosis: See "Childhood Disintegrative Disorder."

DSM: See "Diagnostic and Statistical Manual of Mental Disorders."

D-Team: See "Diagnostic Team."

Duration Recording: A system of measuring how long a behavior lasts.

Early Intervention Programs: Programs for young children that are designed to help prevent or reduce developmental difficulties.

Echolalia: The frequent repetition of what somebody else said.

EI: See "Early Intervention Programs."

Epilepsy: A condition characterized by frequent seizures.

Event Recording: A system of measuring behavior each and every time it occurs. Also called "frequency recording."

Extinction: Making an outcome of a behavior no longer rewarding.

Facilitated Communication: A controversial method of communicating where a facilitator helps steady the hand of the non-verbal individual as he points to letters or words.

FAPE: See "Free and Appropriate Public Education."

FBA: see "Functional Behavior Analysis."

FC: See "Facilitated Communication."

Forward Chaining: A method of teaching where the first step in a task analysis is mastered, followed by the second step, then the third, and so on until the entire task is learned.

Fragile X Syndrome: A potentially autistic-like condition caused by an abnormality in the X-chromosome.

Free and Appropriate Public Education: A component of IDEA that guarantees that students in special education receive an appropriate (not best) education in the public schools without cost to their parents.

Frequency Recording: A system of measuring behavior each and every time it occurs. Also called "event recording."

Frontal Lobe Seizures: Seizures causing a person to experience atypical twitching or odd sensations in the face, hands, or legs.

Functional Behavior Analysis: A systematic approach designed to understand the purpose of behaviors.

Gesture Prompts: A method of teaching that is characterized by using gestures (e.g., pointing) to prompt the student.

Grand Mal Seizures: See "Tonic-Clonic Seizures."

Grandma's Law: See "Premack Principle."

Group Home: A residential option where several individuals with disabilities live together.

Hand-Over-Hand: A method of teaching that is characterized by physically helping the student perform the task.

Heller's Syndrome: See "Childhood Disintegrative Disorder."

High Functioning Autism: see "Asperger's Syndrome."

Home Signs: An informal sign language that is unique to the individual.

Hyperfocus: The ability of many individuals with autism to concentrate on one thing (e.g., a spinning top) for hours on end.

Hypersensitivity: Extreme sensitivity to certain stimuli (e.g., noise, touch, smell).

IDEA: see "Individuals with Disabilities Education Act."

Idiot Savant: An archaic term now considered to be derogatory. See "Savant Syndrome."

IEP: see "Individualized Education Plan."

IFSP: See "Individualized Family Service Plans."

Indirect Verbal Cue: A method of teaching that is characterized by verbally suggesting or prompting the student.

Individualized Education Plan: A formal, written, legally binding contract between the school and parents of students in special education that outlines the goals and services that the student will receive over the course of a year.

Individualized Family Service Plans: A formal written plan that outlines the goals and services provided to a family and child by an early intervention program.

Individualized Written Rehabilitation Plan: A formal plan that outlines the goals of individuals in vocational rehabilitation programs.

Individuals with Disabilities Education Act: A federal law governing many aspects of special education.

IWRP: See "Individualized Written Rehabilitation Plan."

Landau-Kleffner Syndrome: A condition often associated or confused with autism that is characterized by a sudden or gradual loss of language skills.

Latency Recording: A system of measuring the time that elapses between when a behavior should occur and when it actually occurs.

Least Restrictive Environment: The environment that is the most inclusive in which a special education student can receive a free and appropriate public education.

LKS: See "Landau-Kleffner Syndrome."

Lovaas: A behavior modification approach that uses discrete trial training.

LRE: See "Least Restrictive Environment."

Medicaid: A health care program for individuals who have low incomes.

Medicare: A federal health program for people who are sixty-five years or older and people who have been receiving social security disability benefits for more than two years.

Mental Retardation: A developmental disability that is characterized by significantly below average intelligence and poor adaptive skills.

Mitigated Echolalia: The immediate repetition of what somebody else said.

MMR Vaccinations: Inculcations for measles, mumps, and rubella. Often thought to cause autism.

M-Team: See "Multi-Disciplinary Team."

Multi-Disciplinary Team: A committee of educators and other school personnel who officially assess students to determine if they qualify for special education.

Multimodality Teaching: A teaching technique where multiple senses are engaged, such as making a student see, hear, and feel what is being taught.

Myoclonic Seizures: Seizures causing a person to display sudden jerking motions, usually involving one muscle or muscle groups.

Making Autism a Gift

Natural Consequences: A philosophy where individuals with disabilities are allowed to learn from the potential negative outcomes that arise from their own behavior.

Negative Reinforcement: Taking away something that a person doesn't like so that he will continue performing a desired behavior.

Nondiscriminatory Evaluation: A component of IDEA which mandates that schools must assess students using multiple and nonbiased methods.

Obsessive-Compulsive Disorder: A condition characterized by recurring behavior that reduces atypical anxiety caused by recurring thoughts.

Occipital Lobe Seizures: Seizures causing people to temporarily lose all or part of their vision.

OCD: See "Obsessive-Compulsive Disorder."

Parietal Lobe Seizures: Seizures causing a person to experience a tingling feeling throughout the entire body. People may feel as if they are moving, sinking, or being choked.

PDD: See "Pervasive Developmental Disorder."

PDD-NOS: See "Pervasive Developmental Disorder–Not Otherwise Specified"

PECS: See "Picture Exchange Communication System."

Pervasive Developmental Disorder: A developmental disability characterized by chronic and profound impairments in a person's social and communication skills.

Pervasive Developmental Disorder–Not Otherwise Specified: A form of pervasive developmental disorder that is atypical in its development, symptomology, or etiology.

Petit Mal Seizures: See "Absence Seizures."

Pica: A condition characterized by the willful, age-inappropriate, consumption of inedible materials, such as dirt, paint, rocks, hair, and feces.

Picture Exchange Communication System: A system of communicating based upon pictures.

PLOP: See "Present Level of Performance."

Positive Reinforcement: Giving a person something that she likes so that she will continue performing a desired behavior.

Robert Evert Cimera

Premack Principle: A philosophy or teaching strategy where students perform the least desirable activity before they move on to something more desirable.

Pre-Referral Strategies: Strategies that should be employed to correct problems that a student is having in the regular education classroom prior to when the student is formally evaluated for special education.

Present Level of Educational Performance: See "Present Level of Performance."

Present Level of Performance: The section of an IEP that states results from recent assessments. It should also include the student's strengths and the concerns of the parents.

Presentation Punishment: Giving a person something that she does not like so that she will not continue performing an undesirable behavior.

Procedural Due Process: The process through which parents and school officials can arbitrate grievances.

Punishment: Approaches that decrease undesirable behavior.

Reciprocity: The "give and take" in a relationship or conversation.

Response-Cost: Taking away something that a person likes so that he will not continue performing an undesirable behavior.

Rett's Disorder: A degenerative condition where "normal" females develop autistic-like symptoms.

Reward: Approaches that increase desirable behavior.

Savant Syndrome: A "condition" where individuals with autism display dramatic strengths, such as being able to complete complex math problems or play musical instruments.

Schizophrenia: A condition characterized by hallucinations, delusions, and disorganized thoughts or behaviors.

Seizure: A physiological response to errant electrical currents in the brain. Can produce a wide array of symptoms, including convulsions, staring off into space, random movements, and hallucinations.

Self-Injurious Behavior: Intentional behavior that results in harm to oneself.

Self-Stimming: See "Self-Stimulation."

Self-Stimulation: Performing certain repetitious behaviors.

Semi-Independent Living Program: A residential option where individuals with disabilities live in the community and receive whatever supports that they need.

Sensory Integration Therapy: A treatment for individuals with autism thought to reduce self-stimming behaviors.

Sensory Processing Dysfunction: A condition that is characterized by a difficulty in processing information obtained via a specific modality, such as visually or auditorily.

Sheltered Workshop: Segregated programs that provide vocational training.

SI: See "Sensory Integration Therapy."

SIB: See "Self-Injurious Behavior."

Signed English: A form of sign language in which every word is signed.

SILP: See "Semi-Independent Living Program."

SPD: See "Sensory Processing Dysfunction."

Special Education: A federally mandated program designed to provide a free and appropriate public education to qualifying students who are between the ages of three and twenty-one.

Splinter Skills: Abilities that are above those normally displayed by the individuals. Also see "Savant Syndrome."

SSI: See "Supplemental Security Income."

Stereotypic Behavior: Behaviors that occur repeatedly, such as rocking back and forth or flapping the hands.

Superstitious Learning: Believing that one behavior or variable leads to an action when it really doesn't. For example, if you wear a certain hat, you will get a good grade on your math exam.

Supplemental Security Income: A federal program that pays monthly benefits to qualifying individuals.

Supported Employment: Vocational programs through which workers with disabilities obtain and maintain employment within the community.

System of Least Restrictive Prompts: A method of teaching individuals by using a highly structured progression of supports that are gradually faded until the student can perform the activity independently.

Systematic Desensitizing: A gradual process of making a person less sensitive to various stimuli.

TA: See "Task Analysis"

Task Analysis: A written breakdown of all the steps required to complete a task.

Tonic Seizures: Seizures causing a person to suddenly go stiff, as if frozen in stone.

Tonic-Clonic Seizure: Seizures causing rigidity followed by convulsions.

Transition Plan: A plan that outlines the services that a school will provide to prepare a special education student for adult life.

Trigger: A stimuli that elicits a certain, often negative, response.

Vocational Rehabilitation: A program that addresses the vocational needs of adults with disabilities.

Work Adjustment: Vocational programs that teach job seekers skills that they require to obtain and maintain employment within the community.

Wrapping: A technique often used as part of sensory integration therapy where an individual with autism is wrapped in a weighted blanket. It is thought to reduce self-stimming behavior.

Zero Reject: A component of IDEA which says no child who qualifies for special education can be rejected.

Resources

The following are some resources that you might find useful in your quest to help your child. Their inclusion here by no means indicates that I endorse them or vouch for their quality. You'll have to judge their merits for yourself based upon your own needs.

Mission statements for organizations and descriptions of e-groups come directly from their corresponding websites. All information was current at the time of this book's publication.

BOOKS AND PRINTED RESOURCES
General Books on Autism

The Self-Help Guide for Special Kids and Their Parents
Joan Matthews, James Williams
Jessica Kingsley Publishers (August 2000)

Out To Get Jack: Where Do You Draw The Line Between Obedience And Standing Up For Yourself?
James Williams
Kensa (November 2003)

Robert Evert Cimera

Autism Spectrum Disorders: The Complete Guide to Understanding Autism, Asperger's Syndrome, Pervasive Developmental Disorder, and Other ASDs
Chantal Sicile-Kira, Temple Grandin
Perigee Trade (August 31, 2004)

Thinking In Pictures: and Other Reports from My Life with Autism
Temple Grandin
Vintage (October 29, 1996)

The Autism Sourcebook: Everything You Need to Know About Diagnosis, Treatment, Coping, and Healing
Karen Siff Exkorn
Regan Books (October 1, 2005)

When My Autism Gets Too Big! A Relaxation Book for Children with Autism Spectrum Disorders
Kari Dunn Buron
Autism Asperger Publishing Co. (January 2004)

Making Peace with Autism: One Family's Story of Struggle, Discovery, and Unexpected Gifts
Susan Senator
Trumpeter (August 30, 2005)

Toilet Training for Individuals with Autism and Related Disorders
Maria Wheeler
Future Horizons (April 1, 1998)

Making Autism a Gift

Overcoming Autism
  Lynn Kern Koegel, Claire LaZebnik
  Viking Books (April 2004)

The Autism Social Skills Picture Book
  Jed Baker
  Future Horizons (April 16, 2003)

Playing, Laughing and Learning with Children on the Autism Spectrum: A Practical Resource of Play Ideas for Parents and Carers
  Julia Moor
  Jessica Kingsley Publishers (June 2002)

*Biological Treatments for Autism and PDD_*
  William Shaw
  Sunflower Publications; 2nd rev. edition (October 1, 2001)

Facing Autism: Giving Parents Reasons for Hope and Guidance for Help
  Lynn M. Hamilton
  WaterBrook Press (March 14, 2000)

Unraveling the Mystery of Autism and Pervasive Developmental Disorder: A Mother's Story of Research & Recovery
  Karyn Seroussi
  Broadway (January 8, 2002)

Everybody Is Different: A Book for Young People Who Have Brothers or Sisters With Autism
  Fiona Bleach
  Autism Asperger Publishing Co. (February 11, 2002)

Children with Autism: A Parent's Guide
Michael D. Powers
Woodbine House; 2nd edition (July 15, 2000)

Books on Behavior Modification

Enhancing Your Child's Behavior: A Step-By-Step Guide for Parents and Teachers
Robert Evert Cimera
Scarecrow Education (August 2003)

A Treasure Chest of Behavioral Strategies for Individuals With Autism
Beth Fouse, Maria Wheeler
Future Horizons (August 1997)

Behavioral Intervention for Young Children With Autism: A Manual for Parents and Professionals
Catherine Maurice (Editor), Gina Green (Editor), Stephen C. Luce (Editor)
Pro-Ed (May 1996)

Making a Difference: Behavioral Intervention for Autism
Catherine Maurice, Gina Green
Pro-Ed (May, 2001)

Raising a Child with Autism: A Guide to Applied Behavior Analysis for Parents
Shira Richman
Jessica Kingsley Publishers; 1st edition (March 2001)

Making Autism a Gift

Books about *Special Education*

The Truth about Special Education: A Guide for Parents and Teachers
Robert E. Cimera
Scarecrow Education (March 2003)

Negotiating the Special Education Maze: A Guide for Parents and Teachers
Winifred Anderson, Stephen Chitwood, Deidre Hayden
Woodbine House; 3rd edition (May 1, 1997)

Special Education in Contemporary Society: An Introduction to Exceptionality
Richard M. Gargiulo
Wadsworth Publishing (March 29, 2002)

Birth to Eight: Early Childhood Special Education
Frank Bowe
Delmar Thomson Learning (September 1, 2003)

Exceptional Children: An Introduction to Special Education
William Heward
Prentice Hall; 6th edition (July 28, 1999)

Books on *Legal Issues*

Wrightslaw: Special Education Law
Peter W. D. Wright, Pamela Darr Wright
Harbor House Law Press (November 1, 1999)

Robert Evert Cimera

Getting Comfortable with Special Education Law: A Framework for Working with Children with Disabilities
Dixie Snow Huefner
Christopher-Gordon Publications (December 1, 2000)

Special Education Law
Nikki L. Murdick, Barbara C. Gartin, Terry Lee Crabtree
Prentice Hall; 1st edition (May 1, 2001)

The Law and Special Education
Mitchell L. Yell
Prentice Hall; 1st edition (November 10, 1997)

Books on Conditions Related to Autism

Mental Retardation Doesn't Mean "STUPID!": A Guide For Parents and Teachers
Robert Cimera, Ph.D.
Rowman and Littlefield (May 2006)

Mental Retardation
Mary Beirne-Smith, Richard F. Ittenbach, James R. Patton
Prentice Hall; 6th edition (June 5, 2001)

Handbook of Mental Retardation and Development
Jacob A. Burack, Robert M. Hodapp, Edward F. Zigler
Cambridge University Press (February 28, 1998)

Mental Retardation: A Lifespan Approach to People with Intellectual Disabilities
Clifford J. Drew, Michael L. Hardman
Prentice Hall; 8th edition (April 7, 2003)

Making Autism a Gift

Teaching Students with Mental Retardation: A Life Goal Curriculum Planning Approach
   Glen E. Thomas
   Prentice Hall (February 5, 1996)

Understanding Mental Retardation (Understanding Health and Sickness Series)
   Patricia Ainsworth, Pamela C. Baker
   University Press of Mississippi (July 1, 2004)

Asperger's Syndrome: A Guide for Parents and Professionals
   Tony Attwood
   Jessica Kingsley Publishers (January 1998)

Freaks, Geeks and Asperger Syndrome: A User Guide to Adolescence
   Luke Jackson
   Jessica Kingsley Publishers (October 2002)

The OASIS Guide to Asperger Syndrome: Completely Revised and Updated: Advice, Support, Insight, and Inspiration
   Patricia Romanowski Bashe, Barbara L. Kirby, Simon Baron-Cohen, Tony Attwood
   Crown (March 29, 2005)

Asperger Syndrome and Adolescence: Helping Preteens & Teens Get Ready for the Real World
   Teresa Bolick
   Fair Winds Press (June 2004)

Asperger Syndrome: What Teachers Need to Know
   Matt Winter
   Jessica Kingsley Publishers (April 1, 2003)

Robert Evert Cimera

When Autism Strikes: Families Cope With Childhood Disintegrative Disorder
Robert A. Catalano
Plenum Publishing (May 1998)

Obsessive-Compulsive Disorders: A Complete Guide to Getting Well and Staying Well
Fred Penzel
Oxford University Press (August, 2000)

Freeing Your Child from Obsessive-Compulsive Disorder: A Powerful, Practical Program for Parents of Children and Adolescents
Tamar E. Chansky
Three Rivers Press (July 10, 2001)

What to Do When Your Child Has Obsessive-Compulsive Disorder: Strategies and Solutions
Aureen Pinto Wagner
Lighthouse Press (September 15, 2002)

Pathways to Learning in Rett Syndrome
Jackie Lewis, Debbie Wilson
David Fulton Publishers (May 1998)

The Official Parent's Sourcebook on Rett Syndrome: A Revised and Updated Directory for the Internet Age
Icon Health Publications
Icon Health Publications (November 2002)

273

Making Autism a Gift

Pervasive Developmental Disorders: Diagnosis, Options, and Answers
Mitzi Waltz
Future Horizons (September 9, 2003)

Pervasive Developmental Disorder: An Altered Perspective
Barbara Quinn, Anthony Malone
Jessica Kingsley Publishers (April 15, 2000)

The Out-of-Sync Child: Recognizing and Coping with Sensory Integration Dysfunction
Carol Stock Kranowitz, Larry B. Silver
Perigee Trade (March 1, 1998)

Childhood Schizophrenia
Sheila Executor, Evelyn Katz Cantor
Guilford Press (June 3, 1988)

Schizophrenia in Children and Adolescents
Helmut Remschmidt (Editor), Ian M. Goodyer (Series Editor)
Cambridge University Press (February 15, 2001)

Seizures and Epilepsy in Childhood: A Guide
John M. Freeman, Eileen P. G. Vining, Diana J. Pillas
Johns Hopkins University Press; 3rd edition (December 1, 2002)

Growing Up with Epilepsy: A Practical Guide for Parents
Lynn Bennett Blackburn
Demos Medical Publishing (August 1, 2003)

Children with Fragile X Syndrome: A Parents' Guide
Jayne Dixon Weber
Woodbine House (July 15, 2000)

Fragile X Syndrome: Diagnosis, Treatment, and Research
Randi Jenssen Hagerman, Paul J. Hagerman
Johns Hopkins University Press, 3rd edition (April 15, 2002)

Understanding Williams Syndrome: Behavioral Patterns and Interventions
Eleanor Semel, Sue R. Rosner
Lea (January 1, 2003)

Books on Vocational, Residential, and Other Adult Life Issues

Preparing Children With Disabilities for Life
Robert Evert Cimera
Scarecrow Education (February 1, 2003)

Helping Adults with Mental Retardation Grieve a Death Loss
Charlene Luchterhand, Nancy Murphy
Accelerated Development (May 1, 1998)

Supported Employment in Business: Expanding the Capacity of Workers with Disabilities
Paul Wehman
Training Resource Network (July 1, 2001)

Transition and Change in the Lives of People with Intellectual Disabilities
David May
Jessica Kingsley Publishers (December 1, 2000)

Making Autism a Gift

The Road Ahead: Transition to Adult Life for Persons with Disabilities
  Keith Storey, Paul Bates, Dawn Hunter
  Training Resource Network (March 1, 2002)

Beyond High School: Transition from School to Work
  Frank R. Rusch, Janis Chadsey
  Wadsworth Publishing (December 15, 1997)

ORGANIZATIONS AND SUPPORT GROUPS

Organization: National Autistic Society
Mission Statement: The National Autistic Society exists to champion the rights and interests of all people with autism and to ensure that they and their families receive quality services appropriate to their needs. The website includes information about autism and Asperger syndrome, the NAS and its services and activities.
Website: http://www.nas.org.uk/
Contact Information: The National Autistic Society
393 City Road
London EC1V 1NG
UK nas@nas.org.uk

Organization: Autism Society of America
Mission Statement: The mission of the Autism Society of America is to promote lifelong access and opportunity for all individuals within the autism spectrum, and their families, to be fully participating, included members of their community.

Robert Evert Cimera

Education, advocacy at state and federal levels, active public awareness and the promotion of research form the cornerstones of ASA's efforts to carry forth its mission.

Website: http://www.autism-society.org

Contact Information: 7910 Woodmont Avenue, Suite 300

Bethesda, MD 20814-3067

800-3AUTISM

Organization: National Autism Association

Mission Statement: The mission of the National Autism Association is to advocate, educate, and empower. We will advocate on behalf of those who cannot fight for their own rights. We will raise public and professional awareness of autism spectrum disorders. We will empower those in the autism community to never give up in their search to help their loved ones reach their full potential.

Website: http://www.nationalautismassociation.org/

Contact Information: P.O. Box 1547

Marion, SC 29571

877-NAA-AUTISM.

Organization: National Alliance For Autism Research (NAAR)

Mission Statement: The mission of the National Alliance for Autism Research is to aggressively fund global biomedical research accelerating the discovery of the causes, prevention, effective treatments and cure for autism spectrum disorders and

Making Autism a Gift

to educate the public on the critical role research plays in achieving these goals.

Website: http://www.naar.org/
Contact Information: 99 Wall Street, Research Park
Princeton, NJ 08540
888-777-NAAR

Organization: Families for Early Autism Treatment (FEAT)
Mission Statement: This site provides information to parents of children diagnosed with Autism Spectrum Disorders including Autism, Pervasive Developmental Disorder (PDD), and Asperger's Syndrome, and to professionals about FEAT, its goals, organization, and how FEAT can help families, as well as to provide information about other available resources.
Website: http://www.feat.org/
Contact Information: P. O. Box 255722
Sacramento, CA 95865-5722
916-463-5323

Organization: Cure Autism Now (CAN)
Mission Statement: Cure Autism Now (CAN) is an organization of parents, clinicians and leading scientists committed to accelerating the pace of biomedical research in autism through raising money for research projects, education and outreach.
Website: http://www.cureautismnow.org/
Contact Information: 5455 Wilshire Boulevard, Suite 2250
Los Angeles, CA 90036-4234
888-828-8476

Robert Evert Cimera

Organization: Doug Flutie, Jr., Foundation

Mission Statement: The Foundation's mission is to aid financially disadvantaged families who need assistance in caring for their children with autism; to fund education and research into the causes and consequences of childhood autism; and to serve as a clearinghouse and communications center for new programs and services developed for individuals with autism.

Website: http://www.dougflutiejrfoundation.org/

Contact Information: Doug Flutie, Jr. Foundation for Autism
PO Box 767
Framingham, MA 01701
1-866-3AUTISM

Organization: Autism National Committee

Mission Statement: Our organization was founded in 1990 to protect and advance the human rights and civil rights of all persons with autism, Pervasive Developmental Disorder, and related differences of communication and behavior.

Website: http://www.autcom.org/

Contact Information: P.O. Box 6175
North Plymouth, MA 02362-6175

Organization: Rett Syndrome Association

Mission Statement: We are a national organization giving help, advice and support to parents, caregivers, siblings and professionals, in fact anybody involved with a child or adult who has Rett syndrome.

Website: http://www.rettsyndrome.org.uk

Making Autism a Gift

Contact Information: 113 Friern Barnet Road
London N11 3EU U.K.

Organization: National Fragile X Foundation
Mission Statement: The National Fragile X Foundation unites the fragile X community to enrich lives through educational and emotional support, promote public and professional awareness, and advance research toward improved treatments and a cure for fragile X syndrome.
Website: http://www.nfxf.org
Contact Information: P.O. Box 190488
San Francisco, CA 94119
800-688-8765

Organization: National Organization for Rare Disorders (NORD)
Mission Statement: The National Organization for Rare Disorders (NORD), a 501(c)3 organization, is a unique federation of voluntary health organizations dedicated to helping people with rare "orphan" diseases and assisting the organizations that serve them. NORD is committed to the identification, treatment, and cure of rare disorders through programs of education, advocacy, research, and service.
Website: http://www.rarediseases.org
Contact Information: 55 Kenosia Avenue
P.O. Box 1968
Danbury, CT 06813-1968
800-999-6673

Robert Evert Cimera

Organization: Council for Exceptional Children
Mission Statement: The worldwide mission of The Council for
                                 Exceptional Children is to improve educa-
                                 tional outcomes for individuals with excep-
                                 tionalities.
Website: http://www.cec.sped.org
Contact Information: 1110 North Glebe Road, Suite 300
                                 Arlington, VA 22201-5704
                                 888-CEC-SPED

Organization: American Association on Mental Retardation
Mission Statement: AAMR promotes progressive policies, sound
                                 research, effective practices, and universal hu-
                                 man rights for people with intellectual dis-
                                 abilities.
Website: http://www.aamr.org
Contact Information: 444 North Capitol Street, NW, Suite 846
                                 Washington, DC 20001-1512
                                 800-424-3688

Organization: TASH (formerly The Association for Persons
                                 with Severe Handicaps)
Mission Statement: TASH is an international association of peo-
                                 ple with disabilities, their family members,
                                 other advocates, and professionals fighting for
                                 a society in which inclusion of all people in all
                                 aspects of society is the norm.
Website: http://www.tash.org
Contact Information: 29 W. Susquehanna Avenue, Suite 210
                                 Baltimore, MD 21204
                                 410-828-8274

Organization:	The Arc of the United States
Mission Statement:	The Arc of the United States works to include all children and adults with cognitive, intellectual, and developmental disabilities in every community.
Website:	http://www.thearc.org
Contact Information:	1010 Wayne Avenue, Suite 650
	Silver Spring, MD 20910
	301-565-3842

E-GROUPS

E-Groups are online communities where people with similar interests e-mail each other back and forth, sharing resources and experiences. Please keep in mind that the content offered via these groups is often unmonitored, so accuracy cannot be guaranteed. However, they frequently can be a great source of support.

All of the following groups are from www.yahoo.com. Other groups exist from other Internet service providers.

Name of Group:	ABA4ALL
Web Address:	http://groups.yahoo.com/group/ABA4ALL/
Description:	ABA (Applied Behavioral Analysis) is a teaching methodology that can be effective for a variety of children with special needs at varying levels of functioning and development. Children with mental retardation, complex multiple disabilities, and other syndromes/disorders, as well as children with social skills issues, ADD/ADHD, and others who are "high functioning" may benefit from the type of individualized, direct

instruction that ABA offers. ABA programs are designed to meet the individual needs of each child; this may or may not include DTT (discrete trial training).

ABA is best known for being the chosen teaching method for children on the Autism Spectrum, unfortunately this often means that many parents of children with other disability labels never come across ABA in their research; this is disheartening as ABA could very well turn out to be successful for these children and families. ABA4ALL is a place to share ABA information, strategies, and experiences. Most of all, this group should give hope to parents who have watched their child struggle for years and have made little to no progress in their current educational programs.

Name of Group:	Asperger PDD Parents
Web Address:	http://groups.yahoo.com/group/Asperger_PDD_Parents/
Description:	Parents of children with Asperger's Syndrome, High-functioning Autism, or PDD can come here for support, ideas, exchange, discussions of current research, or just assurance that you are not in this parenting journey alone. While this group will frequently focus on Central Texas issues such as parent support meetings or playgroups, we welcome members from other geographic areas to participate in discussions and share their experiences.

Making Autism a Gift

Name of Group: Asperger Support
Web Address: http://health.groups.yahoo.com/group/
                   AspergerSupport/
Description: This group is moderated by a Certified School
                   Psychologist who has done an extensive amount
                   of work with children who have been diagnosed
                   with Asperger/Autistic/PDD. There is also a Li-
                   censed/Certified Speech Language Pathologist
                   with the group. It is a wonderful place for par-
                   ents, educators, and anyone who works with
                   children with these Autism Spectrum Disorders
                   or with children who have some symptoms but
                   are not diagnosed.

Name of Group: Autism Adolescence
Web Address: http://groups.yahoo.com/group/Autism_
                   Adolescence/
Description: There is not a whole lot of research on the net
                   about Autism Spectrum Disorders and adoles-
                   cence. I am the mother of two sons. My older
                   son has Asperger's Syndrome, and is 12. My
                   younger son is 10 and is classified as Autistic. I
                   am hoping to connect with parents who have
                   pre-teen, or teenaged children, though all are
                   welcome here. Please free to share your stories,
                   advice, woes, rants, tears, and especially laughter
                   here with us. We are all in this ship together. I
                   think I can speak for all of us when I say we are
                   in it for the long haul.

Robert Evert Cimera

Name of Group:	Autism Comorbidity
Web Address:	http://health.groups.yahoo.com/group/autism-comorbidity/
Description:	This list is meant for people who have, or are related to someone who has, an Autistic Spectrum Disorder (Autism, Asperger's, PDD, Rett's or CDD) along with one or more comorbid disorders. Common comorbid disorders of ASDs include ADD/ADHD, Tourette's Syndrome and Epilepsy/Seizures, but people who are related to ASDs with additional physical impairments, blindness, deafness, other neurological disorders, learning disabilities, mental retardation, Down Syndrome or other developmental disabilities, psychiatric conditions (depression, bipolar, OCD etc.), chronic illnesses or any other health problem are also welcome, as well as people who have one or more health conditions and assume they may have an additional ASD. Here we can discuss how being autistic affects handling the comorbid disorder(s) and how the comorbid disorder(s) influence an autistic person and his/her needs. Come to share your frustrations, sadness, hope and success, exchange information, and support each other. This list—created by a legally blind adolescent who suspects an additional ASD—is meant for autistics themselves as well as parents, family members, friends, relatives, teachers, professionals and others interested in or related to ASDs and comorbidity.

Making Autism a Gift

Name of Group:	Autism Aspergers
Web Address:	http://health.groups.yahoo.com/group/ autism-aspergers/
Description:	This list is for parents and caregivers of kids with autism and Aspergers, and any other disability. I am the mother of 4 special needs boys, and I created this list to share stories, ideas, treatments, therapies, advice and support. It's a list where we can all make friends and have fun.

Name of Group:	Autism Awareness
Web Address:	http://health.groups.yahoo.com/group/ autismawareness/
Description:	Autism Awareness is about informing concerned parents of the latest breakthroughs in autism, PDD, ADHD and the like. It is a compassionate support system for parents who have been there and are still there. It will inform you on successful remedies parents have been using and doctors are too scared to back. It will allow you to get a glimpse into the mind of your child.

Name of Group:	Autism Awareness Action
Web Address:	http://health.groups.yahoo.com/group/ autism-awareness-action/
Description:	This list is an autism informational list to share and receive information and support on autism. Members on this list are from all across the United States and worldwide. All issues of autism are explored—from diet, supplements, interventions, legislation, treatments, educational

and vocational strategies, and even some off-topic humor. The purpose of this list is to be a well rounded resource for autism and all it encompasses.

As the name implies, this list is about autism, sharing information to keep you aware of what is going on in the world of autism—medically and otherwise, and most of all things you can do to take action in support of legislation. This list will keep you up to date on future autism conferences, hearings, legislation, and how you can participate.

This list will be a positive place for members to learn about autism, as well as to share and seek information—and, of course, to meet new friends on this journey of ASD. There will be off-topic posts, to give us a much needed laughter break now and then. Occasionally a parent will seek support for a situation they need help with. Our main objective however, is for each parent, professional, and family member to come to this list for all the information they need to fight autism! United together we can and will make a difference in autism!

Name of Group:	Autism Downs MR
Web Address:	http://groups.yahoo.com/group/autism_downs_mr/
Description:	This list is for people who are teachers or caregivers (group home workers, etc.) and are interested in learning more about disabilities. This

Making Autism a Gift

list will allow you to explore all of these disorders (autism, downs syndrome, mental retardation, ADD, ADHD and many more). This list is for any person who would like to share theories, opinions, thoughts, and stories about the unique and interesting people they have encountered. I have been working with students and adults for eight years and I can tell you AWARENESS is the KEY. If you feel like this is a list you would like to join please do so. I can't wait to hear your stories and thoughts.

Name of Group: Autism in Girls

Web Address: http://health.groups.yahoo.com/group/
Autism_in_Girls/

Description: Restricted membership! This list is for all parents and professionals who wish to exchange information regarding treatment of autism in girls, how autism effect females in the family, and any other issues dealing with autism and females and/or the comparison of males and females with autism. Other than the restricted membership, the list will not be censored in any way so as to promote the free flow of information between its members.

Name of Group: Birth to Three Support

Web Address: http://groups.yahoo.com/group/Birthto
ThreeSupport/

Description: Support for all parents and professionals in Birth to Three Programs or Early Intervention or ECI

Robert Evert Cimera

programs. We each struggle with the same early issues. We welcome parents of children with any disability or at risk for a disability and professionals who work with these families.

Name of Group:	Children with Autism
Web Address:	http://groups.yahoo.com/group/children_ with_autism/
Description:	My 6 year old son is autistic. We found out when he was 4. I have created this group to help us parents find out more about this disorder. If anyone has info please feel free to post. We are here to help each other and be there so we are not alone in this!!!!! You will find a lot of useful information under our group links. You will find topics such as, SSI, sensory issues, laws for children's education rights, info on autism, and much more.

Name of Group:	High Functioning Autism
Web Address:	http://groups.yahoo.com/group/High FunctioningAutism/
Description:	This is a place where people who have an interest in the life of a child with the diagnosis of high functioning or mild autism, P.D.D., P.D.D.-N.O.S., or semantic pragmatic disorder or have no official diagnosis but have autistic-like traits can come together to: 1. exchange stories, ideas, and information. 2. vent the inevitable frustrations and heartaches of the everyday life experiences involved with a special needs child.

Making Autism a Gift

Name of Group:	Home School Special Needs Kidz
Web Address:	http://groups.yahoo.com/group/Home school_SpecialNeedsKidz
Description:	There is hope! This is a support group for those who live mainly in the USA who are home schooling a "special needs" child, ages preschool to 19. Whether your child has ADHD, a learning disability (LD), dyslexia, emotional or neurological disorder, bipolar, Tourette syndrome, deafness, autism, anxiety disorder, oppositional defiance disorder, blindness, any type of emotional or physical handicap, etc, then this group is for you.

Name of Group:	Mild MR Group
Web Address:	http://groups.yahoo.com/group/mildmrgroup/
Description:	For parents of children with mild mental retardation/challenges, high functioning mentally retarded/challenged, "slow" learners, to pool our minds and experiences in any and all areas of life, allowing us to better help our children, and not feel so all alone while we're at it.

Name of Group:	Moms Of Spec Needs Kids
Web Address:	http://groups.yahoo.com/group/momsofspecneedskids/
Description:	This list was created for mothers of special needs children to have a place to vent about the trials of their every day lives, and talk to other moms in similar situations.

Name of Group: Parent2Parent
Web Address: http://health.groups.yahoo.com/group/
                   parent2parent/
Description: Quick description is that we are all parents,
                   teachers or caregivers of special kids - that is our
                   common bond. Our kids are in special education
                   or will be, are on the spectrum or have other de-
                   velopmental delays. On this group we support
                   each other as people, listening, offering advice in
                   all aspects of life for ourselves as well as on how
                   to help our kids.

Name of Group: PDD-NOS family
Web Address: http://health.groups.yahoo.com/group/
                   PDD-NOSfamily/
Description: PDD-NOS family is for family members or care-
                   givers of children with PDD-NOS and/or
                   autism. We hope to provide encouragement as
                   well as to share vital information regarding
                   treatment options, therapy plans and legislation
                   that will affect our loved ones.

Name of Group: SpecialEDontheWeb
Web Address: http://groups.yahoo.com/group/special
                   edontheweb/
Description: This is your place to go when you want to find
                   information about any topic in Special Educa-
                   tion. Need to find some web resources on a Spe-
                   cial Education topic? Just leave a message and
                   others will try to help you out!

Making Autism a Gift

Name of Group:	Special Educators
Web Address:	http://groups.yahoo.com/group/Special_ Educators/
Description:	In this list you can ask questions and get advice about lesson plans, teaching styles and about the Special Education population. This is also a place to let off some steam after a long day or to share accomplishments of students and even of yourself. If you love teaching or are a teacher, then this is the place for you!

Name of Group:	The Ultimate Advocate
Web Address:	http://health.groups.yahoo.com/group/ TheUltimateAdvocate/
Description:	The focus of The Ultimate Advocate is on those who have a child with an Autistic Spectrum Disorder but EVERYONE is welcome. If you have a question, someone here either has the answer, or can lead you to someone who has. The Ultimate Advocate has been formed to help parents learn to navigate the Special Education "Maze" and to learn how to effectively advocate for their child(ren). Parents need to understand their Rights and Responsibilities under Special Education Laws, as well as what the Educators are required by Law to provide our children. We can help answer questions about IDEA, IEP's, Letter Writing, Complaints and much more. We are here to share information, both locally and globally, and most importantly, to support each other.